A NEW WAY TO DINNER

FOOD52

A NEW WAY TO
DINNER

A playbook of recipes and
strategies for the week ahead

AMANDA HESSER & MERRILL STUBBS

PHOTOGRAPHY BY JAMES RANSOM

TEN SPEED PRESS
BERKELEY

Contents

AMANDA'S SUMMER

THE WEEK AHEAD 71
fish tacos, jasmine rice, blistered tomatoes,
pickled onions, spicy peaches, blueberries

Limeade with Basil 75

Blistered Cherry Tomatoes 76

Jasmine Rice Salad with Blistered Tomatoes,
Tuna, Olives, and Capers 76

Blistered Cherry Tomato Sandwich 76

Spicy Peach Salad 79

Spicy Peaches Wrapped in Prosciutto 79

Thai Steak Salad 80

Steak and Avocado Salad with Crisp Rice
and Cashews 82

Thai Steak Sandwich with Avocado, Cilantro,
and Pickled Onions 82

Steak Sandwich with Pickled Onions,
Blistered Tomatoes, and Spicy Greens 82

Fail Then No-Fail Jasmine Rice 83

Low-Maintenance Fish Tacos 85

Pickled Onions 86

Penne with Blistered Cherry Tomatoes and Corn 88

Blueberry Ice 91

THE WEEK AHEAD 93
oil-poached tuna, couscous, romesco,
braised peppers, brown butter, plums

Grilled Squid Salad with Lemon, Capers,
and Couscous 96

Smoked Paprika Mayonnaise on Grilled Bread 96

Couscous Salad with Zucchini, Pistachios,
and Feta 99

Brown Butter Tomatoes 99

Couscous Salad with Zucchini, Pistachios,
and Poached Tuna 99

Poached Tuna 100

Tuna Salad Sandwich with Hacked Romesco 100

Olive Oil–Braised Peppers 103

Tuna Salad with Peppers and Smoked
Paprika Mayonnaise 103

Summer Evening Pasta 104

Grilled Pork Chops with Hacked Romesco 107

Eggs with Romesco 107

Plum Tart 109

MERRILL'S SUMMER

THE WEEK AHEAD 113
steak, grilled shrimp, farro, mushrooms, arugula,
garlic scape pesto, radishes, strawberries, meringues

Strawberry Rosé Spritzer 116

Strawberry Shakes with Yogurt and Honey 116

Farro Salad with Roasted Mushrooms and Parmesan 119

Steak with Arugula, Lemon, and Parmesan 120

Grain Bowls with Chopped Steak 121

Lime Sriracha Butter 121

Avocado and Radish Tartine with Lime Sriracha Butter 121

Radish and Hummus Tartine 121

Grilled Shrimp with Arugula and Garlic Scape Pesto 123

Farro Salad with Shrimp, Radishes, and Pesto 124

Pesto Toasts 124

Pasta with Pesto and Tuna 124

Avocado Toasts with Pesto, Crispy Bacon,
and Poached Eggs 124

Eton Mess 126

THE WEEK AHEAD 129
crab, meatballs, pasta, tomatoes, zucchini,
green beans, avocado, basil, watermelon,
peaches, black raspberry ice cream

Watermelonade 133

Crab and Avocado Salad 134

Crab Toasties 134

Blistered Tomato, Avocado, and Crab Tartine
with Capers 134

Meatballs with Tomato and Zucchini 136

Meatball Sandwiches with Fresh Mozzarella and Basil 136

Quick Tomato Sauce 137

Boiled Green Beans 137

Pasta with Garlic, Tomatoes, Basil, and Brie 138

My Favorite Tomato Sandwich 138

Black Raspberry Chocolate Chip Ice Cream 141

MERRILL'S FALL

AMANDA'S FALL

INTRODUCTION

You've finished work, you're heading home, and you suddenly realize you haven't given a lick of thought to dinner. There are a few wilting greens and a piece of leftover chicken in the fridge, and no time to shop. Plus you have to help the kids with their homework and do the laundry. Your thoughts turn dark; this is a place you find yourself all too often.

We've been there, too.

Because of what we do, people always ask us, "You must cook all the time, right?"

"Well, no," we say, "we actually do most of our cooking on the weekend."

As parents and as partners running a growing business, we have very little time to cook during the week. If we want to eat well, we need to plan our shopping and cooking for the weekends, and to come up with ways to do it so that family dinners don't become monotonous.

It took us years, working separately, to figure out how to pull this off. There were mistakes. There was take-out pizza. But over time, the small triumphs and the wisdom of experience began to add up. And once we began working on this book, the insights and tips started flowing at a rapid-fire pace, and the pieces came together very quickly. We were onto something, and we could help others.

Here's how we got started.

AMANDA: After my twins were born, I would shop at the Greenmarket on Saturdays and buy whatever looked best. On Sundays, I'd cook all the ingredients simply, with a plan to combine them in enticing ways throughout the week. The problem with this was . . . well, there were several. Cooks in a hurry gravitate toward the path of least resistance—so I was roasting everything. Combining all the roasted fish and beets in a sparklingly original way on a Tuesday night happened pretty much never. Several months in, I realized that not only was I bored, but that I had gotten myself into a deep, depressing cooking rut. What saved me were recipes—I turned the clock back two decades and started following other people's recipes again.

Recipes are a relief when you're busy and not feeling inspired to create. Follow directions and a destination is yours. And recipes, which allow you entry into another creative person's mind, reinvigorated my love of cooking. I was learning again, and the results were surprising and delicious. The only problem? Stand-alone recipes feed you well for a night, but not for a week.

Eventually, I began tying together recipes to form a menu that would carry me through the week. And I started involving my husband, Tad, more in our weekly menu prep, creating a time and space for us to chitchat while we cooked.

MERRILL: I'm newer to the idea of planning meals ahead. It wasn't too long ago that I was still swinging by the grocery store on my way home from work to pick up a whole chicken, some fresh pasta, or whatever looked best for my husband, Jonathan, and me to have that night. Steak au poivre on a Wednesday? You bet. With mashed potatoes and sautéed greens on the side—all served promptly at 10 p.m.

But then baby Clara arrived, followed by Henry three years later, and everything changed. No more eating at 10 p.m. Impromptu dinners became a thing of the past (or at least reserved for weekends), and suddenly the sheer volume of food necessary to get us all through the week became intimidating.

Although I'd never fully drifted away from recipes as inspiration, I started turning to a different breed: recipes that could bear the burden of being stretched and poked and prodded to adapt to different seasons, ingredients, cooking methods, and yields. I began cooking several recipes each weekend with an eye toward efficiency, always on the lookout for winning combinations and permutations.

AMANDA: We approached our weekly menus with our own tics—er, style. Merrill would have loose notes scattered here and there and menus that produced mix-and-match leftovers for work lunches, such as braised chicken and brothy beans. I secretly pined for her lunches and took mental notes on her ideas.

MERRILL: Amanda opted for meticulously handwritten weekly menus and Sunday cooking plans (she's a Virgo), which gave birth to inspired wheat berry and quinoa salads and brussels sprouts with anchovy dressing.

AMANDA: Over our desk lunches or while walking to meetings, we'd talk about what we were cooking and trade tips and recipes—such as Merrill's tip to roast pork shoulder overnight (page 165). Soon, we could see ourselves influencing each other.

We realized there was a flywheel effect happening, with a coherent world view on dinner planning arising from our complex lives. Finally—duh!—it occurred to us that this was the book we should write together. Because it was a topic we cared about deeply, and because so many other people struggle with the same challenge.

We learned from our own failures that the biggest obstacle to eating well isn't the cooking, it's the organizing. That's why we arranged our book by season and menu and layered it with tactical tips and instructions. This new way to dinner will change the flow of your weeks and improve your life. Gone will be that nagging to-do anxiety about what you'll put together for dinner after work. When you get home, you'll know what needs to be done, and you'll have more time with the people you love. You'll sit down to dinners that are varied and good for you. You'll save money on groceries and waste less food. You'll become a faster and better cook while cooking this way. And if you follow every step in this book, you, too, will have two children, run a start-up, and live in Brooklyn.

We'll be with you the whole way—join us!

　　　—Amanda and Merrill

HOW TO USE THIS BOOK

At first glance, our book may seem daunting. It really is a new way to dinner, and this new way may mean altering your shopping and cooking habits. To cook for the week, you'll need to decide on your menu and plan a big shop so you're ready to get in the kitchen over the weekend.

Our plan may take some of the spontaneity out of your cooking, but we feel the benefits far outweigh this. You'll start each week feeling organized and on top of your game. You'll have a detailed plan for five dinners (and many lunches) that anyone can execute, so in case you have to stay late at work or travel, your partner or sitter can take over, and no one's schedules will be compromised.

Most important, you'll head into the week knowing that you'll eat well. There will be a little last-minute prep or cooking some nights—and a lot more time to spend with your friends and family.

A few important points to keep in mind before trying out your first menu:

- When you're first starting out, our menus will probably take longer than the stated cooking time. These are new recipes and our multitasking cooking plan may not come naturally. All our menus were tested and timed by people on our team, so we know they work. Don't be concerned if your timing is slower—once you get the hang of our approach to weekend cooking, it'll come easily to you as well.

- Cooking times represent the active time you spend in the kitchen. Occasionally, you'll be done with your active work time, but a braise or a cake may take an hour or so longer before you remove it from the oven.

- Cooking times also represent the time it would take for one person to complete the menu. If you have someone to help you out, your time in the kitchen should be substantially shorter.

- We haven't accounted for washing dishes or cleanup time, because every cook has his or her own approach. It's helpful to use the "clean as you go" method and wash dishes between recipes or steps. It will make you happier if you finish a menu without having a mountain of dishes to deal with.

- We give you a weekend plan for cooking ahead in one fell swoop, but feel free to spread out the cooking over a couple of days and make it work for you. For instance, make the dessert on Saturday morning and a stew in the evening, then use Sunday to wrap up the smaller recipes. We ourselves don't manage to cook in one sustained burst every week—sometimes our weekend cooking seeps into Monday, or we end up ordering pizza on a night we'd planned to cook. We don't feel guilty about it, nor should you!

- Think of the full menus in the book as Perfect World Menus; they're meant for when you're really in the mind-set to cook and are going to be home for all of the weeknights. They are an ideal that we, too, aspire to, but don't always manage. That's why we offer shortcuts for every menu—ideas on which recipes you can save for another week when you have more time.

- Similarly, if you're only going to be home for a night or two in a week, just make part of a menu.

- You'll notice that the weekend cooking plans will leave you with different configurations of food. Some weeks, you'll have several dishes fully prepared and ready to reheat and serve. Others, you may end up with a collection of stand-alone elements ready to act as building blocks for some light weeknight cooking.

- Our menus are designed to feed a family of four and can usually be scaled up or down to fit your needs (scale down either by halving an individual recipe or by cutting out a dish or two).

- We organized the book seasonally (with an East Coast point of view) so you can take advantage of the best ingredients of each season. This is how we cook—we let the farmers' market guide us, and that's often the first place we start when coming up with a new menu. Please feel free to adjust based on your location.

- If you're concerned about any dishes going bad before you get to eat them, not to worry: We've designed our menus to eliminate this problem. Each plan makes a bounty of food, and if you're not feeding a lot of mouths, you can stock up for another week by sticking some of the prepared dishes in the freezer.

- We've noted which recipes are great for freezing and have given you storage times and tips for everything we could think of.

- We don't call for any esoteric tools or equipment (no spiralizers in this book!), but some menus require multiple large pots and pans. If you don't want to invest in more cookware, borrow from a friend or spread your cooking over a couple of days so you can wash and reuse the same equipment.

- Storage containers—yep, you'll need a lot. Because so many recipes and components are stored until the dinner for which they're needed, your Tupperware drawer and canning jars will get a good workout.

- As we wrote the book, we realized that there were a few staple recipes that should be highlighted in special sections, for easy reference if you decide to freestyle off menu. Thus our sections on salad dressings (page 152), Friday night pastas (page 270), and dishes you can freeze ahead for winter (page 107).

- Mini recipes are either easy basics or simple dishes that build on fuller recipes you've already made for a menu—much like a verbal recipe you might get from a friend. Minis are less detailed, and we thought you'd enjoy the break from conventional recipes now and then. You'll find mini recipes and tips throughout that aren't included in the nightly menu plans. Think of these as bonuses—and further inspiration for creating your own menus!

- We included grocery lists to save you time—so the work of going through all the ingredient lists in a menu is done for you. We hope it's helpful! If you want to do a shortcut plan, don't forget to make adjustments to your grocery shopping.

KITCHEN CONFIDENCE

We've learned a lot from cooking many menus throughout the years, including tricks for storing food efficiently, time-saving tips, and how to keep fresh ingredients at their peak for as long as possible. Here are some of the bits of kitchen wisdom we find ourselves relying on most.

Storing Fresh Ingredients.

Use some of your weekend cooking time to wash all of your herbs and greens for the week. Dry them thoroughly and store them in the fridge in zipper plastic bags lined with paper towels. Amanda presses out all of the air and seals the bags, while Merrill leaves them open at the top. We tested both methods in the Food52 kitchen to see which kept the greens longer, and after five days it was a draw: Both were still going strong, so the choice is yours!

To cut down on waste, wash and reuse 1-gallon zipper bags or recycle clean plastic grocery bags to store greens and other raw prepared vegetables. You can also keep washed salad greens right in the salad spinner (add a few paper towels to absorb any excess moisture) if you have room in your fridge—not likely in our kitchens!

Keep lemons and garlic in light linen bags (or plastic bags lined with paper towels) in a vegetable drawer. Onions, potatoes, and fruits besides berries (like apples, peaches, melons, and so on) hold up well on the counter. Spread them on large platters so little stacking is required.

Store ripe bananas and avocados on the counter (hang bananas if possible), away from other produce. This will help keep them from going brown.

Crusty breads with a delicate crumb (like baguettes) are best the same day you buy them. But if you don't regularly have access to fresh bread, freezing some until you need it is a great alternative. Simply wrap the loaf (you may want to cut it in half crosswise if it's long) tightly in plastic wrap, then in aluminum foil, and freeze. When you're ready to use it, thaw the bread on the counter for an hour or so, then put it (uncovered) in a 350°F (175°C) oven for about 5 minutes to revive the crust.

Storing Cooked Food.

If you blanch or cook vegetables like sugar snaps, asparagus, or green beans before you plan to serve them, store them separately in the fridge in paper towel–lined containers or bags. Make sure to use them within a couple of days; wait much longer, and they will have lost most of their crunch.

As you use up food throughout the week, transfer things to smaller containers. By the end of the week, your fridge will be a lot emptier, making it easier for you to do a good cleanup and purge anything past its prime (it's harder for that bag of wilting greens to hide in an uncluttered crisper).

Whenever possible, refrigerate dishes like stews, braises, baked pastas, and pilafs right in the pan they were cooked in. You'll cut down on dishes, and it makes reheating simple.

You'll see that we call for shaking up most of our salad dressings in a jar. It's the easiest way to emulsify the ingredients, and then you're left with both a handy storage container and one step to re-emulsify the leftovers.

Reheating.

If you're using the oven to reheat cooked foods, most things do well within a range of 250°F to 300°F (120°C to 150°C). If you're trying to reheat something like biscuits or a galette, you'll want to crank up the oven closer to 350°F (175°C) or even 375°F (190°C).

Warm dishes like braises, stews, and baked rice in the oven, covered, at 250°F to 300°F (120°C to 150°C) for 15 to 30 minutes, until heated through. These also typically do well in the microwave: Put the food in a microwave-safe dish, cover with a damp kitchen or paper towel, and heat just to temperature. (Being overzealous with the microwave is a surefire way to ensure a rubbery dinner.)

Reheat sturdier dishes like roasted vegetables and meat in the oven, tented loosely with aluminum foil so they don't steam. If you're reheating meat that has already been sliced (like the pork roasts on page 165 and page 263), dampen the slices with gravy or sauce first to keep them from drying out. Never reheat meat that you'd like to remain pink (like the steak on page 120). You'll be

much happier if you let it sit out for half an hour before dinner and then serve it at room temperature with warm sides.

Always cover fish to reheat it, in a very gentle (250°F/120°C) oven or in the microwave. (An exception is the oven roasted fish on page 32, which you cook partially over the weekend and then broil quickly before serving.)

Set chilled desserts (like puddings) and cheeses out to come to room temperature before dinner. Soften hard ice cream at room temperature for a few minutes to make it easier to scoop.

It's always important to season food to taste, but especially so when reheating and reworking leftovers. A stew that seemed perfectly seasoned when you took it off the stove may need another pinch of salt after a day in the fridge. Taste what you're serving once you've reheated it and then adjust the seasonings.

Freezing.

Although some foods will last longer if they're well wrapped, a good general rule is to limit freezing time to six months or less. Otherwise, you're risking freezer burn.

Make sure to clearly label and date anything you freeze. You may think you'll remember which container you put the homemade chicken stock in, but you probably won't. And frozen chicken stock looks a lot like frozen egg whites.

To freeze small things you'd like to keep from clumping together—like cooked chickpeas, gnocchi, or fresh berries—spread them out in a single layer on rimmed baking sheets and freeze until hard, then transfer them into bags or containers. They won't stick together, and you'll be able to easily remove only what you need.

Freeze pesto in ice cube trays, then pop out the cubes and store in a bag. Freeze tomato sauce, soups, and stews in two-person portions. This way, you can defrost the right amount for however many people you're feeding.

Anytime you juice a lemon or lime, zest it first. Keep the zest in an airtight container or bag and store it in the freezer for another day. Use frozen zest as you would fresh—it thaws almost instantly.

We've tried not to call for a handful of fresh cilantro or parsley leaves without a recommendation for how to use up the rest. If you do end up with leftover herbs, whiz them up into a pesto (page 123) or green sauce (page 198) and freeze as noted earlier.

If you end up with just a sprig or two of herbs, the top of an onion, a nub of carrot, or some clean vegetable shavings, add them to a scraps bag in the freezer. The next time you make stock, toss in whatever is in the bag, straight from the freezer; your stock will thank you.

Cleanup.

Make sure your dishwasher is cleaned and emptied before you start cooking, so you can fill it up without interruption.

If you have a two-compartment sink, keep one filled with hot, soapy dishwater for washing on the fly and use the other for rinsing off dishes. Don't put dirty dishes directly into the soapy water or the water will get greasy very quickly, and you won't get clean dishes.

Spread a kitchen towel on the counter by your sink for drying washed greens and herbs.

Things to Have on Hand.

As you'll see in our menus, we often rely on staples from the pantry, fridge, and freezer to round out a meal. These are things that require little to no preparation and allow you some freedom from the constraint of having already planned every meal at the start of the week. They can help you stretch a menu, or whip up something else if the meal for that night doesn't work for you. Here are some of our workhorses:

- Eggs
- Avocado
- Greek yogurt
- Ricotta
- Good cheese
- Hummus
- Canned beans and chickpeas
- Cured meats
- Bacon
- Sausage
- Good-quality canned fish (tuna, sardines, anchovies)
- Olives
- Pickles
- Bread
- Crackers
- Pasta
- Hunk of Parmesan
- Rice
- Fresh fruit
- Dried fruit
- Nut butters
- Nuts
- Good chocolate
- Ice cream
- Cookies

Merrill's Spring

THE WEEK AHEAD

THE RECIPES

Sugar Snap, Asparagus, and Pea Shoot Salad with Preserved Lemon Cream and Merguez 14

Jonathan's Roasted Asparagus 15

Green Salad with Sugar Snaps, Roasted Asparagus, Ricotta, and Toasted Almonds 15

Lamb Merguez 16

Orecchiette with Merguez and Ramps 19

Merguez Sandwich with Pea Shoots, Goat Cheese, and Green Olives 19

Ramp Butter 20

Green Eggs 20

Ricotta Toasts 20

Crispy Crunchy Oatmeal Cookies 23

HOW THEY COME TOGETHER

DINNER ONE

Orecchiette with Merguez and Ramps

Crispy Crunchy Oatmeal Cookies with chocolate ice cream

TO DO TODAY Make the pasta—and you're nearly done! Serve the ice cream with cookies on the side.

DINNER TWO

Ricotta Toasts with sautéed ramps

Thinly sliced prosciutto

Jonathan's Roasted Asparagus

Good chocolates

TO DO TODAY Roast the asparagus and put half in the fridge for later in the week. Make the toasts and arrange them on a board with the prosciutto. Pass chocolates for dessert.

DINNER THREE

Sugar Snap, Asparagus, and Pea Shoot Salad with Preserved Lemon Cream and Merguez

Ricotta with honey, chocolate chips, dried cherries, and pistachios

TO DO TODAY Thirty minutes before dinner, set out the salad dressing. Fry 1¼ pounds (590g) of the merguez patties, putting whatever you don't serve for dinner in the fridge for lunches. Assemble the salad. Serve small bowls of ricotta with toppings on the side for dessert.

DINNER FOUR

Green Eggs

Ricotta Toasts with lemon zest and honey

Raw pea shoots and blanched sugar snaps with lemon dressing

Chocolate ice cream with salted peanuts and crumbled Crispy Crunchy Oatmeal Cookies

TO DO TODAY Make the toasts and the green eggs, enlisting a helper so everything is ready at once. Dress the pea shoots and sugar snaps with leftover dressing from the sugar snap pea salad. Add the ice cream toppings right before dessert.

DINNER FIVE

Lamb Merguez patties

Toasted country bread with Ramp Butter

Jonathan's Roasted Asparagus with preserved lemon cream

Crispy Crunchy Oatmeal Cookies

TO DO TODAY Fry the remaining 1 pound (450g) of merguez patties. Spread thick slices of toast with ramp butter. Thin the leftover lemon cream with a little milk and drizzle over the asparagus.

BROWN BAG LUNCHES

Merguez Sandwich with Pea Shoots, Goat Cheese, and Green Olives

Green Salad with Sugar Snaps, Roasted Asparagus, Ricotta, and Toasted Almonds

Prosciutto, basil, and Ramp Butter on toast

GAME PLAN

TO MAKE OVER THE WEEKEND

Sugar Snap, Asparagus,
and Pea Shoot Salad with
Preserved Lemon Cream
and Merguez

Ramp Butter

Crispy Crunchy
Oatmeal Cookies

Lamb Merguez

HOW TO PULL IT OFF

This weekend, you can expect to be cooking for about
3 hours. I suggest making the merguez one day and
everything else the next, to spread out your tasks.

• On Saturday (if possible), make the merguez mixture
(page 16). Shape 2¼ pounds (1kg) of the sausage into
patties, keeping 12 ounces (340g) of the sausage loose.
Store it in the refrigerator in separate containers.

• On Sunday, set out all of the unsalted butter to come
to room temperature. Yes, 5¾ sticks is a lot of butter,
but it's all for a good cause.

• Make the preserved lemon cream and the lemon
dressing for the salad (page 14) and put them in
the fridge.

• Clean all of the ramps and trim the root ends.

• Make the ramp butter (page 20) and freeze half to use
for steak or baked potatoes when ramps have gone
for the year. Put the rest of the ramps in the fridge
in a plastic bag lined with paper towels for later in the
week. Refrigerate the rest of the ramp butter.

• Heat the oven to 350°F (175°C) and make the oatmeal
cookies (page 23).

• While the cookies are baking and cooling, wash and dry
the sugar snaps, pea shoots, and asparagus. Remove
the strings from the sugar snaps and trim the tough
ends from the asparagus. Blanch all the sugar snaps
and the asparagus for the salad. Store the vegetables
separately in the fridge.

• Pour yourself a glass of wine and kick back. You're set
for the week!

Take it easy. If you're feeling uninspired by the challenge
of making your own merguez, don't torture yourself—go
ahead and buy it. (It's easiest to find in coils, which you
can just slit open.) Now you're looking at about 2 hours
in the kitchen.

GROCERY LIST

PRODUCE

Asparagus, 4 bunches

Garlic, 7 cloves

Ginger, 1 tablespoon grated

Lemons, 4

Pea shoots, 12 cups (240g) firmly packed

Ramps, 45 large

Sugar snap peas, 2 pounds (900g)

HERBS

Basil leaves, ½ cup (10g) loosely packed

Chives, 1 tablespoon chopped

SPICES

Anise or fennel seeds, 1 tablespoon

Cayenne, ½ teaspoon

Coriander seeds, 1 tablespoon

Cumin seeds, 1 tablespoon

Ground cinnamon, 1 tablespoon plus ¼ teaspoon

Ground turmeric, 2 teaspoons

PANTRY

Extra-virgin olive oil, 1 cup (240ml)

Green olives, for lunch

Harissa, 6 tablespoons (90g)

Honey, 1 teaspoon, plus more for drizzling

Orecchiette or other short pasta, 1 pound (450g)

Preserved lemon, ¼ cup (30g) finely chopped

Flaky salt

Tomato paste, 3 tablespoons

Vegetable oil, for frying

BAKING AISLE

All-purpose flour, 1 cup (125g)

Almonds, for lunch

Baking powder, ¾ teaspoon

Baking soda, ½ teaspoon

Chocolate chips, dried cherries, and pistachios, for dessert

Good chocolates, for dessert

Old-fashioned rolled oats, 2½ cups (225g)

Salted peanuts, for dessert

Light brown sugar, ¼ cup (50g) firmly packed

Sugar, 1 cup (200g)

Pure vanilla extract, 1 teaspoon

DAIRY AND EGGS

Unsalted butter, 2¾ cups plus 2 tablespoons (650g)

Crème fraîche, 1 cup (240ml)

Eggs, 11

Fresh ricotta, 1 pound (450g), plus more for dessert

Milk, a bit

Parmesan, for serving

Soft goat cheese, 1 pound (450g)

MEAT AND SEAFOOD

Ground lamb shoulder, 3 pounds (1.4 kg)—ask your butcher to grind it for you

Prosciutto

FREEZER

Chocolate ice cream

BAKED GOODS

Baguettes, 2

Country bread, 1 loaf

Sugar Snap, Asparagus, and Pea Shoot Salad with Preserved Lemon Cream and Merguez

I first had this salad at Resto in New York City a decade ago, paired with crisp slices of spiced lamb belly. The grassy crunch of pea shoots and sugar snaps and the pucker of Meyer lemon kept the fattiness of the lamb in check. Lamb belly doesn't exactly lend itself to weeknight cooking (I don't know many neighborhood butchers who carry it), but the merguez in this chapter is a capable stand-in. If you've never had pea shoots before, they're the tender young pea vines (with leaves) you see in tangled piles at the farmers' market.

Make Preserved Lemon Cream Your Ally Serve it with asparagus, sliced tomatoes, grilled fish, or green beans. Also, it's great for dinner party first courses: All you have to do is make the lemon cream, smear dollops on plates, and plunk the best in-season vegetable on top.

SERVES 4

PRESERVED LEMON CREAM

12 ounces (340g) soft goat cheese, at room temperature

1 cup (240ml) crème fraîche

¼ cup (30g) finely chopped preserved lemon

Kosher salt and freshly ground black pepper

LEMON DRESSING

¾ cup (175ml) extra-virgin olive oil

6 tablespoons (90ml) freshly squeezed lemon juice (from regular or Meyer lemons)

1 teaspoon honey

Salt and freshly ground black pepper

SALAD

1 pound (450g) sugar snap peas, strings removed

1 bunch asparagus, trimmed

6 cups (120g) firmly packed pea shoots

1 pound (450g) Lamb Merguez patties (page 16), for serving

⅓ cup (13g) loosely packed basil leaves

1 tablespoon chopped chives

1 To make the lemon cream, put the goat cheese in the bowl of a stand mixer fitted with the paddle attachment. Whip on medium speed until light and smooth, about 2 minutes. Beat in the crème fraîche and preserved lemon just until combined. Season with salt and pepper to taste. Store in a covered container in the fridge for up to a week.

2 To make the lemon dressing, combine the olive oil, lemon juice, and honey in a jar with some salt and pepper. Seal the jar and shake well to combine. Taste and adjust the seasoning. Store in a covered container in the fridge for up to 10 days. Let sit at room temperature for 15 minutes before shaking to emulsify and using.

3 Bring a large pot of salted water to a boil and have a bowl of ice water ready. Boil the sugar snaps for 30 seconds. Scoop them out with a slotted spoon and plunge them into the ice water for about 30 seconds. Lay them on a kitchen towel to dry.

4 Return the water to a boil. Cook the asparagus for 3 to 5 minutes, until tender but not floppy. Shock them in the ice water and let dry on a kitchen towel. Store the cooked sugar snap peas and asparagus in paper towel–lined containers or plastic bags in the fridge for up to 3 days.

5 **The day of:** Cut the sugar snaps into 1-inch (2.5cm) lengths and the asparagus into 2-inch (5cm) lengths. Combine the pea shoots, sugar snaps, and asparagus in a large bowl. Sauté the merguez patties (page 16) and keep warm.

6 Toss the salad with ¼ cup (60ml) of the dressing. Season with salt and pepper and toss again. Cut the basil into thin ribbons, add to the salad along with the chives, and toss again.

7 Smear about 2 tablespoons of the lemon cream in the center of each plate and mound some salad on top. Serve with the lamb merguez patties.

Jonathan's Roasted Asparagus

The first thing my husband ever cooked for me was roasted asparagus, and I encourage him to make it often when asparagus is in season. Here's how he does it: Heat the oven to 450°F (230°C). Spread **3 bunches of asparagus** (you washed and trimmed them already, right?) in a single layer on rimmed baking sheets. Drizzle with **extra-virgin olive oil** and sprinkle liberally with flaky sea salt and freshly ground black pepper. Toss and roast for 6 to 8 minutes, jostling the baking sheets halfway through. The asparagus should be tender but still bright green, with burnished tips. Halve **a lemon** and squeeze it over the asparagus before serving. The asparagus will keep in a container in the fridge for 3 or 4 days and is just as good at room temperature.

If you prefer, you can grill the asparagus, which will take less cooking time, so watch them closely. Make sure to use a vegetable grilling grate so you don't lose any precious spears to the embers.

Lunch: Green Salad with Sugar Snaps, Roasted Asparagus, Ricotta, and Toasted Almonds

For lunch, put some sliced **roasted asparagus** and **blanched sugar snaps, a few spoonfuls of fresh ricotta,** and **a handful of chopped toasted almonds** in a container. Pack some **lemon dressing** (opposite) separately. Toss right before eating.

Lamb Merguez

Cathy Barrow, who contributed this recipe to the site, points out that the most important ingredient is the harissa. Make sure to find a brand you like; my favorite is Les Moulins Mahjoub. This is a highly spiced sausage, so a little goes a long way. It's great with pasta and ramps (page 19) or atop a pea shoot and sugar snap salad (page 14). Try tucking the patties into a pita with hummus and vegetables or add some loose sausage to a shakshuka.

The spice blend makes twice as much as you'll need for the merguez, but it keeps for six months. Try adding some to the meatballs on page 136 or rubbing it onto the skin of a chicken before roasting.

Amanda's Take "I remember how elated we were when we first saw this recipe on the site. We thought, 'Our home cooks even make their own sausage!' I often serve sausage with simmered beans (page 264) or mashed potatoes (page 251). This merguez is also great with green rice (page 266)."

Sausage 2.0 If you're feeling ambitious, buy casings and make sausage links or a long coil. They freeze well, too, and you'll impress your friends when you lay a 3-foot (90cm) coil of homemade merguez on the grill!

You can use other meats (pork, turkey, chicken, or a combination) if you don't like lamb. For the best results, buy ground meat that is at least 15 percent fat.

MAKES 3 POUNDS (1.4KG) SAUSAGE, ENOUGH TO SERVE 4 FOR 3 DINNERS, PLUS LUNCHES

SPICE BLEND

1 tablespoon coriander seeds

1 tablespoon cumin seeds

1 tablespoon aniseeds (or fennel seeds, in a pinch)

1 tablespoon ground cinnamon

2 teaspoons turmeric

½ teaspoon cayenne

SAUSAGE

3 pounds (1.4kg) ground lamb shoulder (if possible, get your butcher to grind it for you)

6 tablespoons (90g) harissa

3 tablespoons spice blend (see left)

3 tablespoons tomato paste

6 cloves garlic, minced

1 tablespoon grated fresh ginger

1 teaspoon kosher salt

3 to 6 tablespoons ice water

Vegetable oil, for frying

1   To make the spice blend, toast the coriander, cumin, and aniseeds in a dry skillet over low heat until fragrant, about 1 minute. Let cool, then combine with the cinnamon, turmeric, and cayenne and grind finely in a spice grinder or with a mortar and pestle. Set aside 3 tablespoons for the sausage and transfer the remaining spice blend to an airtight container and store for up to 6 months.

2   To make the merguez, combine all of the ingredients except the ice water in the bowl of a stand mixer fitted with a paddle attachment. Mix on low speed until just combined, about 30 seconds. Add the water a tablespoon at a time, until the sausage just comes together, 30 seconds to 1 minute.

3   Form a small patty and sauté it in a thin film of vegetable oil over medium-low heat. Taste and adjust the seasoning. Put ¾ pound (340g) of sausage in a container for the orecchiette (page 19) and refrigerate.

4   Prepare a bowl of ice water. Dip your hands into the water to keep them from getting sticky as you form the remaining sausage into 3-inch (7.5cm) patties ½ inch (1.3cm) thick. You should have about 2 dozen patties. Pack into an airtight container between layers of waxed paper. Refrigerate for up to 5 days or freeze for up to 3 months; thaw the patties in the fridge before cooking.

5   **The day of:** Warm a little vegetable oil in a large skillet over medium heat. Add the sausage patties and sauté until browned and cooked through, 2 to 3 minutes per side. Serve with a salad (like on page 14) or on their own with roasted asparagus (page 15).

Orecchiette with Merguez and Ramps

This pasta adheres to a basic equation I've turned to time and time again for weeknight dinners: sausage + something green + something oniony + pasta = good. It takes all of twenty minutes to prepare, since you've already done all the heavy lifting by making the merguez ahead of time. You can easily substitute another type of sausage (hot or sweet) and any greens you like, such as leeks, broccoli rabe, kale, or spinach. Just toss in a little garlic or onion right after you brown the sausage if you're not using something from the allium family.

SERVES 4, WITH LEFTOVERS

Kosher salt

1 tablespoon extra-virgin olive oil

¾ pound (340g) Lamb Merguez (page 16) or any loose sausage

6 ounces (170g) ramps (about 15 large), cleaned and trimmed

1 pound (450g) orecchiette or other short pasta

Grated Parmesan, for serving (optional)

1 Bring a large pot of generously salted water to a boil. Warm the olive oil in a large skillet over medium heat and brown the merguez, breaking it up with a wooden spoon as it cooks.

2 Meanwhile, slice the white bulbs of the ramps finely and coarsely chop the leaves, keeping them separate. Add the bulbs to the pan and cook, stirring frequently, until they soften and start to brown, a few minutes. Add the leaves and cook until just wilted, another minute or so. Turn off the heat and set aside. (You can hold the sausage and ramps for up to an hour; reheat gently before you add the pasta.)

3 Cook the pasta until al dente. Reserve 1 cup (240ml) of the cooking water and drain the pasta. Add the pasta to the sausage and ramps and cook briefly over medium heat, stirring through and using some of the cooking liquid to loosen things up and create a silky sauce. (You don't want the pasta to be at all dry or sticky, but you don't want it sitting in a pool of water either.) Serve immediately, with Parmesan if you like.

Lunch: Merguez Sandwich with Pea Shoots, Goat Cheese, and Green Olives

Chop **a few olives** roughly and scatter them over **a halved 6-inch (15cm) piece of baguette** spread with **soft goat cheese.** Add some cooked **merguez patties** (page 16) and **a fistful of pea shoots** and wrap in foil.

Ramp Butter

The epic challenge of ramps is how to preserve them beyond their ridiculously brief season. Pickling is a great option, as is pesto (see page 123 for a recipe in which you can easily substitute ramps for garlic scapes). But I think a simple ramp butter gives the best bang for your buck: It's great for finishing steak or fish or topping baked potatoes, and it will make any sandwich sing.

To make it, soften **2 cups (450g/4 sticks) of unsalted butter** at room temperature. Trim and wash **8 ounces (225g), or about 20, large ramps.** Bring a pot of salted water to a boil and have a bowl of ice water at the ready. Blanch the ramps for 30 seconds, then plunge them into the ice water. Roll the ramps in a kitchen towel to dry them, then chop them finely. Pound the ramps into a thick paste using a mortar and pestle. Add the butter and some salt and pepper and stir vigorously to combine (or use a food processor to chop the ramps and make the butter). Roll the butter into two logs and cover tightly in plastic wrap. Put one in the fridge for this week and the other in the freezer for a damp, dark day months from now when you need a pick-me-up. Store in the fridge for 2 weeks and in the freezer for up to 8 months. (Makes about 2 cups/450g.)

No Ramp Butter Wasted in Amanda's House "If you don't eat the rest of the ramp butter straight from a spoon, it's also great spread on toasted country bread and topped with roasted mushrooms. Or prosciutto. Or mashed avocado. Take your pick."

Green Eggs

Ramp butter makes for delicious scrambled eggs. For 4 people, zest **a lemon** and grate **a fistful of Parmesan.** Whisk **10 eggs** with salt and pepper. Put **a walnut-size lump of ramp butter** (see above) in a nonstick pan over low heat and when it melts, pour in the eggs. Stir constantly until the eggs are softly cooked. Fold in the lemon zest and Parmesan and scoop onto warm plates.

Ricotta Toasts

This is a basic concept that lends itself to endless variations. Brush **¼-inch (6mm) slices of baguette** with **extra-virgin olive oil** and grill or toast in a 450°F (230°C) oven until golden, flipping them once. (Keep an eye on the toasts so you don't burn them, like I usually do.) Rub each toast lightly with a cut **clove of garlic** (you just want the barest whisper of it). Smear the toasts thickly with the best **fresh ricotta** you can find. You can stop here, or keep topping.

When I have them, I like to add sautéed ramps: Coarsely chop **a large bunch of cleaned and trimmed ramps.** Warm **a glug of extra-virgin olive oil** in a pan over medium heat. Sauté the ramps with a pinch of salt, stirring once in a while, until the smell overcomes you, 3 to 5 minutes. Top the ricotta toasts with a little heap of the warm ramps, drizzle with more olive oil, and add a shower of flaky salt and a few grinds of pepper.

I also like to drizzle the toasts with **a few drops of extra-virgin olive oil** and **honey** and sprinkle with **finely grated lemon zest,** freshly ground pepper, and flaky salt. Or layer on a paper-thin **slice of bresaola** or add **a dab of hot pepper jam.** The world is your oyster!

Crispy Crunchy Oatmeal Cookies

When I was growing up, there were always homemade cookies in the jar. My mother had a seemingly endless parade of recipes up her sleeve. One of my favorites was a perfectly crisp oatmeal cookie that was buttery and light with just a whisper of cinnamon. Recently, I asked my mother if she still has the recipe, but she's lost track of it (since my sister and I left the house, she doesn't make as many cookies, it turns out). I managed to find a reasonable facsimile from America's Test Kitchen. There are very few ingredients; it's basically oats held together with a whole lot of butter and sugar. To replicate my mother's, I added cinnamon and left the cookies in the oven a bit longer for maximum crunch.

Save Some for a Rainy Day Most cookies are great candidates for freezing. In fact, I know some people who make cookies for holiday gifts weeks in advance and freeze them right up until they give them out. These are no exception. If you don't think you'll finish the whole batch within a week or so, pack up any extras in a double layer of aluminum foil and put them in a plastic zipper bag (clearly labeled with the date!). Freeze for up to 3 months and thaw at room temperature.

MAKES ABOUT 3 DOZEN COOKIES

1 cup (125g) all-purpose flour

1 teaspoon kosher salt

3/4 teaspoon baking powder

1/2 teaspoon baking soda

1/4 teaspoon ground cinnamon

14 tablespoons (200g) unsalted butter, at room temperature

1 cup (200g) sugar

1/4 cup (50g) firmly packed light brown sugar

1 egg

1 teaspoon pure vanilla extract

2 1/2 cups (225g) old-fashioned rolled oats

1 Heat the oven to 350°F (175°C). Line two baking sheets with parchment paper.

2 In a bowl, whisk together the flour, salt, baking powder, baking soda, and cinnamon.

3 In the bowl of a standing mixer fitted with a paddle attachment, cream the butter and the sugars until light and fluffy, 3 to 5 minutes. Scrape down the sides of the bowl, add the egg, and beat until incorporated, about 30 seconds. Scrape down the bowl and do the same with the vanilla.

4 On low speed, add the dry ingredients and beat until just combined. Fold in the oats by hand, mixing just until there are no more pockets of flour or oats.

5 Form tablespoon-size lumps of dough into balls and place them 2 inches (5cm) apart on the baking sheets. Bake in batches until crisp and lightly golden, about 15 minutes, rotating once so the cookies bake evenly. Let them cool completely on the baking sheets for maximum crispness. The cookies will stay crunchy all week in an airtight container at room temperature.

Make ahead:
biscuits
char w/ herb mayo
frittata - peas?
salad dressing
shortcakes (use biscuits) - rhubarb

frittata
salad
bread
shortcakes

fish
sautéed greens
ice cream

frittata
sausages or bacon
cookies

take ramp butter out of freezer!)

THE WEEK AHEAD

THE RECIPES

Cream Biscuits 28

Frittata on a Biscuit with
Herbed Mayonnaise
and Hot Peppers 28

Frittata with Peas, Spring
Greens, and Ricotta 31

The Best Red Wine
Vinaigrette 31

Oven–Roasted Char with
Herbed Mayonnaise 32

Baked Potatoes 32

Rhubarb Shortcakes 35

Chocolate Toasts 35

Lamb Merguez 16

Ramp Butter 20

Lemony Pasta with
Asparagus 49

Roasted Sausages 213

Garlicky Greens 235

HOW THEY COME TOGETHER

DINNER ONE

Frittata with Peas, Spring Greens, and Ricotta
Green salad with The Best Red Wine Vinaigrette
Crusty bread and good salted butter
Rhubarb Shortcakes

TO DO TODAY Set out the rhubarb compote,
vinaigrette, and salted butter. Warm the frittata.
Slice the bread and toss the salad. Assemble the
shortcakes at the last minute.

DINNER TWO

Oven–Roasted Char with Herbed Mayonnaise
Garlicky Greens, using escarole
Vanilla ice cream with rhubarb compote

TO DO TODAY Make the char, refrigerating
half before you broil it for later in the week.
While it roasts, make the escarole, adding
a squeeze of lemon. Top the ice cream
with the compote for dessert.

DINNER THREE

Frittata with Peas, Spring Greens,
and Ricotta

Roasted sausages or Lamb Merguez
patties from the freezer

Store-bought cookies

TO DO TODAY Roast the sausages or
fry the merguez patties. Warm the frittata.

DINNER FOUR

Oven–Roasted Char with Herbed Mayonnaise

Baked potatoes with Ramp Butter from the
freezer or salted butter

Green salad with The Best Red Wine Vinaigrette

Ricotta with honey and rhubarb compote

TO DO TODAY In the morning, take the ramp
butter out of the freezer. Bake the potatoes.
Broil the leftover char. Dress the salad.
Top the ricotta.

DINNER FIVE

Lemony Pasta with Asparagus
Chocolate Toasts

TO DO TODAY Make the pasta. Assemble
the chocolate toasts for dessert.

BROWN BAG LUNCHES

Frittata on a Biscuit with Herbed Mayonnaise
and Hot Peppers

Garlicky escarole with char, reheated gently

Lemony Pasta with Asparagus (room
temperature) and thinly sliced prosciutto
or soppressata

GAME PLAN

TO MAKE OVER THE WEEKEND

Cream Biscuits

Frittata with Peas, Spring
Greens, and Ricotta

The Best Red Wine
Vinaigrette

Oven–Roasted Char with
Herbed Mayonnaise

Rhubarb Shortcakes

READY, SET, GO!

This weekend, plan to be in the kitchen for about
2½ hours. I've tried to keep you busy with other
prep while things are in the oven so there isn't any
wasted time.

- Heat the oven to 425°F (220°C). Make a batch of
  cream biscuits (page 28).

- Get the rhubarb compote (page 35) for the shortcakes
  on the stove. Save the rest of the rosé to drink with
  dinner this week!

- Do all of your vegetable prep: Shell the peas for the
  frittata; wash and dry the greens; trim and wash the
  asparagus for the pasta. Store what you're not cooking
  today in the fridge.

- Make the frittata (page 31). While it cooks on the
  stovetop, turn on the broiler and start the herbed
  mayonnaise (page 32) for the char.

- Put the frittata under the broiler.

- Finish the herbed mayo. Make the red wine vinaigrette
  (page 31). Whip the cream with the crème fraîche for
  the shortcakes. Put everything in the fridge, including
  the cooled rhubarb compote.

- Once the biscuits are completely cool, freeze half of
  them for next month.

- Give yourself a pat on the back and go for a walk.

Looking for a shortcut? Cut the shortcakes. Skip the
biscuits and the compote and you'll free up about an
hour of your time.

GROCERY LIST

PRODUCE

Asparagus, 2 pounds (900g)

Escarole, 1¼ pounds (570g)

Garlic, 3 cloves

Lemons, 4

Navel orange, 1 large

Rhubarb, 16 large stalks

Russet or sweet potatoes, 4

Salad greens, for 2 dinners

Shelled peas, ¾ cup (110g)

Yellow onion, 1 medium

Young spicy greens (like arugula
or mustard greens), 6 cups (120g)

HERBS

Chives, 1 bunch

Marjoram, 1 large sprig

SPICES

Nutmeg, 1 whole

PANTRY

Extra-virgin olive oil, 1½ cups plus
6 tablespoons (445ml), plus more
to have on hand

Good red wine vinegar,
3 tablespoons

Honey, for dessert

Hot pickled peppers, for lunch

Mayonnaise, ⅔ cup (160ml)

Flaky salt

Sherry vinegar, 1 tablespoon

Spaghetti, 1 pound (450g)

BAKING AISLE

All-purpose flour, 4 cups (500g)

Baking powder, 2 tablespoons

Best dark chocolate, 1 bar

Sugar, 1 tablespoon plus
2 teaspoons

Turbinado sugar, ¾ cup (150g)

DAIRY AND EGGS

Salted butter, 2 tablespoons,
plus more for serving

Crème fraîche, 3 tablespoons

Eggs, 18

Fontina, 4 ounces (115g), grated

Fresh whole-milk ricotta,
3 cups (735g)

Heavy cream, 3 to 4 cups
(710 to 950ml)

Parmesan, for serving

Sour cream, for garnish (optional)

MEAT AND SEAFOOD

Arctic char or salmon fillets,
skin on, 3 pounds (1.4kg)

Sausages or lamb merguez patties
(page 16), for dinner

Thinly sliced prosciutto or
soppressata, for lunch

BOOZE AND SUCH

Rosé, ¼ cup (60ml)

FREEZER

Vanilla ice cream, for dessert

BAKED GOODS

Baguette, 1

Crusty bread, 1 loaf

Store-bought cookies, for dessert

Cream Biscuits

You are either a baker or a cook. Very few people are both. Amanda is one of them, but I am not. I'm not saying I'm completely incompetent, but baking is not my strong suit; if I have to roll out dough or activate yeast, I start to sweat a little. So when I tell you these biscuits are both delicious and foolproof, I hope you will believe me. Marion Cunningham, who wrote *The Fannie Farmer Cookbook*, learned this recipe at one of James Beard's summer cooking classes in Seaside, Oregon, and then, thank goodness, she shared it with the world. Instead of buttermilk, the recipe calls for heavy cream, which rescues the biscuits from any threat of dryness. And more great news for nonbakers: Even after a serious kneading, the biscuits are as tender as can be. The recipe below is for a double batch of biscuits, so you can have plenty for this week and still freeze half for later.

Variations on a Theme The biscuits are perfect vehicles for other flavors: Try adding grated cheddar and chives, or chopped ham and Gruyère. I've also made mini biscuits with fresh dill and sandwiched them with smoked salmon and crème fraîche for a party.

How Amanda Eats Them "You should also put these biscuits on your weekend breakfast list. I serve them warm, with salted butter and honey. Try hot honey if you like to be more alert in the morning. This is also a good moment for Nutella."

MAKES 16 LARGE BISCUITS

4 cups (500g) all-purpose flour	1 teaspoon kosher salt
2 tablespoons baking powder	2 to 3 cups (475 to 710ml) heavy cream
2 teaspoons sugar	2 tablespoons salted butter, plus more for serving

1 Heat the oven to 425°F (220°C). Combine the flour, baking powder, sugar, and salt in a large bowl, stirring with a fork to blend.

2 Slowly add the cream to the dry ingredients, stirring constantly with the fork, until the dough clumps together. Only add as much cream as you need to make the dough come together. Knead gently on a lightly floured surface for 1 minute. Divide the dough in half and pat each half into a round about ½ inch (1.3cm) thick. Use a sharp knife to cut each round into 8 wedges.

3 Place the wedges 2 inches (5cm) apart on 2 ungreased baking sheets. Melt the butter and brush the tops of the biscuits with it. Bake until lightly browned, 12 to 15 minutes. Serve warm with plenty of salted butter or let cool completely on a rack and use for shortcakes (page 35) or freeze.

4 Keep any biscuits you plan to eat within 48 hours in an airtight container on the counter; reheat the biscuits for 5 minutes at 300°F (150°C), and no one will know you haven't just baked them. Wrap the remaining biscuits in a double layer of aluminum foil, put them in freezer-friendly zipper plastic bags, and freeze for up to 6 weeks. Thaw frozen biscuits on the counter for a couple of hours and reheat in a 375°F (190°C) oven for about 10 minutes.

Lunch: Frittata on a Biscuit with Herbed Mayonnaise and Hot Peppers

Toast **a split biscuit,** spread with some of the **herbed mayonnaise** (page 32) from the char, and add **a few hot pickled peppers.** Arrange **a couple of ¼-inch (6mm) slices of leftover frittata** (page 31) on one half of the biscuit, close it up, and wrap in aluminum foil.

Frittata with Peas, Spring Greens, and Ricotta

This frittata is quick and springy—the perfect thing when you need to impress without a lot of fuss. I call for fontina, but pretty much any semisoft cheese you have lying around will do. You can use these proportions as a jumping-off point for different combinations of ingredients: Try broccoli, pancetta, and cheddar, for example, or leeks, asparagus, and some Pecorino.

Frittata Dos and Don'ts Frittatas are forgiving, but there are some rules of the road. Before adding the eggs, you will need to parcook alliums and sturdier vegetables (such as potatoes, carrots, asparagus, and green beans), as well as raw meat like pancetta or bacon. A good rule of thumb is to aim for a 1-to-1 volume ratio of fillings to eggs and cheese. You can err on the side of more eggs, but don't up the filling or your frittata may fall apart on you.

SERVES 4 FOR 2 DINNERS, PLUS LEFTOVERS

2 tablespoons extra-virgin olive oil	18 eggs
1 medium yellow onion, diced	4 ounces (115g) fontina, grated
¾ cup (110g) shelled fresh peas	1 large sprig marjoram, leaves chopped
Kosher salt and freshly ground black pepper	10 chives
6 cups (120g) young greens (such as arugula, spinach, or mustard greens), coarsely chopped	1½ cups (375g) fresh ricotta

1 In a 12-inch (30cm) ovenproof nonstick or cast-iron skillet, warm the olive oil over medium heat. Add the onion and cook until it starts to soften, about 3 minutes. Add the peas and a large pinch of salt and cook for another minute or two, until the peas turn bright green.

2 Add the greens to the pan and cook briefly until they start to wilt. You may need to add them gradually if your pan won't fit them all; add half, and once they've wilted a bit, add the rest. Remove the pan from the heat.

3 In a large bowl, whisk together the eggs, fontina, marjoram, chives, and some salt and pepper. Return the pan to medium heat and pour in the eggs. Stir briefly and then cook the frittata, undisturbed, until the eggs are nearly set but still a little wet, about 10 minutes.

4 Heat the broiler with a rack about 4 inches (10cm) from the flame. Dollop the ricotta evenly over the top of the frittata. Slide the skillet under the broiler and cook until the eggs are set and the ricotta begins to brown, about 5 minutes. Let the frittata cool in the skillet. Cover tightly with plastic wrap, or cut into wedges and refrigerate for up to 5 days.

5 **The day of:** Serve the frittata warm, cold, or at room temperature. To reheat, place it on a baking sheet and warm in a 300°F (150°C) oven for about 10 minutes. Or use the microwave, but go easy. Nuked eggs get tough quickly.

The Best Red Wine Vinaigrette

I used to play the field when it came to vinaigrette. I'd flirt with different vinegars, use honey one night and maple syrup the next, sometimes going heavy on the Dijon mustard and other times favoring lemon juice. Finally, I knuckled down with a big bottle of olive oil with hopes of reaching vinaigrette nirvana. I discovered this simple formula:

Combine **3 tablespoons good red wine vinegar, 1 tablespoon sherry vinegar, 1 cup (240ml) extra-virgin olive oil, 2 teaspoons kosher salt**, and ¼ **teaspoon freshly ground black pepper** in a jar with a tight-fitting lid. Screw on the lid and shake vigorously until emulsified. Taste and adjust the seasoning. You will have about 1¼ cups (300ml) vinaigrette, which keeps in the fridge for up to 2 weeks. Let it come to room temperature and shake again before using.

Oven–Roasted Char with Herbed Mayonnaise

This method for cooking fish is both forgiving and dead simple. After painting the fillets with an herbed mayonnaise to protect them from the dry heat of the oven, you roast them very gently, removing the fish from the oven before it's cooked through. The broiler finishes the cooking and gives the fish a lovely burnished top. You can broil it just after roasting or broil leftover roasted fish a couple of days later—once you've caramelized the surface under the broiler, you won't remember you're eating leftovers.

SERVES 4 FOR 2 DINNERS, PLUS LEFTOVERS

HERBED MAYONNAISE

1 tablespoon finely grated lemon zest

2 tablespoons freshly squeezed lemon juice

2/3 cup (160ml) mayonnaise

3 tablespoons chopped fresh herbs (such as marjoram, chives, flat-leaf parsley, or dill), or use ramps if you have them

Kosher salt and freshly ground black pepper

CHAR

3 pounds (1.4kg) arctic char or salmon fillets, skin on

1 To make the herbed mayonnaise, combine the lemon zest and juice in a small bowl. Stir in the mayonnaise and herbs and season with salt and pepper. Keep in an airtight container in the fridge for up to 10 days.

2 Position a rack in the top third of the oven and heat it to 250°F (120°C). Sprinkle the flesh side of the fish fillets with salt and pepper and slather them with about 1/3 cup (80ml) of the herbed mayonnaise. Arrange the fish, skin side up, in a large, shallow baking dish (use two if necessary). Bake until it starts to look opaque around the edges, 15 to 20 minutes (cooking time will vary depending on the thickness of the fish). Put 2 pounds (900g) in a container and refrigerate for up to 3 days.

3 **The day of:** Heat the broiler and position the rack 4 to 5 inches (10 to 13cm) from the flame. With a spatula or your hands (the fish won't be very hot even if you're broiling it just after baking), gently turn over the fish so that the flesh side is facing up and slather each fillet with another spoonful of the mayonnaise. Broil the fish until the top starts to brown and it sizzles a bit, about a minute. (Don't go much longer, or it will overcook.) Serve immediately.

How to Bake a Potato

Like eggs, a baked potato can save the day. Heat the oven to 450°F (230°C). Rub **4 scrubbed russet or sweet potatoes** with **extra-virgin olive oil,** season with salt, and prick several times with a fork. Bake on an aluminum foil–lined baking sheet until the potatoes yield easily under a sharp knife, 45 to 60 minutes. Split and top with **ramp butter** (page 20) from the freezer, **salted butter, sour cream,** or whatever you please.

Rhubarb Shortcakes

These shortcakes began with a recipe for strawberry rhubarb compote from my friend Avi, whose mother makes it for Passover every year. Her recipe is solid and forthright: strawberries, rhubarb, sugar, water. I skip the strawberries and add a little more sugar, some orange peel, and a glug or two of rosé (why not?). The compote is tart and fresh, with just enough sugar to keep your mouth from puckering. It's good on top of plain Greek yogurt or ricotta, and it's even better with vanilla ice cream. To make shortcakes, I dollop it on my favorite biscuits (page 28) with freshly whipped cream mixed with a bit of crème fraîche.

If Rhubarb Is Nowhere in Sight You can make the compote for these shortcakes with frozen berries if rhubarb hasn't hit the markets yet. If you do, cut down on both the sugar and the cooking time by half.

MAKES 4 SHORTCAKES, PLUS EXTRA COMPOTE

COMPOTE

12 cups (1.5kg) chopped rhubarb (from about 16 large stalks), cut into 1-inch (2.5cm) pieces

¾ cup (150g) turbinado sugar

¼ cup (60ml) rosé

Peel from ½ large navel orange

Pinch of kosher salt

SHORTCAKES

1 cup (240ml) heavy whipping cream

3 tablespoons crème fraîche

1 tablespoon sugar

4 Cream Biscuits (page 28)

1 To make the compote, combine the rhubarb, turbinado sugar, rosé, orange peel, and salt in a saucepan and add ¼ cup (60ml) water. Bring to a simmer over medium heat, stirring to dissolve the sugar. Cook gently for 30 to 45 minutes, stirring occasionally. (You want the rhubarb to cook through and soften without losing all of its structure and the compote to thicken to the consistency of applesauce.) Let the compote cool, then remove and discard the orange peel and transfer the compote to an airtight container. Refrigerate for up to a week.

2 Whip the cream, crème fraîche, and sugar just until it starts to hold soft peaks. Transfer to a container and refrigerate for up to 3 days.

3 **The day of:** Split the biscuits and spoon a few tablespoons of both the compote and whipped cream onto the bottom halves. Add the biscuit tops and serve immediately.

Chocolate Toasts

This is an excellent back-pocket dessert or snack from *Cooking for Mr. Latte* (thanks, Amanda!). To make the toasts, heat the oven to 350°F (175°C). Cut **a slim baguette** into ¼-inch (6mm) slices and arrange them on a baking sheet. Top each with **a thin square of your best dark chocolate.** Bake for a few minutes, until the chocolate softens but still holds its basic shape. Sprinkle with **a few drops of good extra-virgin olive oil** and several grains of flaky salt. Serve the toasts warm, for dessert or a midafternoon snack. (If you make them for breakfast, no one will think less of you.)

Amanda's Spring

THE WEEK AHEAD

THE RECIPES

Roberta's Roasted Garlic Dressing 42

Sliced Chicken, Avocado, and Lemon Salad 42

Chicken Fingers 45

Chicken Finger Sandwich with Pickles and Special Sauce 45

Brandade 46

Brandade Pancakes 46

Lemony Pasta with Asparagus 49

Creamy Cow's Milk Cheese with Crackers and Asparagus Salad 49

Asparagus and Avocado Salad with Shaved Parmesan 49

Tad's Roasted Potatoes 50

Spring Vegetable Jumble 50

Rhubarb Galette 53

Roasted Rhubarb with Clementines and Cardamom 53

Jonathan's Roasted Asparagus 15

HOW THEY COME TOGETHER

DINNER ONE

Chicken Fingers

Tad's Roasted Potatoes

Jonathan's Roasted Asparagus with Roberta's Roasted Garlic Dressing

Rhubarb Galette

TO DO TODAY Reheat the chicken fingers and the potatoes. Dress the asparagus.

DINNER TWO

Brandade

Salad with Roberta's Roasted Garlic Dressing

Rhubarb Galette

TO DO TODAY Reheat the brandade. Make a salad and dress it.

DINNER THREE

Lemony Pasta with Asparagus

Affogato

TO DO TODAY Cook the pasta. Make the affogato = pour hot espresso over vanilla ice cream.

DINNER FOUR

Sliced Chicken, Avocado, and Lemon Salad

Roasted Rhubarb with Clementines and Cardamom plus vanilla ice cream

TO DO TODAY Put the salad together and dress it. Let the rhubarb come to room temperature before serving (or warm it in the microwave if you prefer it hot).

DINNER FIVE

Brandade Pancakes

Spring Vegetable Jumble

Good chocolates plus milk for the kids and bourbon for the adults

TO DO TODAY Make pancakes with the remaining brandade. Reheat the jumble.

BROWN BAG LUNCHES

Creamy Cow's Milk Cheese with Crackers and Asparagus Salad

Chicken Finger Sandwich with Pickles and Special Sauce

Asparagus and Avocado Salad with Shaved Parmesan

GAME PLAN

TO MAKE OVER THE WEEKEND

Roberta's Roasted Garlic
Dressing

Chicken Fingers

Brandade

Spring Vegetable Jumble

Tad's Roasted Potatoes

Half recipe of Jonathan's
Roasted Asparagus (page 15)

Rhubarb Galette

Roasted Rhubarb with
Clementines and Cardamom

HOW TO GET IT ALL DONE OVER THE WEEKEND

Plan on 3 to 3½ hours in the kitchen to focus on the
pleasures of trimming, chopping, and aromatherapy.

• On Friday night or Saturday morning, make the rhubarb
galette dough (page 53) and chill it in the fridge. Begin
soaking the salt cod for the brandade (page 46).

• When you're ready to cook, heat your oven to 450°F
(230°C). Slice the chicken (page 45), coat it with
panko, and roast it. Let the chicken fingers cool, then
store in the fridge.

• Roast 1½ pounds (680g) of the asparagus. The asparagus
needs just a few minutes to roast, so keep an eye on it.
When it's done, remove it from the oven and reduce
the heat to 375°F (190°C). Roast the potatoes (page
50)—and while they cook, roast the garlic for Roberta's
roasted garlic dressing (page 42) as well. Your oven is
now a multitasking queen. While they roast, prepare
the brandade (page 46) through step 6, and store it in
the fridge.

• Meanwhile, make the galette. Prepare the filling
(cutting the rhubarb for the roasted rhubarb as well
and setting it aside), then roll out the dough and
assemble the galette. Put it in the fridge until all
of the savory dishes are out of the oven. Then bake
the galette.

• Mix the rhubarb for roasted rhubarb (page 53)
with the other ingredients, and roast it while the
galette bakes.

• While the desserts bake, simmer the spring vegetable
jumble (page 50). Make the salad dressing in your food
processor. Aaaaannnnddd ... you're out!

If your time is short, meet your new best friend: the grill.
The grill can help you quickly trim down the cooking
you do on warm-weather weekends. Make the sides
and Roberta's dressing on the weekend, and instead of
chicken fingers and brandade, grill chicken thighs and
fish in the evenings. Also save the rhubarb desserts for
an easier week. This will trim your weekend cooking time
down to an hour.

GROCERY LIST

PRODUCE

Asparagus, 4 pounds (1.8kg)

Avocados, 2

Clementines, 3

Garlic, 1 head plus 14 cloves

Lemons, 4

Limes, 1

Meyer lemons, 2

Pre-washed salad greens like arugula, mizuna, or baby kale, 6 to 8 cups (120 to 160g)

Rhubarb, 16 stalks

White potatoes, 4½ pounds (2kg)

Yellow onions, 2

HERBS

Basil, chives, or tarragon, for garnish

Oregano, 3 teaspoons finely chopped from 5 or 6 sprigs

Sage, 1 bunch

Thyme, 1 bunch

SPICES

Allspice berries, 3

Bay leaf, 1

Black peppercorns, 10

Cayenne, a pinch

Clove, 1

Ground cardamom, a pinch

Ground cinnamon, 2 pinches

Nutmeg, 1 whole

PANTRY

Anchovy fillets, 5

Cider vinegar, 1½ teaspoons

Crackers, for lunch

Dijon mustard, 2 tablespoons plus more for lunch

Extra-virgin olive oil, 2½ cups (590ml)

Hot sauce, for lunch

Ketchup, for lunch

Mayonnaise, for lunch

Panko, 5 cups (300g)

Pickles, for lunch

Coarse salt

Flaky salt

Sherry vinegar, 2 tablespoons

Spaghetti, 1 pound (450g)

Vegetable oil, ¾ cup (175ml)

White wine vinegar, 1½ tablespoons

BAKING AISLE

All-purpose flour, about 3¼ cups (405g)

Baking powder, ⅛ teaspoon

Good chocolates, for dessert

Sugar, 1¾ cups (350g)

DAIRY AND EGGS

Unsalted butter, 1½ cups plus ½ tablespoon (350g)

Cream cheese, 3 ounces (85g)

Creamy cow's milk cheese, for lunch

Crème fraîche or heavy cream, ½ cup plus 2 tablespoons (150ml)

Eggs, 8

Fresh ricotta, ½ cup (125g)

Milk, 1½ cups (355ml), plus more for sipping

Parmesan, 1 cup (100g) grated from a wedge, plus more for serving

MEAT AND SEAFOOD

Bacon, 4 slices

Boneless, skinless chicken thighs or breasts, 3 pounds (1.4kg)

Boneless, skinless salt cod, 1½ pounds (680g)

BOOZE AND SUCH

Bourbon, for sipping

Espresso, for dessert

FREEZER

Frozen artichoke hearts, 1 (9-ounce/260g) box (no sauce)

Frozen peas, 1½ cups (210g)

Vanilla ice cream, for dessert

BAKED GOODS

Croutons, for lunch

Soft rolls, for lunch

Roberta's Roasted Garlic Dressing

Adapted with admiration from *Roberta's Cookbook*. My kids eat this creamy, pungent dressing by the spoonful. They've been known to dip everything in it, including steak. To make it, you roast a head of garlic to sweeten and mellow it, then blend it with fresh garlic, a dose of bracing vinegars, egg yolks, anchovy, and lemon. The resulting dressing is dense like a green goddess—so much so that I've used it as a mayonnaise on sandwiches.

Merrill's Minus "Some people in my house (we won't name names) are a little sensitive about 'fishy fish.' Even if you decide to omit the anchovies, as I sometimes do, this dressing will still rock your world. I've also left out the egg yolks with no ill effects."

MAKES 1½ CUPS (355ML)

1 head garlic, with 1 clove peeled and set aside

¾ cup plus 1 tablespoon (190ml) extra-virgin olive oil, plus a splash for the garlic

2 tablespoons Dijon mustard

2 tablespoons sherry vinegar

1½ tablespoons white wine vinegar

2 egg yolks

5 anchovy fillets

Juice of ½ lemon, plus more if needed

Kosher salt and freshly ground black pepper

1 Heat your oven to 375°F (190°C). Cut ¼ inch (6mm) off the head of garlic and place the head, cut side up, on a big square of aluminum foil. Give it a splash of water and a splash of olive oil. Bring the corners of the foil up over the garlic to make a loosely wrapped little package. Bake for about 45 minutes. Remove the garlic from the oven and let it cool in the foil. Squeeze the roasted garlic out of 4 or 5 cloves and set the rest aside for the brandade (if you're not making the brandade, the garlic is really good spread on grilled bread with salted butter).

2 Put the roasted garlic, the raw garlic clove, mustard, vinegars, egg yolks, anchovies, and lemon juice into a blender or food processor and blend for 30 seconds or until combined.

3 With the machine running, add the olive oil in a slow, steady stream until it's incorporated and the dressing looks smooth. Taste and add salt, pepper, and more lemon juice as desired. The dressing will keep for a week in the refrigerator.

Sliced Chicken, Avocado, and Lemon Salad

Mix together a few **handfuls of lettuce** (pre-washed arugula or kale works well) and spread them in a large, shallow serving dish. Scatter **sliced chicken fingers** (page 45), **avocado wedges, roasted potatoes** (page 50), and **crumbled bacon** over the greens. Top the salad with **supremes from a Meyer lemon.** Spoon **Roberta's dressing** (above) over the salad and let someone mix it at the table.

Chicken Fingers

Full disclosure: This recipe for the best chicken fingers on earth is Merrill's. Made with chicken thighs (more flavorful than breasts), seasoned with both Parmesan and oregano, and rolled in a bed of crisp panko, they please like chicken fingers are meant to, but don't feel dumbed down. I make them so often that I snuck them in among my menus. Merrill didn't notice until we were almost done with the book, and she kindly let it slide. I know who's going on runs to the coffee shop this year.

Merrill's Childhood Chicken Fingers "I grew up eating these chicken fingers, and requesting them for every birthday. (I also discovered early on that, like pizza, they're just as good cold, when they've lost their crispness.) Add leftovers to a salad or sandwich (see Amanda's recipes below and on the previous page), or warm them gently, cut them into bite-size pieces, and scatter them over a pizza bianca with fresh arugula and chile oil."

MAKES ROUGHLY 3 DOZEN CHICKEN FINGERS

1½ cups (190g) all-purpose flour

Salt and freshly ground black pepper

3 cups (215g) panko

1 cup (100g) grated Parmesan

3 teaspoons finely chopped fresh oregano

6 large eggs

3 pounds (1.4kg) boneless, skinless chicken thighs (or breasts), cut lengthwise into 1-inch strips

Vegetable oil

About 4 tablespoons unsalted butter

1 Heat your oven to 450°F (230°C). Put the flour in a medium bowl and season generously with salt and pepper—stir through with a fork.

2 Put the panko in a second medium bowl, add the Parmesan and oregano, and season generously with salt and pepper. Stir through until everything is well-combined.

3 Crack the eggs into a third bowl and beat them lightly with the fork. You will need two large baking sheets for cooking the chicken. If you have a third baking sheet, use it to set the coated chicken on top of; otherwise use a couple of large plates. Drop a handful of the chicken strips into the seasoned flour, toss to coat, then shake off any excess. Dip them all at once in the egg mixture, folding them into the egg to thoroughly coat them; and then in the panko, pressing lightly so that the panko adheres. As you finish each handful, set them out on the baking sheet or plates. Doing this a handful at a time is a little messier but much faster; get in there and give it a try!

4 Generously coat the base of two baking sheets with vegetable oil; add two tablespoons butter to each. Place the baking sheets in the oven to heat. When the butter has finished foaming and just starts to brown, gently lay the chicken strips on the baking sheets. Cook for 10 minutes, until the bottoms are golden brown and crispy. Use tongs to turn them over and cook for another 10 minutes, until both sides are evenly browned and the chicken is cooked through. Add more butter and oil as needed.

5 Let the chicken fingers cool, then store in a covered container in the fridge.

6 **The day of:** Reheat the chicken fingers uncovered on a baking sheet in a 300°F (150°C) oven.

Lunch: Chicken Finger Sandwich with Pickles and Special Sauce

Make special sauce by combining **mayonnaise** with **a little Dijon mustard, ketchup,** and **hot sauce.** Layer **a soft roll** with special sauce, thinly sliced **chicken finger, pickles,** and **greens.**

Brandade

If you've never made brandade—a garlicky potato and salt cod gratin—I want you to try it. Working with salt cod is remarkably easy, and it's pleasing to be able to cook fish that you keep in your pantry. I buy salt cod at Whole Foods, and as long as you have a well-stocked spice cabinet, brandade is a nifty, thrifty dish. Some versions are loose, almost like dip. This one (adapted from a recipe by David Tanis in the *New York Times*) is a heartier casserole—buttery and fragrant, with some kick—designed for dinner.

MAKES ENOUGH FOR 2 DINNERS, EACH SERVING 4

1½ pounds (680g) skinless, boneless salt cod

1½ cups (355ml) milk

2 thyme sprigs

1 bay leaf

10 black peppercorns

3 allspice berries

1 clove

1½ pounds (680g) white potatoes, peeled and cut in 1-inch (2.5cm) cubes

8 cloves garlic, peeled

Leftover roasted garlic cloves, from Roberta's Dressing (page 42)

3 tablespoons extra-virgin olive oil

1 teaspoon finely grated lemon zest

Pinch of cayenne

Large pinch of grated nutmeg

½ cup plus 2 tablespoons (150ml) crème fraîche or heavy cream

Kosher salt and freshly ground black pepper

4 tablespoons (60g) cold unsalted butter

¾ cup (45g) panko

1 Rinse the salt cod well and rub off any salt. Soak in 2 quarts (1.9L) cold water for at least 8 hours. Drain and change the water every few hours (an overnight soak without changing is fine).

2 In a saucepan, heat the milk plus 1½ cups (355ml) water over medium-high heat. Add the cod, thyme, bay leaf, peppercorns, allspice berries, and clove. Adjust the heat to maintain a bare simmer. Cook until the fish flakes easily, about 15 minutes. Remove the fish and hold at room temperature.

3 Meanwhile, in a separate pot, cover the potatoes with water and bring to a boil. Add the garlic and a good pinch of salt. Boil the potatoes until they're soft, about 15 minutes, then drain the potatoes, reserving the cooking liquid.

4 Put the potatoes and roasted garlic in a large bowl. With your fingers, flake the cod on top. With a potato masher, roughly blend the potatoes and cod. Add the olive oil, lemon zest, cayenne, and nutmeg to taste. Switch to a wooden spoon and stir in ½ cup (120ml) of the crème fraîche and beat well to combine. Beat in about ½ cup (120ml) of the potato cooking liquid (strained) to lighten the mixture so it has the texture of soft mashed potatoes. Taste and adjust the seasoning; it will probably need salt and pepper.

5 Use 1 tablespoon of the butter to grease a low-sided 3-quart (2.8L) baking dish. Transfer the brandade mixture to the buttered dish and smooth with a spatula. Paint the top with the remaining 2 tablespoons crème fraîche and sprinkle with the panko. Dot the top with the remaining 3 tablespoons butter. Cover and store in the fridge.

6 **The day of:** Bring the brandade to room temperature, then heat the oven to 400°F (200°C). Bake until golden and bubbling, about 20 minutes.

Brandade Pancakes

Form **leftover brandade** into hamburger-size pancakes, dip into a plate of **panko**, and press the panko all over to coat. Fry the pancakes in **extra-virgin olive oil,** in a nonstick pan, until golden brown and warmed through, about 3 minutes per side. (See finished dish on page 51.)

Lemony Pasta with Asparagus

I love lemony spaghetti as much as I love asparagus, so I thought I'd combine these two flavors in this dead-simple pasta. No blanching is necessary for the asparagus—unless it's directly from a farm and contains grit, in which case blanch you must! Just sauté the asparagus in olive oil while the spaghetti cooks, tossing in garlic and lemon zest. Reiterate the lemon flavor later on by sprinkling the juice over the spaghetti. Grate some Parmesan, dollop on some ricotta, and your vibrant and grassy dinner is ready.

Merrill's Riffs "If asparagus isn't in season, I like to make this pasta with broccoli cut into bite-size florets, or even small brussels sprouts, quartered."

SERVES 4

Salt and freshly ground black pepper

2 pounds (900g) asparagus, trimmed

6 tablespoons (90ml) extra-virgin olive oil

2 cloves garlic, smashed

Finely grated zest and juice of 2 lemons (Meyer, if possible)

1 pound (450g) spaghetti

4 tablespoons (60g) unsalted butter

Grated Parmesan, for serving

½ cup (125g) fresh ricotta

1 Bring a large pot of generously salted water to a boil. Cut the asparagus where the tip and stalk meet. Cut the stalks into ½-inch (1.3cm) pieces.

2 Meanwhile, warm the oil in a large sauté pan over medium heat. Add the garlic and cook for 1 minute, until softened on the edges. Add the asparagus and season with salt. Cook, stirring to turn and distribute the asparagus, until crisp-tender, 6 to 8 minutes. Stir in the lemon zest. Remove from the heat.

3 When the water comes to a boil, add the spaghetti and cook until al dente. Scoop out about ⅓ cup (80ml) pasta water and set aside. Drain the spaghetti and add it to the asparagus along with the butter. Place over medium heat. Use tongs to toss and melt the butter. Add half of the lemon juice and toss again. Taste and adjust the seasoning, adding more lemon juice and salt if needed. If the spaghetti is dry, fold in some of the pasta water.

4 Divide among 4 plates. Season with pepper and sprinkle with Parmesan. Drop a dollop of ricotta on top. Devour.

Lunch: Creamy Cow's Milk Cheese with Crackers and Asparagus Salad

Slice **roasted asparagus** (page 15) into 1-inch (2.5cm) pieces. Pack the asparagus with a **lemon wedge** separately from the **cheese** and **crackers,** so nothing gets mushy!

Lunch: Asparagus and Avocado Salad with Shaved Parmesan

Thinly slice the **roasted asparagus** (page 15). Combine with **chopped avocado** and **croutons,** if you have good ones around (otherwise something like cooked quinoa or barley works well). Season with **extra-virgin olive oil** and **lime juice.** Top with **shaved Parmesan.**

Tad's Roasted Potatoes

This is my husband Tad's specialty. His first version of this recipe was pure potato, but over time, he added chopped yellow onion, which underlines the earthy sweetness in the potatoes.

Tad roasts the potatoes and onions in two cast-iron pans with lightly smashed whole garlic cloves and whatever herbs are in the fridge. He blankets them with olive oil, scatters on coarse salt and coarsely ground pepper, and then sticks the pans in a hot oven. The real secret isn't this technique, though. It's using potatoes that have been hanging around in the pantry or fridge for a month or two, as they brown more deeply. (See finished dish on page 44.)

Merrill's Rules of the Roast "I find that most starchy root vegetables roast perfectly well at any temperature between 350°F and 425°F (175°C and 220°C). They'll take a bit longer at a lower heat and lose a little more moisture from the extra time spent in the oven (which means they'll be extra crunchy). They'll brown faster in a hotter oven; cover them with foil if they're getting too dark. This adaptability makes roasted vegetables great oven mates for other dishes that are more finicky, like cookies, saving you valuable cooking time."

SERVES 4 AS A SIDE DISH, WITH ENOUGH LEFTOVERS FOR THE CHICKEN SALAD

3 pounds (1.4kg) old white potatoes, scrubbed and cut into ¾-inch (2cm) cubes

2 medium yellow onions, coarsely chopped

Extra-virgin olive oil

12 herb sprigs (any combination of thyme, sage, and rosemary)

4 cloves garlic, skins left on and lightly smashed

Kosher salt and coarsely ground black pepper

1 Heat the oven to 375°F (190°C). Spread the potatoes and onions in two well-seasoned 12-inch cast-iron pans—they should fit comfortably in one layer. Douse with olive oil, like you're marinating them. Add the herbs and garlic and season generously with salt and pepper. Toss the potatoes a few times to mix in the herbs and seasoning.

2 Roast in the oven. Let the potatoes get nicely browned on the bottoms, about 25 minutes, before scraping up and turning them. Continue roasting, turning the potatoes every 10 minutes or so, until they are well caramelized and tender, another 35 to 45 minutes.

3 **The day of:** Reheat the potatoes in a cast-iron skillet in a 300°F (150°C) oven for about 15 minutes.

Spring Vegetable Jumble

In a large saucepan, combine **1 (9-ounce/260g) box frozen artichoke hearts** (no sauce) with **¼ cup (60ml) extra-virgin olive oil** and place over medium heat. When the artichokes are thawed and their juice has mostly cooked off, 5 to 10 minutes, add **8 ounces (225g) trimmed and thinly sliced asparagus** and **1½ cups (210g) frozen peas or lima beans.** Bring to an active simmer over medium-high heat. Season with salt and pepper. Cook just until the asparagus is tender, about 5 minutes. Top with **chopped chives, basil, or tarragon.**

The day of: Warm the jumble in a saucepan over medium heat, stirring often. Serve with the brandade pancakes (page 46).

Rhubarb Galette

This galette dough is one I've used and written about many times. Made with cream cheese, it's extremely tender and delicious. The original recipe comes from Rose Levy Beranbaum's *The Pie and Pastry Bible*. I've slimmed down the process to make it faster, and here I've used the dough as the nest for a bright rhubarb filling.

Pastry Rules If there's a premade pastry dough you like, buy it. Or if you have a favorite pastry recipe, by all means, use that. To feel even more organized, double the recipe and freeze half of the dough so you can easily pull off another galette weeks from now.

Merrill's Pear Variation "In the fall, I like to make this with pears. If they're ripe and you slice them thinly enough, they soften beautifully within the relatively short cooking time. To make 4 to 5 cups (560 to 700g) of sliced pears (preferably Anjou), peel and thinly slice (no thicker than ¼ inch/6mm) 3 or 4 pears. Use the pears in place of the rhubarb for the filling, reduce the sugar to ¼ cup (50g), and add a few pinches of ground nutmeg. Bake following the instructions for the rhubarb galette. Don't forget to pass a pitcher of cream with the galette, which I reheat in a 300°F (150°C) oven for 5 to 10 minutes before serving."

MAKES ONE 12-INCH (30CM) GALETTE

CRUST
1⅓ cups (165g) all-purpose flour

⅛ teaspoon salt

⅛ teaspoon baking powder

3 ounces (85g) cold cream cheese, cut into cubes

½ cup (110g) cold unsalted butter, cut into cubes

1½ tablespoons ice water

1½ teaspoons cider vinegar

FILLING
5 cups (610g) sliced rhubarb (from about 12 stalks)

1¼ cups (250g) sugar

5 tablespoons (35g) all-purpose flour

2 pinches of ground cinnamon

1½ tablespoons unsalted butter

1 To make the crust, place the flour, salt, and baking powder in a food processor and process for a few seconds to combine. Add the cream cheese to the flour. Process for about 20 seconds, or until the mixture resembles coarse meal. Add the butter and pulse until none of the butter is larger than the size of a pea.

2 Add the ice water and vinegar. Pulse until most of the butter is reduced to the size of small peas, and the mixture holds together when pressed between two fingers. Place the dough onto a work surface, knead it together, and press into a flat disk.

3 Cover the dough in plastic wrap and refrigerate for at least 45 minutes, preferably overnight.

4 Heat your oven to 375°F (190°C). To make the filling, blend the rhubarb, sugar, flour, and cinnamon in a large bowl.

5 Roll out the dough into a 13-inch (33cm) circle that's ⅛ inch (3mm) thick and transfer to a baking sheet. Spread the filling on top, leaving 2 to 3 inches (5 to 7.5cm) of dough around the edge. Fold the edges over the filling to form a border. Dot with the butter. Bake until the filling is bubbling and the edges are golden brown, about 30 minutes.

Roasted Rhubarb with Clementines and Cardamom

Juice **2 clementines;** slice **another clementine** into 8 wedges. Cut **4 rhubarb stalks** into 3-inch (7.5cm) pieces and toss them with the clementine wedges and **¼ cup (50g) sugar** and **a large pinch of cardamom.** Spread out in a large baking dish and dot with **1 tablespoon butter.** Roast at 375°F (190°C) until the rhubarb is beginning to brown on the edges and is tender, about 45 minutes. Immediately sprinkle the reserved clementine juice over the roasted rhubarb. Serve warm or at room temperature with **vanilla ice cream.**

monday
asparagus revueltos
chocolate ice cream
w/ brioche + almonds

tuesday
chicken w/ chermoula
spring veg w/ garlic
scape ricotta
schlumpf

wednesday
steak tacos
lime ice cream

thursday
grain salad
schlumpf

friday
garlic scape
quesadillas
radishes w/ salt
lime pie ice cream

on sunday
grain salad
marinate chicken
garlic scape pesto
wash turnips, radishes,
etc.
schlumpf
toast brioche
lime ice cream

THE WEEK AHEAD

DINNER TWO

Chicken Cutlets with Charmoula
and Preserved Lemon

Spring Vegetables with Salt or
Garlic Scape Ricotta

Bread

Schlumpf

TO DO TODAY Stir together the ricotta dip and
serve alongside a plate of sliced turnips, radishes,
and carrots. Grill the chicken and serve with the
charmoula and bread. Recrisp the schlumpf
under the broiler.

THE RECIPES

Asparagus Revueltos 58

Grain Salad with Asparagus,
Baby Turnips, Feta, and
Preserved Lemon Dressing 61

Spring Vegetables with Salt
or Garlic Scape Ricotta 61

Chicken Cutlets with
Charmoula and Preserved
Lemon 62

Steak and Charmoula
on a Kaiser Roll 62

Garlic Scape Pesto
Quesadillas 65

Schlumpf 66

Chocolate Ice Cream with
Toasted Brioche Crumbs,
Almonds, and Salt 66

Low-Maintenance Steak
Tacos 86

Pickled Onions 86

Lime Ice Cream 268

Lime Pie Ice Cream 268

DINNER THREE

Low-Maintenance Steak Tacos
with Pickled Onions

Lime Ice Cream

TO DO TODAY Set out the cilantro, pickled onion,
sliced avocado, and hot sauce. Broil or grill the
steak and toast the tortillas.

DINNER FOUR

Grain Salad with Asparagus, Baby Turnips,
Feta, and Preserved Lemon Dressing

Schlumpf

TO DO TODAY In a serving bowl, mix together the
salad ingredients and dress the salad. Recrisp
the schlumpf under the broiler.

HOW THEY COME TOGETHER

DINNER ONE

Asparagus Revueltos

Toasted country bread

Chocolate Ice Cream with Toasted Brioche
Crumbs, Almonds, and Salt

TO DO TODAY Sauté the asparagus, saving half
for the grain salad you'll make later in the week.
In the same pan, finish cooking the revueltos.
After dinner, serve up the ice cream.

DINNER FIVE

Garlic Scape Pesto Quesadillas

Radishes with salt

Lime Pie Ice Cream

TO DO TODAY Whip up the lime pie ice cream;
also whip cream. Chill both. Assemble and cook
the quesadillas.

BROWN BAG LUNCHES

Steak and Charmoula on a Kaiser Roll

Grain salad with more charmoula

GAME PLAN

TO MAKE OVER THE WEEKEND

Grain Salad with Asparagus, Baby Turnips, Feta, and Preserved Lemon Dressing

Chicken Cutlets with Charmoula and Preserved Lemon

Garlic Scape Pesto (page 123)

Pickled Onions (page 86)

Spring Vegetables with Salt or Garlic Scape Ricotta

Schlumpf with rhubarb

Chocolate Ice Cream with Toasted Brioche Crumbs, Almonds, and Salt

Lime Ice Cream (page 268)

OFF WE GO!

This week is a zippy 90 minutes in the kitchen.

- Mix together the lime ice cream base (page 268) and freeze in a container, stirring now and then until it firms up.

- Scrub the baby turnips, radishes, and carrots, and wash and spin dry the cilantro. Store, layered between paper towels, in a plastic bag or container.

- Pull out your food processor and make the charmoula (page 62), followed by the garlic scape pesto (page 123). Use half of the charmoula to marinate the chicken, then store the marinated chicken and the remaining charmoula (in a separate container) in the fridge. Put the garlic scape pesto in the fridge as well. Feel the power of having completed two major menu components in less than 30 minutes.

- Heat your oven to 350°F (175°C). Get the rhubarb schlumpf (page 66) ready to go in the oven. Say "schlumpf" aloud a few times as you're making it. Try not to laugh. Then bake the schlumpf. Feel the schlumpf. BE THE SCHLUMPF!

- Bring a large pot of salted water to a boil. Cook the grains for the salad (page 61). Drain and store in a container in the fridge.

- Meanwhile, toast the brioche crumbs for the chocolate ice cream (page 66).

- Make the pickled onions (page 86), then put into a container and store in the fridge.

- Get outside and enjoy the day!

Looking for a speedier version? Pass on making the dessert—put together the lime pie ice cream (page 268) with store-bought ice cream (lime if you can find it) and pick up cookies for the nights the schlumpf is on the menu. Also skip the garlic scape pesto; instead, double the charmoula and use half for the quesadillas. The rest is a breeze, about 1 hour of your time.

GROCERY LIST

PRODUCE

Arugula, 8 cups (160g) loosely packed

Asparagus, 1 pound (450g)

Avocado, 1

Baby carrots (real baby carrots!), a few for dipping

Baby turnips, 2 bunches

Garlic, 1 clove

Garlic scapes, ½ cup (50g) chopped, from about 3 scapes

Lemons, 4

Limes, 7

Radishes, 1 bunch

Red onions, 2

Rhubarb, 8 cups (960g) sliced from about 20 stalks, or 8 cups (1.2kg) fresh or frozen blueberries

Scallions, 2

HERBS

Cilantro, 2 bunches

Flat-leaf parsley leaves, 1 cup (20g)

SPICES

Aleppo pepper or crushed red pepper flakes, large pinches

Ground ancho chile or ground chipotle, ¼ teaspoon

Ground cinnamon, ⅜ teaspoon

Ground cumin, ¾ teaspoon

Red pepper flakes, a pinch

PANTRY

Cider vinegar, 1½ cups (355ml)

Dijon mustard, 1 tablespoon

Extra-virgin olive oil, 2¼ cups (530ml)

Graham crackers, 3

Hot sauce (we like Cholula), for seasoning

Jasmine rice, 1 cup (185g)

Preserved lemon, 4 tablespoons chopped

Quinoa, ½ cup (85g)

Red wine vinegar, 2 tablespoons

Flaky salt

Unsweetened shredded dried coconut, ¾ cup (60g)

Wheat berries, 1 cup (180g) soft (or hard)

BAKING AISLE

All-purpose flour, 2¼ cups (280g)

Almonds, a handful, chopped

Honey, 2 tablespoons

Roasted and salted almonds, 3 tablespoons

Light brown sugar, 1 cup (220g)

Sugar, 1¾ cups plus 2 tablespoons (375g)

Pure vanilla extract, ¼ teaspoon

DAIRY AND EGGS

Salted butter, 1 cup plus 2 tablespoons (250g)

Crumbled feta, ½ cup (75g)

Eggs, 10

Fresh ricotta, ¾ cup (190g)

Sharp cheddar cheese, 4 cups (440g) grated from a wedge

Heavy cream, 3½ cups (830ml), plus more for whipped cream

Mayonnaise, for lunch

Pecorino, ⅓ cup (35g) grated from a wedge

MEAT AND SEAFOOD

Boneless, skinless chicken cutlets, 6

Flank steak, 1½ to 2 pounds (680 to 900g)

FREEZER

Chocolate ice cream, for dessert

BAKED GOODS

Brioche, 1 loaf (freeze the extra)

Country bread, for dinner

Kaiser rolls, for lunch

White corn tortillas, 28 small

Asparagus Revueltos

Revueltos are scrambled eggs' raggedy Spanish cousin. I prefer them to their tidier American counterparts, as the eggs are less uniform and the flavors more pure—no milk, cream, or cheese gets in the way. Buy the best asparagus and eggs you can find, and you'll see that even the simplest quick dinner can be exceptional.

A Million Variations Keep this technique in your back pocket for weeks when you have a less organized life menu. Try it with garlic scapes or pancetta or shrimp or chorizo or a handful of mushrooms.

SERVES 4

10 eggs

2 tablespoons extra-virgin olive oil

1 pound (450g) asparagus, trimmed and thinly sliced into ⅛-inch (3mm) circles

Pinch of Aleppo pepper

Salt and freshly ground black pepper

1 Crack the eggs into a large bowl; do not stir. Warm the olive oil over medium-high heat in a 12-inch (30cm) well-seasoned skillet or a nonstick pan. When it shimmers, add the asparagus and toss to coat in the oil. Add the Aleppo pepper and season with salt and black pepper. Sauté until crisp-tender, about 2 minutes, then remove half of the asparagus to a container. Let this portion cool and store in the fridge for the grain salad (page 61) later in the week.

2 Keep the remaining asparagus in the pan. Increase the heat to high and pour in the eggs. Working very quickly, use a spatula to break up the eggs and move them around the pan. Season with salt. You will get sheets and curds and streaks of yolk and white—exactly what you want. The eggs are done when they're still soft and glistening, not raw yet not fully cooked, about 2 minutes. Serve immediately.

Grain Salad with Asparagus, Baby Turnips, Feta, and Preserved Lemon Dressing

I went on a grain cooking binge this past year, and one of the things I learned is that there's no need to cook grains separately. I get bored eating a single grain, so I like salads that mix wheat berries, rice, barley, and what have you (quinoa—a seed, technically, I'm looking at you!). The trick to cooking them together is to work out the time each grain needs and then add the grains sequentially to the boiling water. They'll more or less finish cooking at the same time and you'll have just a single pot to wash.

SERVES 4 FOR DINNER, PLUS LUNCHES

PRESERVED LEMON DRESSING	SALAD
¼ cup (60ml) extra-virgin olive oil	Salt
2 tablespoons charmoula (from Chicken Cutlets, page 62)	1 cup (180g) soft (or hard) wheat berries
1 tablespoon chopped preserved lemon	1 cup (185g) jasmine rice
1 tablespoon Dijon mustard	½ cup (85g) quinoa, rinsed
Juice of 1 lemon	8 ounces (225g) sautéed thinly sliced asparagus (from Asparagus Revueltos, page 58)
Pinch of sugar	8 baby turnips, scrubbed and cut into small wedges
Lots of freshly ground black pepper	Leftover chicken or steak, cut into small pieces (you'll want a cup or two)
	½ cup (75g) crumbled feta

1 To make the dressing, combine all of the ingredients plus lots of freshly ground pepper in a mason jar. Cover the jar and shake it like a madman! Taste and adjust the seasoning. Store in the fridge until later in the week.

2 Bring a large pot of salted water to a boil. Add the wheat berries and cook at a gentle boil for 30 minutes. Stir in the rice, then 5 minutes later, stir in the quinoa. Cook the grains until they're tender but not soft, about 5 minutes more. Drain and let cool. Store in the fridge for later in the week.

3 **The day of:** Get out a big bowl and mix together the cooked grains, asparagus, turnips, and chicken or steak. Give the dressing a good shake to re-emulsify it, then pour half of it over the grains. Fold together. Taste the salad, and add more dressing as you see fit. Top with feta.

Spring Vegetables with Salt or Garlic Scape Ricotta

You could call this one of my warm-weather cop-outs if you're a glass-half-empty person, or see it as an appreciation of spring produce if you usually see the glass half full. I'm going with the latter interpretation. Turnips, radishes, cucumbers, baby greens, beans, peppers, and carrots are so tender and sweet this time of year, my preferred way of eating them is dipped into flaky sea salt. We eat them either before the main course or with it. With **turnips** and **radishes,** I wash and trim them, but keep the greens on if they're in good shape. If you're using beans, blanch them. **Carrots,** I scrub (don't peel), trim, and slice, depending on their size. Great vegetables need no other accompaniment than salt, but if you like, you can add **ground chile** to the salt and put a dish of **extra-virgin olive oil** on the side.

If you want to make a tiny bit more effort, you can serve spring vegetables with garlic scape ricotta: In a shallow serving bowl, mix together ¾ **cup (190g) ricotta** with **a tablespoon of extra-virgin olive oil** and **3 tablespoons garlic scape pesto** (page 123) or **charmoula** (page 62). Season to taste.

Chicken Cutlets with Charmoula and Preserved Lemon

Charmoula is a North African green sauce scented with preserved lemons, cumin, chile, and garlic. You'll want to slather it on everything. On many a summer week, when I don't have a complete menu planned and am feeling short on ideas, I'll make a green sauce of some sort—like this one or the green sauce on page 198. Then I know all I have to do is cook fish (like Merrill's baked fish on page 259) or a good steak (like her grilled steak on page 120).

I first came across this chicken dish on Food52, in a recipe contributed by Lisanne Weinberg Lubitz. Her version includes a recipe for curing and cooking lemons with a cinnamon stick and bay leaves. It's an exceptional recipe but one that I found too taxing for efficient weekend cooking, so I've revamped it to skip the lemon preservation.

Also, if you need to break free from chicken cutlets, go crazy and try boneless thighs!

SERVES 4, WITH LEFTOVERS

CHARMOULA

1 cup (20g) packed fresh flat-leaf parsley leaves

1 cup (20g) packed fresh cilantro leaves and stems

2 scallions, trimmed and chopped

1 clove garlic, peeled

¼ teaspoon ground cumin

⅛ teaspoon ground cinnamon

¾ teaspoon kosher salt

Large pinch of Aleppo pepper or crushed red pepper flakes

Finely grated zest of 1 lemon

¾ cup (175ml) extra-virgin olive oil

2 tablespoons red wine vinegar

CHICKEN

6 boneless, skinless chicken cutlets

3 tablespoons chopped preserved lemon

Salt and freshly ground black pepper

1 To make the charmoula, combine the parsley, cilantro, scallions, garlic, cumin, cinnamon, salt, Aleppo pepper, and lemon zest in the bowl of a food processor. With the machine running, add the olive oil in a slow, steady stream, stopping once or twice to scrape down the sides of the bowl. Pulse in the vinegar. The charmoula should be loose enough to drop from a spoon; if not, add more oil. Taste and adjust the seasoning. Store one-third of the charmoula in a container for the grain salad and other uses. Set aside the remaining charmoula while you prepare the chicken cutlets.

2 Flatten the chicken cutlets between sheets of parchment paper until ⅓ inch (8mm) thick. Mix half of the reserved charmoula with the preserved lemon and spread it all over the cutlets. Cover and place in the fridge until you're ready to eat. Reserve the remaining charmoula for serving.

3 **The day of:** Heat the grill to medium-high. Grill the cutlets, turning once when the bottom side is browned and cooked around the edges, about 3 minutes. Grill until just cooked through, another 3 minutes, then put the cutlets on a serving platter. Top with a few spoonfuls of the reserved charmoula and season with salt and pepper.

Ingredient Swap Charmoula and lamb make good bedfellows; try lamb shoulder chops if you're looking for an alternative to chicken.

Get-Ahead Tip You can grill these cutlets over the weekend. The chicken can be rewarmed in a covered dish in a 250°F (120°C) oven, or enjoyed at room temperature. Top with the reserved charmoula at the table.

Lunch: Steak and Charmoula on a Kaiser Roll

Spread both halves of a **kaiser roll** with **mayonnaise** and **charmoula**. Lay down a few slices of leftover **flank steak** (page 86). Top with **pickled onions** (page 86) and press the two halves together.

Garlic Scape Pesto Quesadillas

These truly take no time or brainpower. You've probably made many a quesadilla in your life, but you might not have thought to toss garlic scape pesto into a tortilla with cheese. If you don't feel like making the garlic scape pesto—I get it—then use the leftover charmoula (page 62). Clean out your fridge and make dinner in a snap. Boom.

A Bigger Dinner If this is too light a main course for you, make a salad with avocado to go along with the quesadillas.

SERVES 4

16 small white corn tortillas

4 cups (440g) grated sharp cheddar cheese

8 tablespoons (125g) garlic scape pesto (page 123) or charmoula (page 62)

1 Heat the oven to 250°F (120°C). Warm a large well-seasoned cast-iron pan or nonstick pan over medium heat. Place 2 tortillas in the pan. Let them warm through, about 1 minute, then flip and warm the other side, about a minute more.

2 Sprinkle ¼ cup (30g) cheese on each tortilla, then spoon ½ tablespoon of garlic scape pesto over the cheese. When the cheese begins showing signs of melting, fold the tortilla in half, cover the pan, and let the cheese melt and the tortilla crisp up. Transfer to a baking sheet and keep warm in the oven while you finish cooking the remaining quesadillas.

Schlumpf

All my life, I've secretly hated crumbles, bettys, and crisps. Then, midlife and mid-Food52, I met schlumpf, and things changed forever. No longer would I have to suffer through gooey layers of fruit that burned my tongue or feel betrayed by a leaden biscuity cap masking victimized fruit. Now I could have a lofty bed of jammy fruit merely veiled by a crisp layer of crumble. Schlumpf may lack grace in its name but not in its execution.

I learned about schlumpf from Marian Bull, a beloved, madcap former Food52 editor, who shared her family recipe for blueberry schlumpf on our site. It quickly became a community favorite, as well as my go-to summer dessert, not only because everyone who eats it loves it, but because it takes about ten minutes to prepare.

Over time, I've tried different fruits (rhubarb and blueberries are my favorite), spices, and toppings, like the cinnamon and coconut here. I even temporarily lost my mind and put quinoa in the crumble. You'll forgive me, won't you, Marian?

MAKES ENOUGH FOR 2 DINNERS PLUS
MIDAFTERNOON SPOONFUL SNACKS

TOPPING

2 cups (250g) all-purpose flour

1 cup plus 2 tablespoons (255g) cold salted butter, cut into cubes

1 cup (220g) packed light brown sugar

3/4 cup (60g) unsweetened shredded dried coconut

FILLING

8 cups (960g) thinly sliced rhubarb (from about 20 stalks) or 8 cups (1.2kg) fresh or frozen blueberries

1/4 cup (30g) all-purpose flour

1/4 cup (50g) sugar

1/4 teaspoon ground cinnamon

1/4 teaspoon pure vanilla extract

Whipped cream or pitcher of cream, for serving

1 Heat your oven to 350°F (175°C). To make the topping, combine the flour, butter, and brown sugar in a bowl. Using your fingers, roughly blend the butter into the dry ingredients until crumbly. The mixture should remain lumpy. Set the bowl in the fridge until the filling is ready.

2 Stir together all of the filling ingredients and spread on a baking sheet. Sprinkle the topping, followed by the coconut, over the rhubarb filling. Bake until bubbling in the center and golden brown on top, about 30 minutes. Let cool, then cover with plastic wrap and leave in the pan until serving.

3 **The day of:** Heat your broiler and recrisp the schlumpf for a minute or two. Scoop into bowls and top with poufy clouds of whipped cream.

Schlumpf Shelf Life Confession: Schlumpf is best served the day it is made, when the topping is crisp and the filling is like a snug rhubarb pudding. This is particularly pertinent in humid climates, which wreak havoc on the schlumpf crumble. Since I'm instructing you to make it on the weekend and serve it a day or more later, I want you to know the risks! Still, I've made schlumpf enough times to tell you that it's still damn good on day three during a humid East Coast summer. If you want to crisp up the top, put it under the broiler for a minute.

Chocolate Ice Cream with Toasted Brioche Crumbs, Almonds, and Salt

Heat the oven to 350°F (175°C). Tear **4 large slices of brioche** into walnut-size pieces. In a baking dish, combine the brioche with **a handful of chopped almonds.** Drizzle the brioche and almonds with **1 to 2 tablespoons of honey** and sprinkle with **flaky sea salt.** Bake until golden, about 7 minutes. Let cool, then store in a container, and serve over **chocolate ice cream.** Store for up to a week. Save remaining brioche for weekend French toast.

Amanda's Summer

monday

limeade
thai steak salad
jasmine rice
blistered tomatoes
blueberry ice

tuesday

fish tacos
peach salad
chocolate ice cream
w/ cinnamon i chile

wednesday

penne w/ tomatoes i corn
strawberry ice cream

thursday

steak i avocado salad
blueberry ice

friday

jasmine rice salad
cantaloupe

to-do

thai steak salad
jasmine rice
pickled onions
roast tomatoes
limeade
blueberry i

THE WEEK AHEAD

THE RECIPES

HOW THEY COME TOGETHER

DINNER ONE

Limeade with Basil

Blistered Cherry Tomatoes

Thai Steak Salad

Fail Then No-Fail Jasmine Rice

Blueberry Ice

TO DO TODAY Bring half the steak salad and cherry
tomatoes to room temperature. Reheat the rice. At
dessert time, scrape the ice into glasses or coupes.

DINNER TWO

Low-Maintenance Fish Tacos
with Pickled Onions

Spicy Peach Salad

Chocolate ice cream topped with
cinnamon and chile dust

TO DO TODAY Roast the fish, toast the tortillas,
slice the avocado, and set out the other taco
toppings. Take the peach salad out of the fridge to
warm to room temperature. Scoop the ice cream
and dust with the spices—use a chile like piment
d'Espelette, if possible.

DINNER THREE

Penne with Blistered Cherry
Tomatoes and Corn

Strawberry ice cream from the store

TO DO TODAY Make the pasta using tomatoes
that you roasted over the weekend.

DINNER FOUR

Steak and Avocado Salad with
Crisp Rice and Cashews

Blueberry Ice

TO DO TODAY Fry the rice and assemble
the salad. Scrape the ice into dessert glasses
or coupes.

DINNER FIVE

Jasmine Rice Salad with Blistered Tomatoes,
Tuna, Olives, and Capers

Cantaloupe with chiles, lime, and salt

TO DO TODAY Set the salad out 20 minutes before
serving, so it warms up a little. Slice the cantaloupe
and serve seasoned with piment d'Espelette or any
finely ground chile you like, lime, and salt.

BROWN BAG LUNCHES

Spicy Peaches Wrapped in Prosciutto

Thai Steak Sandwich with Avocado, Cilantro,
and Pickled Onions

Steak Sandwich with Pickled Onions, Blistered
Tomatoes, and Spicy Greens

Blistered Cherry Tomato Sandwich

GAME PLAN

TO MAKE OVER THE WEEKEND

Spicy Peach Salad

Thai Steak Salad

Fail Then No-Fail Jasmine
Rice

Jasmine Rice Salad with
Blistered Tomatoes, Tuna,
Olives, and Capers

Pickled Onions

Blistered Cherry Tomatoes

Limeade with Basil

Blueberry Ice

SUMMERTIME, AND THE COOKIN' IS EASY

This weekend's kitchen time is a cool 1½ to 2 hours.

- Heat your oven to 425°F (220°C). I know, it's hot out; you'll forgive me later.

- Get the cherry tomatoes ready to go in the oven (page 76), then roast until blistered and browned. Let them cool and store in a container in the fridge.

- While the tomatoes roast and blister, make the blueberry syrup for the ice (page 91), as well as the sugar syrup for the limeade (page 75). Pickle the onions for the tacos (page 86). Put together the peach salad (page 79) and store in a container in the fridge.

- Wash the cilantro for the tacos; spin it dry and store in a zipper plastic bag lined with paper towels.

- Pour the blueberry syrup into a baking pan and begin the freezing and scraping process. Juice the limes and assemble the limeade in a pitcher, then store in the fridge.

- Start the jasmine rice (page 83).

- Let the rice cool. Put half of it in a container in the fridge. Save the other half to make jasmine rice salad with blistered tomatoes, tuna, olives, and capers (page 76), once the tomatoes are done roasting. Then put this rice salad in a separate container in the fridge.

- Heat the broiler or your grill (whichever way you prefer to cook the steak). Cook the steak for the Thai steak salad (page 80) and while it rests, prepare the rest of the salad. Combine the steak and the other salad ingredients, then store in a container in the fridge.

- You're all done. If the blueberry ice needs more scraping, do it at your leisure. Nothing bad will happen!

Overscheduled this week? Leave the limeade, peach salad, pickled onions, and blueberry ice off the menu. Pick up some great ricotta and a baguette and serve the blistered tomatoes with ricotta toasts (page 20) in place of the pasta. Buy blueberries and serve with whipped cream or ice cream. You'll save a good 45 minutes.

GROCERY LIST

PRODUCE

Avocados, 4 firm, ripe

Blueberries, 9 cups (1.4kg)

Cantaloupe, 1 ripe

Cherry (and/or Sun Gold!) tomatoes, 12 cups (1.7kg) of the tiniest, sweetest you can find

Corn, 6 ears

Garlic, 11 cloves

Lemons, 4

Limes, 22

Peaches, 6 just-ripe

Radishes, 8 small

Red chiles (bird's eye preferred), 1 to 2

Red onions, 2 large

Scallions, 2

Watercress and/or arugula, 7 cups (140g)

Yellow onions, 3

HERBS

Basil leaves, 1 bunch

Chives, 3 tablespoons chopped

Cilantro leaves, 1 bunch plus 2 handfuls

Flat-leaf parsley leaves, 1 handful

SPICES

Ground ancho chile or ground chipotle, ¼ teaspoon

Ground cinnamon, a pinch

Ground cumin, ½ teaspoon

Piment d'Espelette or other ground chile, ¼ teaspoon, plus more for sprinkling

PANTRY

Capers, 1 tablespoon chopped

Cider vinegar, about 1½ cups (355ml)

Extra-virgin olive oil, about 2 cups (475ml)

Fish sauce, 8½ tablespoons (125ml)

Hot sauce (such as Cholula), for seasoning

Jasmine rice, 5½ cups (1kg)

Mango juice, for lunch

Mayonnaise, for lunch

Penne rigate, 1 pound (450g)

Pitted olives, a handful of your favorite

Potato chips, for lunch

Coarse salt

Flaky salt

Salted roasted cashews, ½ cup (65g)

Tuna in oil, 1 (7-ounce/200g) jar

Vegetable oil, about ½ cup (120ml), for frying

BAKING AISLE

Raw sugar, ¾ cup (150g)

Sugar, about 1¾ cups (350g)

DAIRY AND EGGS

Parmesan, for serving

MEAT AND SEAFOOD

Flank steak or top sirloin, 2½ pounds (1.1kg)

Pollack or hake or other good white fish, 1 pound (450g)

Prosciutto, for lunches

FREEZER

Chocolate ice cream, for dessert

Strawberry ice cream, for dessert

BAKED GOODS

Baguette, 1 for lunch

Country bread (like ciabatta), 1 loaf for lunches

Sandwich bread, 1 loaf for lunch

White corn tortillas, 12 small

Limeade with Basil

Crisp, bright, and herbal—everything I want in a summer drink. Add gin or vodka for a party. I call for raw sugar, which contributes a rounder caramel sweetness. If you don't have it, regular sugar will work, but use less, just ½ cup (100g).

Merrill's Method for Crushing Ice "To crush ice at home, nest one sturdy plastic freezer bag inside another and fill the inner bag about two-thirds full with ice cubes. Seal both bags, squeezing out most of the air. Use a heavy mallet or a hammer to pound the bags, crushing the ice. Note: Do this on a sturdy surface that you don't mind roughing up a bit—not on your marble countertop!"

SERVES 8 TO 10

¾ cup (150g) raw sugar

13 limes, 12 rinsed and dried and 1 thinly sliced into wheels

12 large fresh basil leaves

1 Spread the sugar in a wide, shallow bowl. Working with one lime at a time, pick up a handful of sugar and firmly rub the sugar all over the lime, holding your hands over the bowl so that the sugar doesn't scatter everywhere. The sugar essentially scratches the lime peel and extracts some of its flavor. Bring 2 cups (475ml) of water to a boil and pour just enough water over the sugar to cover it by ¼ inch (6mm). Add the basil leaves and stir to dissolve the sugar.

2 Halve the limes and juice into a pitcher, using a fine-mesh strainer to catch any seeds. Pour the sugar syrup, a little at a time, through the strainer and into the lime juice. Stir to combine. Continue to add syrup until the limeade tastes good to you. Store in the fridge for up to 5 days. If you have leftover syrup, save it for another batch of limeade—it will keep for at least a week.

3 **The day of:** Serve the limeade over crushed ice with a lime wheel. If you want to stretch it a little, add sparkling water.

Blistered Cherry Tomatoes

These blistered tomatoes have become my default cure to any summer food ailment. Need more flavor? Add blistered tomatoes. Need a veg? Toss them in. Hungry for a snack? Cheese and deliciously shriveled tomatoes will do the trick.

This week, they accompany steak salad (page 80), spread sweetness through a briny rice and tuna salad (right), and act as the cornerstone of a summery tomato and corn pasta (page 88). I couldn't stop there—they're also a vital part of the romesco (page 107) in my next menu. Keep them in your fridge like you would a salad dressing or pickle. At some point you'll be in need, and they'll cheerfully, sweetly, come to the rescue.

An Impromptu Dinner from Merrill "These tiny, sweet roasted tomatoes are truly nature's candy. Here's one way I use them to create a quick, summery dinner: Warm leftover Israeli couscous over low heat with a splash of water, several chopped kalamata olives, some boiled green beans (page 137) cut into 1-inch (2.5cm) lengths, a handful of blistered cherry tomatoes, and a drizzle of olive oil. Stir in chopped fresh basil and a pinch of finely grated lemon zest, then top with an over-easy egg."

Tomato Iteration Longtime Food52 recipe tester Anna Gass blends these tomatoes into aioli; she also uses them as a topping for a margherita pizza.

MAKES 4 TO 6 CUPS (760G TO 1.1KG)

12 cups (1.7kg) of the tiniest, sweetest cherry (and/or Sun Gold!) tomatoes you can find

6 cloves garlic, lightly smashed

Extra-virgin olive oil, for roasting

Coarse salt

1 Heat the oven to 425°F (220°C). Pour the tomatoes onto two heavy baking sheets or roasting pans; they should fit in a single layer (if not, add a third pan). Add the garlic. Pour a generous layer of olive oil over the tomatoes, enough so that a thin layer of oil pools in the baking sheet. Season generously with salt. Bake until the tomatoes are blistered and deflated and release their juices, 20 to 30 minutes. Remove from the oven, discard the garlic, and let cool. Make sure to save all the oily juices! Store in a container in the fridge for up to 10 days.

Jasmine Rice Salad with Blistered Tomatoes, Tuna, Olives, and Capers

Combine **4 cups (630g) cooked jasmine rice** (page 83), **1½ cups (285g) blistered tomatoes** plus some of their juices, **1 (7-ounce/200g) jar tuna in oil** (drained and broken into chunks), **a handful of your favorite pitted olives, 1 tablespoon chopped capers,** and **a handful of chopped flat-leaf parsley and basil** in a big bowl. Add just enough **extra-virgin olive oil** to dress the rice, then gently fold everything together. Taste and adjust the seasoning, adding salt, pepper, **chile, lemon juice,** and more oil as needed.

Lunch: Blistered Cherry Tomato Sandwich

Spread **sandwich bread** with **mayonnaise.** Top with **blistered cherry tomatoes.** Grind some fresh pepper on top. Press the sandwich together and enjoy!

Spicy Peach Salad

This salad lies somewhere between salad and dessert. I use peaches that are just ripe, not soft, and season them with piment d'Espelette, lime juice, crunchy salt, and the tiniest whiff of sugar. The heat and salinity merely underline the peaches' sweetness and remind us how refreshing they can be. I like this salad best as a chaser to aromatic foods like tacos (pages 85 and 86) or Thai steak salad (page 80).

Each Peach Pear Plum You can make this same salad with firm plums, pears, or mangoes. Adjust seasoning as desired and enjoy fiery fruit year-round.

SERVES 4, PLUS LEFTOVERS

6 just-ripe peaches

¼ teaspoon piment d'Espelette or other ground chile

1 teaspoon sugar

1 lime, halved

Flaky sea salt

1 Halve and pit the peaches, then cut each half into 4 wedges. In a large bowl, toss the peaches with the piment d'Espelette, sugar, and the juice from 1 lime half. Season with salt. Store, covered, in the fridge for up to 2 days.

2 **The day of:** Place the salad in a wide, shallow serving bowl and let it come to room temperature. Cut the remaining lime half into wedges and pass at the table.

Lunch: Spicy Peaches Wrapped in Prosciutto

Merrill got me hooked on this as a summer desk lunch. She'd wrap **peach slices** with **thin ribbons of prosciutto** and eat them with **a piece of country bread.** An exceptional desk mate, she often shared them with me, and soon they were a regular lunch for both of us. If you have leftovers of the spicy peach salad, wrap the peaches in thinly sliced prosciutto the next day for lunch. Serve with country bread.

Thai Steak Salad

This recipe from our Food52 community member Merav Shikler changed the way I thought about making steak salad. Instead of marinating and then cooking the steak, you broil this one before any seasonings are added. The steak, which goes under the broiler (or on the grill) dry, browns well and hangs on to its lightly charred flavor. Only after cooking is it layered with pungent fish sauce, lime juice, onions, and chile—all of which stay bright and feisty.

MAKES ENOUGH FOR 2 DINNERS, PLUS LUNCHES

2½ pounds (1.1kg) flank steak or top sirloin

5 cloves garlic, peeled

1 to 2 fresh red chiles (bird's eye preferred)

½ cup (120ml) freshly squeezed lime juice

½ cup (120ml) fish sauce

2 tablespoons sugar

3 yellow onions, thinly sliced

3 tablespoons sliced fresh chives

Large handful fresh cilantro, coarsely chopped

4 cups (630g) cooked jasmine rice (page 83)

1 Heat the broiler (or your grill) and position the rack 4 to 5 inches (10 to 13cm) from the flame. Put the steak in a cast-iron skillet or other heavy pan and broil until well browned, about 3 minutes. Flip the steak and cook until medium-rare, about 3 minutes more. If grilling, cook directly on a rack over hot coals for about 3 minutes per side. The internal temperature of the steak should be 130°F (55°C). Let the steak rest while you prepare the rest of the salad.

2 With a mortar and pestle, mash together the garlic and chiles to create a paste. Scrape the paste into a large bowl and add the lime juice, fish sauce, and sugar. Stir well to dissolve the sugar. Toss in the onions, chives, and cilantro.

3 Carve the steak across the grain into thin, even slices and add to the salad. Mix again thoroughly and let marinate for at least 30 minutes for the flavors to meld. Store the salad, covered, in the fridge for up to 4 days. Half will be used for this dish; the remaining half will be used for the steak and avocado salad (page 82) and lunches.

4 **The day of:** Let half of the salad come to room temperature. Serve with hot rice (page 83) rewarmed in the microwave.

Steak and Avocado Salad
with Crisp Rice and Cashews

This is a good week to buy extras and make the most of them. As you saw in the Thai steak salad (page 80), I've had you make twice what you'll need for that salad. And since you're already buying avocados for the tacos, why not toss two more into your grocery cart? This salad pairs the marinated steak with avocado and watercress and then gives them a pungent and crunchy topping with scallions, fried rice, and chopped cashews. Another way to serve this is to skip the watercress and buy a beautiful head of butter or Bibb lettuce in its stead. Separate the leaves and pass them at the table to make lettuce rolls filled with the salad.

SERVES 4

Vegetable oil, for frying

1 cup (160g) cooked jasmine rice (opposite)

6 cups (120g) watercress and/or arugula (mix in whatever proportions you prefer)

About 12 ounces (340g) leftover steak, thinly sliced

2 firm, ripe avocados, thinly sliced

8 small radishes, cut in wedges

2 scallions, thinly sliced

½ cup (65g) salted roasted cashews, chopped

¼ cup (60ml) extra-virgin olive oil

Juice of 1 lime

½ teaspoon fish sauce

Pinch of piment d'Espelette or other ground chile

Salt

1 Heat 1½ inches (4cm) of vegetable oil in a small saucepan over medium-high heat until shimmering. The oil is ready when a cooked rice grain dropped into the oil sizzles immediately. Add the cooked rice and fry, stirring gently to separate the grains, until light brown and crisp, 1 to 2 minutes. With a slotted spoon, transfer the crisp rice to paper towels and let cool.

2 Arrange the watercress and/or arugula on a platter. Top with the steak and avocado and sprinkle the radishes, scallions, and cashews over the top.

3 Whisk together the olive oil, lime juice, fish sauce, and chile in a bowl. Taste and season with salt and more lime juice if needed.

4 Pour just enough dressing over the salad to lightly coat and scatter the crisp rice on top.

Lunch: Thai Steak Sandwich with Avocado, Cilantro, and Pickled Onions

Spread a split **baguette** with **mayonnaise** and layer with slices of **leftover steak, slivered avocado, fresh cilantro leaves,** and **pickled onions** (page 86). Don't forget to pack **potato chips** and a **mango juice.**

Lunch: Steak Sandwich with Pickled Onions, Blistered Tomatoes, and Spicy Greens

Spread **country bread** with **blistered cherry tomatoes** (page 76) and their juices, then top with thin slices of **leftover steak, pickled onions** (page 86), and **spicy greens** like watercress or mustard greens.

Fail Then No-Fail Jasmine Rice

Here's how to make no-fail jasmine rice: Buy a rice cooker.

I kid, but it really is the most foolproof way to cook rice if you're a rice rube like me. Still, I'm not one to cower from the threat of mushy rice. Short of a rice cooker, I cannot be bothered with measurements, as I've never found them to work. As far as I can tell, successful rice cookery depends a lot on the type of pan you have, the strength of your stove, and most of all, the wisdom that comes with experience. Get ready to fail a bunch at first, and then to eventually get the hang of it.

Put the rice in a fine-mesh sieve and rinse it under cold water for a minute. Let it drain, then drop the rice into a heavy saucepan. Add enough water to cover the rice by 1 inch (2.5cm). Season the water with a large pinch of salt. Put a lid on the pan and bring to a boil over medium-high heat, then lower the heat to a mellow simmer and cook for 15 minutes. Remove the lid and toss with a fork.

I like to make enough for both steak salads and a rice salad later in the week, so I start with 5 cups (925g) uncooked jasmine rice, which should produce just over 8 cups (1.3kg) of cooked rice. When ready to eat, just reheat it in the microwave.

Merrill's Simple Baked Rice

Unlike Amanda, I cling to precise measurements like a life raft when I make rice. (If this sounds like you, read on.) Pierre Franey's baked rice is the only method I've found that yields perfect results every time. It's pilaf-style, infused with onion, garlic, and butter, which makes it a great stand-alone side. If you're looking for something more pure to blend with other flavors, try Amanda's version.

To make Pierre's rice, heat the oven to 400°F (200°C). Melt **a tablespoon of butter** in a heavy saucepan over medium-low heat. Add **¼ cup (40g) finely chopped yellow onion** and **1 minced clove of garlic** and cook until translucent, about 3 minutes. Stir in **1 cup (185g) long-grain white rice,** cook for 1 minute, then add **1½ cups (355ml) chicken stock** or water and ½ teaspoon kosher salt. Cover tightly and bake for exactly 17 minutes. Remove the pan from the oven and let the rice sit, covered, for 3 to 5 minutes. Uncover and fluff with a fork. Stir in **1 tablespoon butter** and season with more salt to taste.

Low-Maintenance Fish Tacos

I came late to tacos, which I long associated with too many bowls and a marathon of chopping. And while I could eat a fish taco every day, the purist in me never wanted to make them at home. You'd have to deep-fry. For a taco.

I also came late to the realization that I can do what I want in life. And in this life, I'm not going to fry the fish for my fish tacos. I'm also not going to chop much for them. So now we have delicious fish tacos every few weeks.

Roasting the fish is the key to Zen fish tacos. By roasting, you can control the speed of cooking and keep the fish moist. The lost crunch from the frying can be made up for with crisp pickled red onions. The onions get a bowl, as does the avocado, which turns out to be conveniently soft and sliceable by kids. Cilantro sprigs and lime wedges—I serve them in a pile right on the countertop—and Cholula hot sauce make up the rest of the toppings.

If I make the pickled red onions over the weekend, I can have fish tacos ready in fifteen minutes. While the fish, rubbed with cumin and ancho chile, roasts, I toast the corn tortillas in a dry pan. My kids slice the avocado, and my husband pours lemonade and opens beers. You can guess who gets what.

Got Leftovers? Make Merrill's salpicon (page 260) with any extra fish.

SERVES 4

1 pound (450g) pollack or hake or other white fish

Kosher salt

½ teaspoon ground cumin

¼ teaspoon ground ancho chile or ground chipotle

1 tablespoon extra-virgin olive oil

Pickled onions (page 86), for serving

1 avocado

2 limes, each cut into 6 wedges

1 bunch cilantro, washed and dried

12 small white corn tortillas

Your favorite hot sauce (we like Cholula), for garnish

1 Heat the oven to 350°F (175°C). Season the fish with salt, followed by the cumin and chile. Lay the fish in a baking dish and sprinkle with the olive oil.

2 Meanwhile, set out the pickled onions. Cut the avocado lengthwise into ⅛-inch (3mm) slices and put it in a bowl (I like to squeeze a little lime juice over it so it doesn't brown). Pile the cilantro sprigs and lime wedges on the counter.

3 When the oven is hot, bake the fish until just cooked through, about 10 minutes.

4 While the fish roasts, warm a large skillet over medium-high heat. Place as many tortillas in it as you can fit in a single layer—probably 2 or 3—and toast just enough to warm through, about a minute or two on each side. Be careful not to let the tortillas dry out. Pile them under a kitchen towel to keep warm.

5 When the fish is cooked, serve it with the warm tortillas and all the fixings. Let everyone make the fish tacos of their dreams.

Variation: Low-Maintenance Steak Tacos

To make the fish tacos recipe with steak, I buy inexpensive, flavorful **flank steak** (hanger or skirt will work well too). If you want leftovers for lunches, buy 1½ to 2 pounds (680 to 900g). Season the steak as you would the fish (I add a little more of the spices on the steak) and let it come to room temperature before cooking. To broil the steak, heat the broiler and position the rack 4 to 5 inches (10 to 13cm) from the flame. Put the steak in a cast-iron skillet or other heavy pan and broil until well browned, about 3 minutes. Flip and cook until medium-rare, about 3 minutes more. The internal temperature of the steak should be 130°F (55°C). If you're more of a griller, feel free to grill the steak as well. Either way, let the steak rest for 5 to 10 minutes after cooking (this is when I toast the tortillas), then thinly slice it across the grain.

Leftover Steak Some weeks I'll cook a bunch of steak for tacos, and either use the leftovers for the Thai steak salad (page 80) or serve the steak cold with a sauce (a blend of mayo, Dijon mustard, Worcestershire, and Tabasco), sliced tomatoes, and steamed corn.

Pickled Onions

I usually make a big batch of these and then use the leftovers for lunches and any other excuse I can find. This recipe will make enough for the tacos and lots of salads and sandwiches to get you through the week.

If you don't have a microwave, bring the water, vinegar, salt, and sugar to a boil and pour over the onions.

MAKES 3 TO 4 CUPS (540 TO 720G)

2 large red onions	2 tablespoons sugar
1 tablespoon kosher salt	1½ cups (355ml) cider vinegar

Slice the onions very thinly and put them in a microwave-safe container. Add the salt and sugar. Combine the cider vinegar and ¾ cup (175ml) water, then pour over the onions, making sure they're submerged.

Microwave for 1 minute, then stir and microwave for 1 minute more. Continue microwaving and stirring until the liquid is hot and the onions begin to soften—it usually takes me 3 to 4 minutes total, but may depend on your microwave. Let cool, transfer to a jar, then refrigerate overnight. The onions will keep for up to 2 weeks.

Our Pickled Onion Addiction Our kids cottoned to these sweet and salty pickled onions, a recipe from one of our earliest Food52 community members and now friend, Abbie Argersinger, when they were about four years old. Now nine years old, they eat them plain as a snack, and sometimes my son will go for seconds at dinner and come back with a plateful of pickled onions.

As I began making them more often, I found it handy to have them around pretty much all the time. They perk up a sandwich, add a noteworthy crunch to a burger, and infuse salads with pungency and verve. So if you're wondering why you keep finding recipes that call for them (from me and Merrill), now you know!

I keep them in a container in the fridge. A batch will last up to two weeks—more than enough time to find ways to use them.

Penne with Blistered Cherry Tomatoes and Corn

Every August, we hunker down in Wainscott, New York, for a couple of weeks, where I split most of my time between farm stands and antique stores. I make this recipe every year when we're there—tripling the batch for Tad's large family. It scales up and down and pleases just about everyone.

A Corn Tip from Merrill "Here's a great trick that Amanda and I learned from our creative director, Kristen Miglore, that makes removing corn kernels from their cobs a snap (and creates virtually no mess).

Lay a shucked ear of corn flat on your cutting board, with the pointy end facing away from you. Using a very sharp knife, slice off a strip of kernels down one side of the ear. Turn the ear so it's lying on the flat strip you've just created (this will stabilize it), and slice another strip of kernels off the cob. Keep rotating the ear until you've removed all the kernels, then use the back of your knife to scrape the milk into a bowl if you like. No flying kernels!"

An Even Simpler Summer Pasta Skip the tomato roasting. Try Merrill's pasta with garlic, tomatoes, basil, and Brie on page 138. I often make it with cubed mozzarella, burrata, or ricotta instead of Brie. If you and cheese aren't friends, you can add jarred tuna or poached tuna (page 100). I like to play around with the pasta shapes as well. Small shells, penne rigate, and radiatori are a few winners.

SERVES 4 (CAN EASILY BE DOUBLED, TRIPLED, SEPTUPLED)

Salt

2 generous cups (380g) Blistered Cherry Tomatoes (page 76)

6 ears corn

1 pound (450g) penne rigate

Handful torn fresh basil leaves

Grated Parmesan, for serving

1 Bring a large pot of generously salted water to a boil. Meanwhile, warm the tomatoes over medium heat in a saucepan, then pour them into a large serving bowl. Cut the corn from the cobs and add it to the tomatoes.

2 Cook the penne until al dente, about 8 minutes, reserving ⅓ cup (80ml) of the pasta cooking water. Drain the pasta and add it to the tomatoes and corn. Fold it all together—the heat of the pasta should soften the corn, and the tomato juices should blanket the pasta like a salad dressing. If it's at all dry, add a little oil and some pasta water. Stir in the basil. Serve the pasta in wide, shallow bowls and pass the Parmesan at the table.

Blueberry Ice

When I'm not making schlumpf (page 66), I stick to blueberry desserts that are as pure as possible. Blueberries and cream is always okay at our house. This is another purity-preserving recipe—a simple ice that extracts blueberry's fresh flavor and makes it even more vibrant with a blast of lemon juice. If you want to mess around with the flavor, you could add lemon verbena to the hot syrup, but I like it as is.

1½ cups (300g) sugar, plus more as needed

9 cups (1.4kg) fresh blueberries

Juice of 3 lemons, plus more as needed

1 Combine 4 cups (950ml) of water and the sugar in a large saucepan. Bring to a boil, then reduce the heat and simmer until the syrup thickens slightly, about 15 minutes. Add the blueberries and stir until their skins soften and the berries are broken down, just a few minutes; crush with a potato masher if needed. Stir in the lemon juice. Let cool. Taste and add more lemon juice or sugar if you like.

2 Pour the blueberry mixture into a lasagna pan (or similar pan)—the mixture shouldn't be more than 1 inch (2.5cm) or so deep. Freeze uncovered for 1 hour, then use a sturdy fork to scrape any bits of ice that have formed. Return the pan to the freezer and stir up the frozen bits every 30 minutes or so, until you have blueberry shards, like a shaved ice you get on the street. Cover the pan with plastic wrap and keep in the freezer for up to a week.

3 **The day of:** Before serving, scrape the ice once more. Spoon into small glasses.

THE WEEK AHEAD

THE RECIPES

HOW THEY COME TOGETHER

DINNER ONE

Grilled Squid Salad with Lemon, Capers,
and Couscous

Smoked Paprika Mayonnaise on Grilled Bread

Plum Tart

TO DO TODAY Warm the couscous you reserved
for this salad. Grill the squid and toast the bread (also
on the grill). Finish the squid salad and spread the
grilled bread with the paprika mayo. Whip cream
for the tart (optional).

DINNER TWO

Grilled Pork Chops with Hacked Romesco

Couscous Salad with Zucchini, Pistachios, and Feta

Peaches and basil

TO DO TODAY Season the pork chops in the morning.
When you're ready to eat, set out the couscous salad to
warm up and grill the pork chops. Cut the peaches into
paper-thin slices and arrange on plates. Dress with olive oil,
salt, raw sugar, torn fresh basil, and a squeeze of lemon juice.

DINNER THREE

Summer Evening Pasta

Plum Tart

TO DO TODAY Make the pasta.

DINNER FOUR

Poached Tuna

Olive Oil–Braised Peppers

Hacked Romesco

Boiled Potatoes

Coconut ice cream with plums

TO DO TODAY In a wide, covered saucepan, warm
the tuna (and its cooking oil), sliced potatoes, and the
peppers, breaking the tuna into large chunks. Serve
with romesco on the side. At dessert time, slice plums
to serve with the coconut ice cream.

DINNER FIVE

Brown Butter Tomatoes

Tuna Salad with Peppers and Smoked
Paprika Mayonnaise

Country bread and good salted butter

Greek yogurt with peaches and honey

TO DO TODAY Put together the tuna salad.
Just before sitting down, make the brown butter
tomatoes. For dessert, put a big dollop of yogurt
in each bowl. Top with sliced peaches and a swirl
of honey.

BROWN BAG LUNCHES

Couscous Salad with Zucchini, Pistachios,
and Poached Tuna

Tuna Salad Sandwich with Hacked Romesco

Eggs with Romesco

GAME PLAN

TO MAKE OVER THE WEEKEND

Grilled Squid Salad with Lemon, Capers, and Couscous	Poached Tuna
	Boiled Potatoes (page 152)
Smoked Paprika Mayonnaise on Grilled Bread	Olive Oil–Braised Peppers
	Half recipe of Blistered Cherry Tomatoes (page 76)
Couscous Salad with Zucchini, Pistachios, and Feta	Hacked Romesco
	Plum Tart

TURN ON YOUR FAVORITE PODCAST AND SHARPEN YOUR CHEF'S KNIFE

Prepare yourself for 2½ to 3 hours of meditative cooking.

- The day before cooking, make the tart dough, press it into the pan, cover, and refrigerate until needed.

- Heat your oven to 425°F (220°C). Prep the plum tart (page 109) and get it in the oven. Then roast a half recipe of the cherry tomatoes (page 76) for the romesco (page 107). Smash 5 more cloves of garlic—you'll need them for other recipes.

- While the tart and tomatoes are roasting, boil the potatoes (page 152), poach the tuna (page 100), and cook the braised peppers (page 103). This sounds like a lot to do at once but they're all stovetop and pretty low maintenance. It's a fun challenge, I promise.

- When the tart is done, let it cool. When the tomatoes are finished cooking, set them aside to cool. Soak the ancho chile for the romesco.

- Cook the couscous for the grilled squid salad (page 96) and the couscous salad (page 99). Mix the couscous with the dressing for the squid salad, then divide in half. Put the half for the squid in a container in the fridge. With the other half, finish making the couscous salad, then store in a container in the fridge.

- Put the tuna and its cooking oil in a container in the fridge; do the same with the boiled potatoes and half of the peppers.

- With the other half of the peppers, whirl together the romesco (page 107) in your food processor. Store it in the fridge.

- Stir together the smoked paprika mayonnaise (page 96).

- And . . . you're pretty much done. I usually take a shower, open a beer, and check my e-mail. In case you want to be as exciting as me.

A quicker way to the finish line. Don't make the romesco—season the pork chops with smoked paprika instead. And rather than taking the time to make a plum tart, serve the plums with cream and honey and top with chopped mint. You'll still be a kitchen hero. And you'll save 45 minutes.

GROCERY LIST

PRODUCE

Baby lettuce leaves, 1 cup (30g)

Baby white potatoes, 1 pound (450g)

Beefsteak tomatoes, 2 or 3 small, ripe

Cherry (and/or Sun Gold!) tomatoes, 6 cups (840g) of the tiniest, sweetest you can find

Corn, 2 ears

Crunchy vegetables (such as radishes, turnips, what have you), for lunch

Garlic, 1 head

Italian or other firm-flesh plums, 12 to 15 small, plus more for snacking and dessert

Lemons, 6

Peaches, 8 to 10

Red and yellow bell peppers, 3 pounds (1.4kg)

Red onion, ½ small

Yellow summer squash, 3 medium

Zucchini, 2 small

HERBS

Basil, 2 tablespoons coarsely chopped, plus 8 more leaves for dessert

Flat-leaf parsley leaves, ¾ cup (15g) packed

Thyme, 12 sprigs

SPICES

Ancho chile, 1 dried

Red pepper flakes, 3 pinches

Sweet smoked paprika, 1 teaspoon

Za'atar, ½ teaspoon

PANTRY

Aged sherry vinegar, 1 to 2 tablespoons

Almonds, ¼ cup (35g)

Capers, 2½ tablespoons

Extra-virgin olive oil, about 4 cups (1L), plus more to have on hand

Honey, for dessert

Large couscous, 2½ cups (425g)

Mayonnaise, 1½ cups (355ml)

Orecchiette or small shells, 1 pound (450g)

Pistachios, ½ cup (60g) chopped, toasted

Preserved lemon, 1 tablespoon chopped

Quinoa, ¼ cup (40g) uncooked

Flaky salt

Vegetable or canola oil, ¼ cup (60ml)

BAKING AISLE

All-purpose flour, 1½ cups plus 2 tablespoons (205g)

Almond extract, ½ teaspoon

Raw sugar, about 2 teaspoons

Sugar, ¾ cup plus 1 teaspoon (155g)

DAIRY AND EGGS

Salted butter, for bread

Unsalted butter, ½ cup (110g)

Eggs, for lunch

Feta, ½ cup (75g) crumbled

Greek yogurt, for dessert

Heavy cream, for whipping

Milk, 2 tablespoons

Parmesan, for serving

MEAT AND SEAFOOD

Bacon, 6 slices

Bone-in pork chops, 4 large

Squid, 12 ounces (340g)

Tuna, 2 pounds (900g)

FREEZER

Coconut ice cream

BAKED GOODS

Airy country bread, 1 loaf

Baguette, for lunch

Rolls, for lunch

Grilled Squid Salad with Lemon, Capers, and Couscous

Every cook has dishes that she orders when in a restaurant but never makes at home. Call these barrier recipes. In the spirit of trying to get past my own barrier recipes—which usually involve shellfish or a grill—I've re-created the squid salad that I order every time we go to Motorino in Manhattan. I grill the squid to give it a little char and then tumble it together with whole parsley leaves, some capers, red pepper flakes, and a douse of lemon. (If you don't have a grill, you can broil the squid in a cast-iron skillet, 3 to 4 inches/7.5 to 10cm from the flame.)

I usually make it with potatoes, but for this week's menu I opted for couscous (and I grill the bread at the same time I grill the salad). Either way, it takes fifteen minutes. Once I actually made the dish and discovered this, I felt pretty dumb for not tackling it sooner. Watch out, clams: I'm coming after you next!

SERVES 4, WITH ENOUGH COUSCOUS FOR A SECOND SALAD (PAGE 99)

2½ cups (425g) uncooked large couscous, made according to package instructions (I prefer Moulins Mahjoub brand)	Finely grated zest of 1 lemon
	Juice of 1 or 2 lemons
5 tablespoons extra-virgin olive oil, plus more if needed	2½ tablespoons capers, coarsely chopped
½ small red onion, very thinly sliced	⅛ teaspoon red pepper flakes, plus more to taste
¾ cup (15g) packed fresh flat-leaf parsley leaves	Salt and freshly ground black pepper
	12 ounces (340g) squid, rinsed (if gritty) and dried

1 Cook the couscous according to the package instructions. Mix the warm couscous with ¼ cup (60ml) of the olive oil, the onion, parsley, lemon zest, lemon juice, capers, and red pepper flakes. Season with salt and pepper. Let cool. Divide the couscous into 2 containers, reserving one for the couscous salad with zucchini, pistachios, and feta, and refrigerate for up to 4 days.

2 **The day of:** Heat the grill to medium-high—if you have a fine grate or vegetable or shellfish basket for the grill, this is the moment to use it. While the grill heats up, toss together the squid with the remaining 1 tablespoon olive oil and warm the couscous in the microwave.

3 Grill the squid. The bodies will steam and fill with liquid; I lift the pieces with tongs and pour the liquid into the fire as they grill, so they char and don't steam. The squid should take 2 to 3 minutes to char and cook through. Transfer to a plate. (If you don't have a grill, you can broil the squid in a cast-iron skillet, 3 to 4 inches from the flame.)

4 Cut the squid bodies into ½-inch (1.3cm) rings. In a large bowl, toss the warm squid rings and heads with the couscous. Taste and adjust the seasoning. Let sit for 10 minutes. Taste again and adjust the seasoning one last time with lemon juice, salt, and pepper. Serve!

Smoked Paprika Mayonnaise on Grilled Bread

Blend **1 cup (240ml) mayonnaise, 1 smashed and chopped large garlic clove, 1 teaspoon smoked sweet paprika,** and a fat squeeze of **lemon juice;** add more paprika to taste. Grill **8 thick slices of airy country bread** on the outer perimeter of the grill grate until well toasted, about 5 minutes. Brush or sprinkle the grilled bread with **extra-virgin olive oil** and season with flaky salt. Reserve ½ cup (120ml) mayonnaise for the tuna salad (page 103); serve the rest with the grilled bread at the table.

Couscous Salad with Zucchini, Pistachios, and Feta

I don't like salads that involve cooking a bunch of ingredients separately, so my salads tend to involve more chopping and assembling. Many cooks don't realize that if you cut zucchini or summer squash small enough, there's no need to cook it. Especially if you buy young, firm zucchini, which holds up and doesn't get lost in a salad. I like a couscous salad that pairs the mellow grain pasta with sharp, independent flavors like preserved lemon, feta, and za'atar—there is no pushover salad here.

SERVES 4, PLUS EXTRA FOR LUNCHES

About 3 cups (620g) cooked and dressed couscous (page 96)	Salt and coarsely ground black pepper
2 small zucchini, trimmed and cut into ⅛-inch (3mm) dice	Juice of ½ lemon (optional)
½ cup (60g) chopped toasted pistachios	Extra-virgin olive oil, as needed
1 tablespoon chopped preserved lemon	½ cup (75g) crumbled feta
2 teaspoons chopped fresh thyme	¼ cup (40g) uncooked quinoa, toasted in a pan (optional)
	½ teaspoon za'atar

1 Fold together the couscous, zucchini, pistachios, preserved lemon, and thyme in a large bowl. Season with salt and pepper and add lemon juice and olive oil if needed. Store in a container in the fridge for up to 5 days.

2 **The day of:** Spoon the couscous into a serving dish, and sprinkle with the feta, quinoa, and za'atar.

Brown Butter Tomatoes

Don't ask, just try these butter-sizzled tomatoes, which taste oddly reminiscent of lobster. They're a little puzzling and extremely delicious.

Core **2 or 3 small ripe beefsteak tomatoes** and cut them into ⅓-inch (8mm) slices. Divide the tomato slices among 4 plates, overlapping them just a little.

Place **6 tablespoons (85g) unsalted butter** in a small heavy saucepan and cook over medium-low heat until completely melted. It will begin bubbling. Continue to let the butter simmer away, cooking off its water, until it begins to smell nutty and brown. Swirl the pan every 30 seconds or so. When the butter turns the color of a hazelnut (this should take 5 to 7 minutes), remove it from the heat. Use a soup spoon to ladle the brown butter over the tomatoes. They'll sizzle! You want to dress the tomatoes with the butter as if you were pouring ganache over a cake—be generous!

Season the tomatoes with flaky sea salt and coarsely ground pepper, then rush the plates to the table so everyone can taste the tomatoes while the butter is still hot! Mop up the butter and tomato juices with **good country bread.**

The Scoop on Brown Butter from Merrill "Amanda and I are serious about brown butter. I've been a lucky taste tester for her brown butter raspberries, which uses the same technique as these tomatoes, just without the salt and pepper. We have big plans to try this on other ripe, soft fruits: Peaches and plums are next on our list."

Lunch: Couscous Salad with Zucchini, Pistachios, and Poached Tuna

If you have leftover **couscous salad,** it makes an excellent lunch, topped with **poached tuna** (page 100).

Poached Tuna

You're going to think I'm lazy—and you're right. I like olive oil, I like vegetables, and I like warm salads. So when I'm not feeling particularly inventive or energetic, I like to throw them all together in a single dinner. I cook the vegetables, poach the fish in oil (an old standby for me), and throw in a squeeze of lemon and some dried chile to give everything a kick in the pants. Without much thought or effort, I have a comforting—and pretty delicious—dinner on the table.

This tuna with braised peppers and potatoes is a constant in my kitchen. Other combinations that I often lean on are tuna with sliced potatoes and blanched green beans and tuna with potatoes and roasted yellow squash. And when I'm not in the mood for potatoes, I make couscous (page 96).

What to Do with All That Oil? Dip bread in it. Use it to make a tuna sauce for pork chops or cutlets (à la vitello tonnato). Whisk it into a grapefruit vinaigrette. Mix together a mayonnaise and spread it on pan bagnat (the French tuna, olive, and anchovy sandwich).

Another Use for Poached Tuna from Merrill "I was thrilled to learn about Amanda's simple method for poaching perfect fish, and I often use the leftovers for salads, like this one: Break the fish into large chunks, then pile the chunks on top of salad greens and sliced jicama; squeeze a lime over the top, drizzle with a little of the olive oil you used to cook the fish, and season with salt and freshly ground pepper. Add a handful of pickled onions (page 86), toss gently, and serve."

Your Bread and Butter The simplest, and might I add most satisfying, way to cut yourself a break when cooking meals from scratch is to serve bread and butter. There are so many excellent country breads and cultured salted butters available. Take advantage of the convenience and appreciate the good work that others are doing to make better food available to all of us.

SERVES 8, ENOUGH FOR 2 DINNERS
AND FOR LEFTOVERS

2 pounds (900g) tuna, cut 1 inch (2.5cm) thick (probably 2 or 3 pieces)

6 thyme sprigs

2 cloves garlic, lightly smashed

Pinch of red pepper flakes

Salt

Olive oil, for poaching

1 lemon, cut into 4 quarters, for serving

1 Place the tuna in a single layer in a saucepan that's just big enough to fit the pieces snugly (you may cut the tuna to fit, if needed). Wedge the thyme, garlic, and red pepper flakes wherever they'll fit. Season the tuna with salt, then generously douse the tuna with olive oil until it comes up to about ¼ inch (6mm) in the pan. Lift a corner of each piece of tuna and tilt the pan so the oil spreads under the fish as well.

2 Place the pan over low heat (medium-low if your stove is shy) and gently cook the tuna, spooning the hot oil over the top of the tuna from time to time—the oil should never boil. As soon as the tuna pieces are halfway cooked, 5 to 7 minutes, turn them and cook the other side for about 5 minutes more. When it's done, the tuna will be faintly pink in the center. Transfer the tuna to a container to cool, leaving the oil in the pan. When the oil cools to room temperature, pour it over the top of the tuna and store in the fridge.

3 **The day of:** In a wide covered saucepan, warm the tuna (and its cooking oil); break the tuna into large chunks.

Lunch: Tuna Salad Sandwich with Hacked Romesco

I often mash up any leftover **poached tuna** with **mayonnaise** and any **crunchy vegetables** I have on hand—**radishes, turnips,** what have you (finely chopped). Layer it on a **baguette** (or the like) with more mayonnaise and some **romesco** (page 107).

Olive Oil–Braised Peppers

I don't have the patience to slowly braise peppers, so I came up with this method based on braised fennel (page 185). Like the pickled onions (page 86), you're likely to find these braised peppers in my fridge throughout summer and fall. They're a clutch ingredient in sandwiches and salads. Sometimes, for dinner, I'll serve roasted potatoes topped with these peppers and fried eggs. Other times, I'll use them to put together a quasi ratatouille with roasted eggplant that I like to serve alongside steak or chicken.

Market Dinner This is the season of the year when I would like to freeze time and eat just a few more tomatoes and peaches. So I've squeezed as many of them as possible into this menu.

Here, I've also included some of my most treasured conquer-the-week recipes—a pared-down romesco (page 107) that I like putting on everything from pork chops (page 107) to toasts; a pasta with grated summer squash and corn (page 104); a poached tuna (page 100) that I make every couple of weeks throughout the year; and a plum tart (page 109) that's dead simple to throw together.

Even when I'm committed to a menu, I like knowing that I always have the option to simply slice and season some farmers' market tomatoes, pick up a ball of mozzarella, and call it dinner.

SERVES 4 AS A SIDE, PLUS ENOUGH FOR THE ROMESCO AND TUNA SALAD LEFTOVERS

½ cup (120ml) extra-virgin olive oil

3 pounds (1.4kg) red and yellow bell peppers, seeded and very thinly sliced

4 thyme sprigs

2 cloves garlic, smashed

Salt

1 Combine the olive oil, peppers, thyme, and garlic in a large saucepan or Dutch oven. Season generously with salt. Place over medium-high heat, giving the peppers a stir to coat them with oil, and cover the pan. Cook, stirring every couple of minutes so the peppers don't burn. You want the peppers to cook down quickly, steaming and letting go of their juices, without browning. Adjust the heat as needed to make sure the juices are bubbling rapidly but not uncontrollably. Braise the peppers until they're limp and silky and the olive oil and pepper juices have fused, 15 to 20 minutes. Adjust the seasoning. Set aside ½ cup (100g) for the tuna salad (below) and 1 cup (200g) for the romesco (page 107). Serve the rest with the poached tuna.

Tuna Salad with Peppers and Smoked Paprika Mayonnaise

Break half of the **poached tuna** (page 100) into small pieces. Chop the reserved **½ cup (100g) olive oil–braised peppers**. Add a few handfuls of **baby lettuce (a cup/30g or so)**. Loosen the **½ cup reserved smoked paprika mayonnais**e (page 96) with **lemon juice** and a sprinkle of water, so it's more dressing than mayo. Fold ½ cup (120ml) of the dressing into the salad, adding more as needed. Taste and adjust the seasoning.

Summer Evening Pasta

My husband, Tad, and I are often working on a pasta dish—there is no beginning and there is no end. It's a once-a-week dinner that we—well, mostly he—have been making for years, and each time we tweak it depending on what's in season, what's in the fridge, and what's going on in our work-addled heads.

The pasta usually begins with bacon or pancetta. When Tad's at the helm, canned tomatoes will likely find their way into the pan, and if it's my turn, a pinch of crushed chile. We've drifted from penne to rigatoni to orecchiette to shells—any shape our kids can easily spear with a fork. Sometimes eggs get tossed in for a little carbonara effect. And occasionally, Tad will slip in goat cheese in his mother's honor (she made an excellent pasta with goat cheese and asparagus). There's never a precise recipe because we never stop the music, we never let the ingredients race to their seats to get counted.

But a few summers ago, we hit a summer variation that was pretty nifty—and it was time to put a pasta on record. We'd gotten into cooking with grated summer squash, which nestles into orecchiette's little cups. Stirring squash into hot pasta is an excellent way to produce soggy pasta, however. To drain the swamp, we salt the grated squash, which draws out its water, then squeeze out as much liquid as we can before adding it to the steaming pasta.

The base is bacon, of course, with a pinch of red pepper flakes and a smashed garlic clove. To underline the sweetness and freshness of the dish, we fold in some just-scraped fresh corn and chopped basil. The dish is part vegetable, part pasta—buoyant, bright, and just what we crave on a steamy summer evening (see finished dish on page 68).

For more pastas, all Tad's, see page 270.

SERVES 4

3 yellow summer squash, trimmed

Salt

6 slices bacon, cut into ¼-inch (6mm) slices

1 clove garlic, smashed

Pinch of red pepper flakes

1 pound (450g) orecchiette or small shells

2 ears corn, kernels cut from the cobs, juices and all (see Merrill's tip on page 88)

2 tablespoons coarsely chopped or torn fresh basil

Freshly ground black pepper

Extra-virgin olive oil, as needed (optional)

Grated Parmesan, for serving

1 Grate the summer squash on a box grater. Gather the gratings in a bowl. Add about 1½ teaspoons salt and toss to combine. Let sit for at least 10 minutes and up to 30 minutes.

2 Bring a large pot of generously salted water to a boil. Meanwhile, spread the bacon in a large sauté pan and add the garlic. Cook over medium heat until the bacon is crisp and its fat has rendered, about 8 to 10 minutes. Turn off the heat and stir in the red pepper flakes.

3 When the water comes to a boil, add the pasta and cook until al dente. Drain the pasta but don't shake it; you want a little pasta water to help create a sauce. Pour the pasta back into the pot off the heat.

4 A fistful at a time, squeeze the salted squash as firmly as possible to extract any liquid, then add to the pasta. Continue until all of the squash has been squeezed. Scrape the corn into the pot. Transfer the bacon to the pot with a slotted spoon; discard the garlic clove. (If there is less than 2 tablespoons rendered fat in the pan, I usually add the bacon and all of the fat to the pasta.) Toss the pasta, then adjust the seasoning, adding more salt if needed. Add the basil, season with pepper, and toss again; sometimes I splash in a few tablespoons of olive oil. Spoon into shallow bowls and top with a scattering of Parmesan.

Grilled Pork Chops with Hacked Romesco

Romesco is one of the great sauces, and this recipe, which makes use of the peppers that you're already cooking this week, is a quickie version. If you want to take an extra step, you can toast the almonds, but the sauce will live—and so will you—if you don't.

Meet Romesco, Sauce Hero Romesco gets along with just about everything in the kitchen. You can mix and match it with lots of other recipes in this book. Here are a few to start with: brandade (page 46), Merrill's grilled steak (page 120), and her grilled shrimp (page 123). Romesco can also act as a marinade. Anna Gass, one of our recipe testers, uses it to marinate chicken kebabs before grilling them.

MAKES 2 1/2 CUPS (590ML)

ROMESCO

1 dried ancho chile

1 cup (190g) Blistered Cherry Tomatoes (page 76)

1 cup (200g) Olive Oil–Braised Peppers (page 103) or store-bought roasted peppers (in oil, not vinegar)

1/4 cup (35g) almonds

1 clove garlic, smashed and chopped

1/2 to 3/4 cup (120 to 175ml) extra-virgin olive oil

Salt

1 to 2 tablespoons aged sherry vinegar

PORK

4 large pork chops

Salt and freshly ground black pepper

1 Soak the chile in very hot water for 20 minutes.

2 Remove the seeds and stem from the chile and discard. Combine the chile, tomatoes, peppers, almonds, and garlic in the bowl of a food processor. Pulse a few times to blend. Then, with the processor running, add the olive oil in a slow, steady stream and process until the sauce becomes thick and creamy, like a mayonnaise. About 1/2 cup (120ml) of oil should be enough, but add up to 1/4 cup (60ml) more as needed. To sharpen the flavor, season with salt and add vinegar to taste. Store in the fridge for up to a week.

3 In the morning of the day you will make the pork chops, place them on a plate or small baking sheet and season with salt and pepper. Place, covered, in the fridge.

4 When you're ready to cook, heat your grill so it has a nice big bed of hot coals. Grill the pork chops until light pink in the center, about 5 minutes per side. The internal temperature should be 145°F (63°C) for medium rare. (If you don't have a grill, you can broil the chops in the oven, 5 inches/13cm from the flame, about 4 minutes per side.)

5 You can top the pork with the romesco or serve it on the side, depending on your personality type. Not judging!

Lunch: Eggs with Romesco

Put some halved **hard-boiled eggs** in a container and top with **romesco.** And pack **a good roll** to sop up all the tasty sauce.

Have Extra Time on Your Hands? This is the best time of year to preserve and freeze summer's bounty for the winter months. Here is a handful of recipes that you can make batches of now.

- Quick Tomato Sauce (page 37)
- Charmoula (page 62)
- Green Sauce (page 98)
- Hacked Romesco (page 107)
- Lime Sriracha Butter (page 121)
- Garlic Scape Pesto (page 123)
- Meatballs with Tomato and Zucchini (page 136)
- Slow-Cooked Pork Tacos (page 263)
- Ginger Syrup (page 268)

Plum Tart

Every cook needs a good dessert recipe that can be whipped up anywhere, especially when you're away from your kitchen with its mixer and rolling pin and other comforting tools. This tart is that recipe for me. To make it, all you need is a knife, a bowl, and some kind of pan. A tart pan ideally, but I've even made it on a baking sheet with one side shored up with aluminum foil. And when I've been without a bowl, I've mixed the dough right in the pan.

The tart dough is made with oil, milk, and almond extract and is pressed into the pan. No blind baking nonsense! Just top the dough with the fruit, shower it with a sugary, salty crumble, and send it on its merry way into the oven.

I got the original recipe, which is a peach tart, from my mother, who uses all vegetable oil in the crust. I use half vegetable oil and half olive oil. She neatly peels her peaches. I do not. Hers is probably better, but you are stuck with me. I can promise you, however, that whoever you serve this to will not mind.

MAKES ONE 11-INCH (28CM) TART; SERVES 4, TWICE!

1½ cups plus 2 tablespoons (205g) all-purpose flour, plus more if needed	2 tablespoons milk
	½ teaspoon almond extract
¾ teaspoon kosher salt	2 tablespoons cold unsalted butter
¾ cup (150g) plus 1 teaspoon sugar	12 to 15 small Italian plums, pitted and cut into ½-inch (1.3cm) wedges
¼ cup (60ml) vegetable or canola oil	
¼ cup (60ml) extra-virgin olive oil	Whipped cream, for serving (optional, but is it?)

1 Heat the oven to 425°F (220°C). In a large bowl, stir together 1½ cups (190g) of the flour, ½ teaspoon of the salt, and 1 teaspoon of the sugar. (Stirring enables the salt and sugar to sift the flour, so you don't need to sift it in advance.) In a small bowl, whisk together the oils, milk, and almond extract, then pour into the dry ingredients. Mix gently with a fork, just enough to dampen, then press together with your hands; do not overwork the dough.

2 Transfer the dough to an 11-inch (28cm) tart pan (you can use a smaller one if needed). Use your hands to pat the dough so that it covers the bottom of the pan, pushing it up the sides until it meets the edge. Pat firmly and confidently; do not curl your fingertips into the dough. The dough should be about ⅛ inch (3mm) thick all around; trim and discard excess dough. Refrigerate.

3 In a separate bowl, combine the remaining ¾ cup (150g) sugar, 2 tablespoons flour, and ¼ teaspoon salt. (If your plums are especially juicy, add 1 tablespoon additional flour.) Add the butter, and, using your fingers, pinch the butter into the dry ingredients until crumbly, with a mixture of fine granules and tiny pebbles.

4 Starting on the edge, arrange the plums on the dough in a concentric circle, overlapping them. Fill in the center in whatever pattern you like. The plums should fit snugly. Sprinkle the pebbly butter mixture over the top (it will seem like a lot). Bake until shiny, thick bubbles begin enveloping the fruit and the crust is slightly brown, 35 to 45 minutes. Transfer to a rack to cool. Store, covered, at room temp, for up to 4 days.

5 **The day of:** Cut into wedges and serve with generous dollops of whipped cream.

Peach and Other Tart Variations You can use any kind of fruit with a structured flesh in place of the plums. Peaches are particularly great here. White and yellow peaches work equally well (you'll need about 5 ripe peaches); I've even made it with doughnut peaches. About 5 Macoun apples are also a smart substitute. Slice them thinly and don't bother arranging them; just mound them into the tart shell. They'll cook down, don't worry.

Merrill's Summer

THE WEEK AHEAD

THE RECIPES

Strawberry Rosé Spritzer 116

Strawberry Ice Cream
Floats 116

Strawberry Shakes with
Yogurt and Honey 116

Farro Salad with Roasted
Mushrooms and
Parmesan 119

Steak with Arugula, Lemon,
and Parmesan 120

Grain Bowls with Chopped
Steak 121

Lime Sriracha Butter 121

Avocado and Radish
Tartine with Lime
Sriracha Butter 121

Radish and Hummus
Tartine 121

Grilled Shrimp with Arugula
and Garlic Scape Pesto 123

Farro Salad with Shrimp,
Radishes, and Pesto 124

Pesto Toasts 124

Pasta with Pesto and
Tuna 124

Avocado Toasts with Pesto,
Crispy Bacon, and Poached
Eggs 124

Eton Mess 126

Meringue Cookies 126

HOW THEY COME TOGETHER

DINNER ONE

Strawberry Rosé Spritzer

Radishes with Lime Sriracha Butter

Grilled Shrimp with Arugula and
Garlic Scape Pesto

Farro Salad with Roasted Mushrooms
and Parmesan

Meringue cookies

TO DO TODAY Marinate the shrimp and bring the
farro salad to room temperature. Set out the radishes
and lime Sriracha butter and mix some spritzers.
Grill the shrimp. Pass the cookies for dessert.

DINNER TWO

Steak with Arugula, Lemon, and Parmesan

Pesto Toasts

Eton Mess

TO DO TODAY In the morning, salt the steaks and
put them back in the fridge uncovered. Before dinner,
heat the grill and assemble the Eton mess. Grill and
assemble the steak and the toasts. Serve the Eton
mess in pretty glasses.

DINNER THREE

Pasta with Pesto and Tuna

Arugula and parsley with lemon juice
and olive oil

Eton Mess

TO DO TODAY Make the pasta. Toss the arugula
with some torn parsley leaves and dress them.
Finish up the Eton mess.

DINNER FOUR

Avocado Toasts with Pesto, Crispy Bacon,
and Poached Eggs

Strawberry Shakes with Yogurt
and Honey

TO DO TODAY Poach the eggs and make the
avocado toasts. Whiz up the shakes for dessert.

DINNER FIVE

Grain Bowls with Chopped Steak

Strawberry Ice Cream Floats

TO DO TODAY Make the grain bowls. Assemble
the floats when you're ready for dessert.

BROWN BAG LUNCHES

Tartines

Farro Salad with Shrimp, Radishes, and Pesto

GAME PLAN

TO MAKE OVER THE WEEKEND

Strawberry Rosé Spritzer

Farro Salad with Roasted
Mushrooms and Parmesan

Lime Sriracha Butter

Grilled Shrimp with Arugula
and Garlic Scape Pesto

Eton Mess

SUMMER'S HERE, AND IT'S TIME TO GRILL

This weekend, you're looking at about 3 hours of cooking
time—a little more or less, depending on how often you
pause to look longingly out the window.

- In the morning, set out the butter for the lime Sriracha
  butter (page 121) and separate the eggs for the Eton
  mess (page 126). Cover and leave out the whites;
  refrigerate the yolks.

- Heat the oven to 450°F (230°C)—not for long,
  I promise! Put the mushrooms for the farro salad
  (page 119) into the oven to roast.

- Get the farro boiling.

- Wash and dry the arugula for the week. Scrub and trim
  the radishes so they're ready for eating. Put everything
  in the fridge.

- Drain the farro and let it cool.

- Rinse, dry, and hull all the berries for the week, halving
  2 cups (300g) of them for the Eton mess (page 126)
  and freezing 3 cups (450g) for shakes (page 116).

- Whip up the meringue. When the mushrooms are done,
  lower the oven to 225°F (107°C) and put the meringues
  in the oven.

- Mix the strawberries and sugar for the spritzer
  (page 116) and let them sit for an hour.

- Chop the Parmesan and parsley for the farro salad
  (page 119) and mix up the salad, reserving half of
  the cooked farro for grain bowls (page 121) later
  in the week. Store the salad and the extra farro in
  the refrigerator.

- Make the lime Sriracha butter (page 121) and garlic
  scape pesto (page 123) and put them in the fridge.

- Whip the cream for the Eton mess (page 126) to the
  softest of soft peaks and refrigerate. Yes, you can
  partially whip cream ahead of time and refrigerate
  it (see page 126)!

- Whiz up the strawberry puree for the spritzers and
  put it in the fridge.

- Now, scram!

Cabin fever? If beautiful weather is beckoning
you outside, forgo the lime Sriracha butter and the
strawberry puree and make a pot of plain farro. I simply
will not allow you to skip the Eton mess. This shortened
plan should take you about 1½ hours.

GROCERY LIST

PRODUCE

Assorted mushrooms (use your favorites), 1 pound (450g)

Avocados, 3

Baby arugula, 22 cups (440g) loosely packed

Garlic, 2 cloves

Garlic scapes, ½ cup (50g) chopped

Lemons, 8

Lime, 1

Radishes, 4 bunches

Raspberries, 2 cups (245g)

Scallions, 4

Strawberries, 8 cups (1.2kg)

HERBS

Flat-leaf parsley leaves, ½ cup (10g) loosely packed

Thyme leaves, 1 teaspoon finely chopped

SPICES

Cayenne, a pinch

Red pepper flakes, 2 pinches

PANTRY

Farro, 4 cups (720g) uncooked

Honey, 6 to 8 tablespoons (120 to 160g)

Extra-virgin olive oil, 2 cups (475ml), plus more for dressing

Flaky salt

Short pasta (such as penne or rigatoni), 1 pound (450g)

Soy sauce, 1 tablespoon, plus more for serving

Sriracha, 2 teaspoons, plus more for serving

Toasted sesame oil, 3 drops

Tuna in oil, 1 (7-ounce/200g) can

Vegetable oil, 1 tablespoon

BAKING AISLE

Cream of tartar, ¼ teaspoon

Roasted and salted almonds, 3 tablespoons

Sugar, ½ cup plus 2 tablespoons (125g)

Superfine sugar, 1½ cups (340g)

Vanilla bean, ½ (optional)

Pure vanilla extract, 1 teaspoon

DAIRY AND EGGS

Unsalted butter, 1 cup (225g)

Eggs, 10

Greek yogurt, 1⅓ cups (315ml)

Heavy cream, 2 cups (475ml)

Milk, ½ cup (120ml)

Parmesan, 3 ounces (85g), plus more for serving

Pecorino, ⅓ cup (35g) grated from a wedge

MEAT AND SEAFOOD

Bacon, 8 ounces (225g)

Jumbo shrimp, 1½ pounds (675g) (16 to 20 count)

T-bone steak, 2 (about 3½ pounds/1.6kg and at least 1½ inches/4cm thick)

BOOZE AND SUCH

Rosé, 12 fluid ounces (355ml)

Soda water, for cocktails

FREEZER

Strawberry ice cream

BAKED GOODS

Country bread, 2 loaves

Whole-grain bread, 1 loaf (freeze extra)

PREPARED FOODS

Hummus, for lunch

Strawberry Rosé Spritzer

As soon as the temperature hits 75°F, all I want to drink is rosé. Add some homemade strawberry puree and a little soda water to that rosé, and I'm even happier.

MAKES 4 DRINKS, WITH ABOUT 1¼ CUPS (300ML) EXTRA STRAWBERRY PUREE

STRAWBERRY PUREE

2⅔ cups (1.2kg) strawberries

½ cup (100g) sugar (more or less, depending on the sweetness of your berries)

SPRITZER

¾ cup (6 fluid ounces/175ml) strawberry puree

12 fluid ounces (355ml) dry rosé

Soda water

1 To make the puree, rinse and hull the strawberries and combine them with the sugar in a large bowl. Depending on the sweetness of the berries, you can use more or less sugar. Let the strawberries sit until they're nice and juicy, about an hour.

2 Puree the strawberries and sugar in a blender or using an immersion blender, then strain through a fine-mesh sieve, discarding the seeds. Keep the puree in a jar in the fridge for up to a week. You should have about 2 cups (475ml) of puree. You'll use ¾ cup (175ml) for the spritzers, with 1¼ cups (300ml) left over for ice cream floats (see right).

3 Put 4 or 5 ice cubes into four 8-ounce tumblers. Add 1½ fluid ounces (45ml) of puree and 3 fluid ounces (90ml) of rosé to each glass and stir gently to combine. Top with soda water and stir again.

Some Variations You can make this spritzer with pretty much any fruit. Adjust the sugar depending on the sweetness of the fruit, and make sure to remove all peels and pits. Peaches and raspberries are both nice, and if you only have white wine around, don't let that stop you!

For a kid-friendly rendition, stir about a ¼ cup (60ml) strawberry puree into 1 cup (240ml) soda water to make a fresh strawberry soda.

For a homemade float, add a scoop of strawberry ice cream to the soda above.

Throw a Party This is a great drink to make into batch cocktails for a group. Scale up the ingredients to match the number of drinks you're making. Combine the strawberry puree and rosé in a pitcher and stir well. Keep this in the fridge until you're ready to serve (up to 6 hours), then pour about ½ cup (120ml) into tumblers filled with ice and top them with ¼ cup (60ml) of soda water.

Strawberry Shakes with Yogurt and Honey

I'm happy to drink one of these any time of day, at any stage of any meal. At breakfast, it's a smoothie; at dinner, it's dessert. The key is to freeze berries at the peak of ripeness, for the most concentrated fruit flavor and sweetness. And because you're starting with frozen fruit, you won't need to dilute your shakes with ice.

To make 4 shakes, combine **3 cups (450g) frozen strawberries, 1⅓ cups (315ml) Greek yogurt, ½ cup (120ml) milk,** and **6 to 8 tablespoons (120 to 160g) honey** (depending on the sweetness of your berries) in a blender. If you happen to have **half a vanilla bean** lying around, scrape some of the seeds in there as well. Blend until thick and creamy, pour into glasses, and pass the straws! For a richer shake, use ice cream instead of Greek yogurt.

Farro Salad with Roasted Mushrooms and Parmesan

Before Food52 had a real office, the gracious staff at Morandi in the West Village allowed Amanda and me to camp out with our laptops for most of the day, greeting us with patient smiles each morning. We consumed countless lattes, ordering food as we got hungry. My lunch of choice was an earthy salad of farro, roasted mushrooms, and Parmesan. What really won me over was the unusual texture of the Parmesan: It wasn't grated but crumbled into tiny pebbles, creating hundreds of chewy bursts of umami. Now I make my version of this salad at home.

Eat It All Year Long In autumn, fold roasted vegetables such as brussels sprouts (page 196), cauliflower (page 169), or small cubes of sweet potato into the salad. In the spring, try blanched fresh peas, swap marjoram or mint for the thyme, and use Pecorino instead of Parmesan.

Make It Dinner One of my favorite one-dish meals is a bowl of this salad with a poached egg: The egg yolk becomes a silky sauce for the farro as you eat it. Set the salad out at room temperature about 30 minutes before you eat, or warm it briefly in the microwave. Identify the best egg poacher in the house and put him to work. Serve everyone a mound of farro with a poached egg on top and hot sauce on the side.

SERVES 4 AS A SIDE FOR 2 DINNERS, PLUS LEFTOVERS

4 cups (720g) uncooked farro

Kosher salt and freshly ground black pepper

1 pound (450g) assorted mushrooms (use your favorites), trimmed and wiped clean

1 teaspoon finely chopped fresh thyme leaves

⅓ cup plus 2 tablespoons (110ml) extra-virgin olive oil

3 ounces (85g) Parmesan

½ cup (10g) loosely packed flat-leaf parsley leaves

¼ cup (60ml) freshly squeezed lemon juice

1 Heat the oven to 450°F (230°C). Line a rimmed baking sheet with parchment paper.

2 Put the farro in a large pot and add enough cold water to cover. Add several big pinches of salt and bring to a boil. Simmer until it's tender but still has some bite, 20 to 25 minutes.

3 Cut the mushrooms into bite-size pieces and combine them in a large bowl with the thyme and 2 tablespoons of the olive oil. Season with salt and pepper and toss gently. Spread out on the prepared baking sheet and roast, stirring once, until crisp around the edges and tender, about 20 minutes. Let the mushrooms cool slightly on the baking sheet.

4 Meanwhile, drain the farro and spread it out on another baking sheet to cool.

5 Chop the Parmesan until it's pebbly (it should look like small Grape-Nuts)—you want about ½ cup (85g). Coarsely chop the parsley.

6 Combine half of the farro with the mushrooms in a large bowl. Reserve the remaining farro for the grain bowls (page 121). Add the lemon juice, the remaining ⅓ cup (80ml) olive oil, the Parmesan, and parsley. Season with pepper and fold gently. Taste and adjust the seasoning. Keep the salad in the fridge for up to 5 days.

7 **The day of:** Reheat the farro salad gently in the microwave for about a minute, or let sit at room temperature for 20 to 30 minutes.

Steak with Arugula, Lemon, and Parmesan

Any Tuscan trattoria worth its salt offers a T-bone steak big enough for a family of four. It's seasoned with lots of salt and pepper, cooked over an open flame, and served thickly sliced, with a river of olive oil and lemons for squeezing. The best bistecca fiorentina I can recall arrived with a mountain of arugula and paper-thin wisps of Parmesan wobbling precariously atop it. The juices from the steak merged with the lemon and oil, creating a warm, tangy dressing for the peppery greens. This is a perfect one-platter meal to enjoy outside all spring and summer long—and even into fall. I owe my seasoning and grilling techniques to steak guru Kenji López-Alt; there are also instructions for cooking the steak in the oven if you don't have a grill. (See finished dish on page 112—and the cover!)

Steak Swap You don't need to break the bank with an expensive cut to make this dish. Rib eye, strip, or flank work nicely too; just make sure to slice less tender cuts more thinly. The most important thing is to season your meat well and do what Kenji says!

SERVES 4, PLUS LEFTOVER STEAK

2 T-bone steaks, at least 1½ inches (4cm) thick, about 3½ pounds (1.6kg)

Kosher salt and coarsely ground black pepper

8 cups (160g) loosely packed baby arugula

2 lemons

Extra-virgin olive oil, for drizzling

Flaky salt

Parmesan, for serving

1 In the morning, put the steaks on a plate or small baking sheet and season with plenty of salt. Refrigerate uncovered until you're ready to cook them.

2 If you're using a grill, heat your grill, banking the coals so that one side is very hot and the other is cooler. Pat the steaks dry with paper towels and grill them on the cooler side with the cover down for 5 to 7 minutes per side, or until the internal temperature reaches 125°F (52°C). Move the steaks over to the hot side of the grill and cook them uncovered for 2 to 3 minutes more on each side, until a nice crust forms and the internal temperature reaches 135°F (57°C) for medium-rare. If you don't have a grill, heat the oven to 375°F (190°C) and warm a well-seasoned cast-iron skillet over high heat on the stovetop. Place the steaks in the pan and cook until well browned, 2 to 3 minutes per side. Slide the pan into the oven and cook for 7 to 10 minutes, until the internal temperature reaches 135°F (57°C) for medium-rare. If all the steaks don't fit in the pan, brown them in batches and transfer them to a baking sheet before finishing them in the oven. Let the steaks rest on a cutting board for 5 to 10 minutes.

3 Pile the arugula onto a large platter and cut the lemons into wedges. Carve the steaks from the bones, then cut one of the steaks across the grain into ⅓-inch (8mm) slices, corralling any juices that try to escape. Reserve the remaining cooked steak in a container and keep in the fridge for up to 5 days.

4 Drizzle olive oil over the arugula, followed by a generous squeeze of lemon juice and plenty of flaky salt and pepper. Arrange the sliced steak on top of the arugula and drizzle the reserved juices over the steak and greens, with some more lemon juice and pepper. Use a vegetable peeler to shave curls of Parmesan over everything. Arrange the rest of the lemon wedges on the edges of the platter and serve right away.

Grain Bowls with Chopped Steak

To make dinner for 4, cut ¾ **pound (340g) cooked steak** into bite-size pieces, chop **4 scallions,** and mince a **large clove of garlic.** Heat **1 tablespoon vegetable oil** in a large skillet or wok over medium-high heat. Add **3 drops toasted sesame oil,** the garlic, and half the scallions, and cook for 30 seconds. Add **2 ⅔ cups (425g) cooked farro** (or substitute other cooked grains like barley or rice) and heat through, stirring well. Add the steak and **1 tablespoon soy sauce** and stir through. Serve with the remaining scallions on the side. Pass soy sauce and **Sriracha** at the table. This is a good time to add any lingering **arugula** or **herbs**—even fry **an egg** for the top.

Lime Sriracha Butter

Radishes, butter, and salt are a classic trio. I thought it was time to shake things up a bit so I came up with this flavored butter. Use leftover butter to finish steak or fish, stir into rice, or melt and pour over popcorn.

To make 1 cup (225g) of butter, let **1 cup (225g) unsalted butter** soften at room temperature. Zest and juice **1 lime.** Put the zest and 2 teaspoons lime juice into a bowl. Add the softened butter, **2 teaspoons Sriracha,** and **a pinch of cayenne** and stir vigorously until everything is combined. (Or use a food processor or stand mixer.) Mound a third of the butter into a bowl and cover with plastic wrap. Form the rest into a log and roll tightly in plastic wrap. Refrigerate until you're ready to use it. Well wrapped, the butter will keep in the fridge for a few weeks or in the freezer for up to 6 months. To serve with radishes, remove the bowl of butter from the fridge and let it soften a bit before setting it out with about 20 trimmed and scrubbed radishes and a small dish of flaky salt.

Lunch: Avocado and Radish Tartine with Lime Sriracha Butter

Thinly slice **country bread** and spread with softened **lime Sriracha butter** (above). Top with thinly sliced **avocado** and **radishes,** flaky salt, and plenty of cracked pepper.

Lunch: Radish and Hummus Tartine

Thinly slice **country bread** and spread with **hummus.** Slice **2 or 3 radishes** and layer them on top. Sprinkle with flaky salt and cracked pepper.

Grilled Shrimp with Arugula and Garlic Scape Pesto

Pesto is a make-aheader's dream. It's a means for cleaning out your fridge and pantry, it freezes beautifully, and it plays nice with everything from meat and fish to pasta and grains to soups and vegetables. It's also a great way to extend the life of your Greenmarket haul. Garlic scapes have a short season and yield a vibrant, kicky pesto, so they're the perfect contender. I've used the garlic scape pesto as a marinade for tender shrimp, simply grilled, but as you'll see below, it has many other applications.

Make Your Scapes Last Put any pesto you don't use this week into ice cube trays and freeze. Transfer the frozen cubes to a plastic freezer bag and freeze for up to 6 months. Toss into soups, or thaw them for pesto toasts (page 124), pasta (page 124), or avocado toasts (page 124).

How Amanda Uses the Pesto "This lively pesto goes well with a number of other dishes in the book. Toss it with the ricotta gnocchi (page 200), or serve it as a condiment with the pan-roasted chicken (page 184) or the lamb blade chops (page 196), or slather it on quesadillas (page 65)."

SERVES 4, PLUS LEFTOVER SHRIMP AND PESTO

PESTO

½ cup (50g) chopped garlic scapes

2 lemons

1 fat clove garlic

8 cups (160g) loosely packed arugula

⅓ cup (35g) grated Pecorino

3 tablespoons roasted, salted almonds

Pinch of red pepper flakes

Kosher salt and freshly ground black pepper

1 cup (240ml) extra-virgin olive oil, plus more as needed

SHRIMP

1½ pounds (680g) jumbo shrimp, peeled and deveined, with the tail on

1 To make the pesto, put the garlic scapes in the bowl of a food processor. Zest and juice 1 lemon into the food processor, straining out the seeds. Add the garlic, arugula, Pecorino, almonds, red pepper flakes, ¼ teaspoon salt, and black pepper to taste. Pulse everything until it's finely chopped, scraping down the sides of the bowl. (If you have a small food processor, you may need to add the arugula in batches.)

2 With the food processor running, add the olive oil in a slow, steady stream and process until everything is blended into a paste. Taste and add more salt, black pepper, or lemon juice, if needed. Transfer the pesto to a container and refrigerate for up to 10 days or freeze for up to 6 months.

3 **The day of:** Toss the shrimp with ⅓ cup (80g) of the pesto. Put in the fridge for at least 20 minutes and up to 3 hours.

4 Heat the grill. Thread the shrimp onto long metal skewers and grill until they're just pink, about a minute per side. Remove the shrimp from the skewers. Pile 1 pound (450g) of the shrimp onto a platter. Put the remaining shrimp in a container and keep in the fridge for up to 2 days. Cut the remaining lemon into wedges and add to the platter before serving.

Lunch: Farro Salad with Shrimp, Radishes, and Pesto

Slice several **radishes** and toss them with **arugula**, leftover **cooked farro** (page 119), and **a spoonful of pesto** (page 123). Top with **grilled shrimp** (page 123) and pack **a couple of lemon wedges** to squeeze on top.

Pesto Toasts

For a simple starter or side, cut **country bread** into ¼-inch (6mm) slices and spread one side with **garlic scape pesto** (page 123) or another pesto of your choice. Toast in a 375°F (190°C) oven for 3 to 5 minutes, until browned and crisp.

Pasta with Pesto and Tuna

To make dinner for 4, bring a pot of salted water to a boil and cook **1 pound (450g) short pasta** (penne and rigatoni are my standbys). Open and drain **a can of good oil-packed tuna**, then use a fork to break it into chunks. Drain the pasta, reserving 1 cup (240ml) of the cooking water, and return it to the pot. Over low heat, fold ⅓ **cup (80g) garlic scape pesto** (page 123) into the pasta, adding a few spoonfuls of the pasta water to loosen it up. Fold in the tuna, **a handful of grated Parmesan**, and some ground pepper and serve. Tuna noodle casserole, all grown up!

Avocado Toasts with Pesto, Crispy Bacon, and Poached Eggs

I can't imagine avocado toast with eggs ever getting old—especially this version, amped up with pesto and bacon. To make avocado toast for 4, fry **8 ounces (225g) sliced bacon** until crisp. Mash **2 avocados** with **2 tablespoons pesto** (the garlic scape version on page 123, or whatever you have on hand) and **a pinch of red pepper flakes**, keeping the avocado chunky. Poach **4 eggs** and toast **4 slices of whole grain bread.** Mound some avocado onto each slice of toast, crumble some bacon over it, and perch an egg on top. Serve the toasts right away, with **hot sauce** on the side.

Yes, You Can Cook Bacon in the Oven I haven't made bacon on my stovetop in at least a decade. When I lived in London, my flatmates taught me to lay the strips on a rimmed baking sheet and crisp them in the oven at 325°F (165°C). There's no splatter and the bacon cooks evenly, with less risk of burning (always a plus for me, a burning aficionado). Turn the bacon with tongs every 10 minutes or so. Depending on the thickness, you can expect it to be done in 20 to 30 minutes.

Eton Mess

If I had to commit to a long-term relationship with a dessert, Eton mess would be it: a berry-scented cloud of cream flecked with shards of crunchy meringue. Like its close cousin the Pavlova, this dessert has endless permutations. Feel free to switch it up with other fruit, like mashed kiwis or peaches. You'll need six egg whites to make the meringue; reserve the yolks to whisk with whole eggs before scrambling for a really special breakfast.

A Secret About Whipped Cream You can whip cream part of the way and keep it in the fridge for a day or two. Whisk the cream until it just forms soft peaks. When you're ready to use it, whisk it a couple more times to get it to the perfect consistency.

SERVES 4 FOR 2 DESSERTS, PLUS EXTRA MERINGUES

MERINGUE	MESS
6 large egg whites, at room temperature	2 cups (300g) fresh strawberries, washed
1 teaspoon pure vanilla extract	2 cups (475ml) heavy cream, plus more if needed
¼ teaspoon cream of tartar	2 tablespoons sugar
1½ cups (340g) superfine sugar	2 cups (190g) fresh raspberries, washed

1 To make the meringue, heat the oven to 225°F (107°C). Line 2 baking sheets with parchment paper.

2 In the bowl of a stand mixer fitted with the whisk attachment, beat the egg whites on low speed until foamy, 1 to 2 minutes. Add the vanilla and cream of tartar and beat until incorporated. With the mixer running, gradually add the superfine sugar and continue to beat until the whites hold soft peaks, 2 to 3 minutes.

3 Pile half of the whipped egg whites onto one of the prepared baking sheets in a rough circle; it should be about 1½ inches (4cm) high (don't worry too much about the shape, since you'll be crumbling the meringue later). Smooth the top with a spatula. Using two large spoons, drop dollops of the remaining whipped egg whites onto the second prepared baking sheet (each dollop should be about 3 tablespoons), placing them 1½ inches (4cm) apart.

4 Put both baking sheets in the oven and bake for about an hour, until the meringues are crisp on the outside but not browned. You don't want them completely dry, but they shouldn't be too wet in the center either. Remove them from the oven, slide the parchment paper onto racks, and let cool completely. Store the smaller meringues separately from the larger one; both will keep in airtight containers at room temperature for up to 5 days. You'll use the larger meringue for the mess and the smaller ones for other desserts.

5 While the meringues bake, hull and halve the strawberries (if they're large, quarter them). Whip the cream. When it starts to thicken, sprinkle in the sugar. Continue to whip just until the cream starts to hold very soft peaks when you lift a spoonful from the bowl. (Do not overbeat, as you will be working it more later.) Refrigerate the whipped cream and strawberries for up to 24 hours.

6 **The day of:** Break the large meringue into bite-sized pieces and set aside. In a large bowl, fold together the whipped cream, strawberries, and raspberries. Gently fold in the meringue. The mixture should be soft and not too dense; you can add more liquid cream if it seems tight. Spoon it into a large bowl and serve right away or refrigerate until serving time. The mess is best eaten within 2 hours, but it will still be good the next day.

Meringue Cookie Variations Add some chocolate chips or chopped toasted nuts after you've formed the larger meringue for the Eton mess, and your smaller meringue cookies will disappear twice as fast.

THE WEEK AHEAD

THE RECIPES

HOW THEY COME TOGETHER

DINNER ONE

Crab and Avocado Salad

Blistered Cherry Tomatoes

Watermelon

TO DO TODAY Let the tomatoes and the lemon
mustard dressing for the crab salad come to
room temperature. Assemble the salad. Serve
cold sliced watermelon for dessert.

DINNER TWO

Meatballs with Tomato and Zucchini

Quick Tomato Sauce

Spaghetti

Boiled Green Beans with lemon
mustard dressing

Black Raspberry Chocolate Chip Ice Cream

TO DO TODAY Boil the green beans and cool them.
Cook a pound of spaghetti, warm the meatballs in the
tomato sauce, and toss it all together. Serve with grated
Parmesan. Drizzle some of the lemon mustard dressing
from the crab salad over half of the beans, refrigerating
the rest. Soften the ice cream a bit before scooping.

DINNER THREE

Watermelonade

Crab Toasties

Peaches with sour cream and brown sugar

TO DO TODAY Make the crab toasties and mix up
the watermelonade. Top sliced peaches with dollops
of sour cream and brown sugar for dessert.

DINNER FOUR

Pasta with Garlic, Tomatoes, Basil, and Brie

Boiled Green Beans with lemon mustard dressing

Black Raspberry Chocolate Chip Ice Cream

TO DO TODAY In the morning, start the sauce
for the pasta. Before dinner, dress the green
beans and finish up the pasta.

DINNER FIVE

Meatball Sandwiches with Fresh Mozzarella
and Basil

Watermelon or peaches

TO DO TODAY Make the meatball sandwiches.

BROWN BAG LUNCHES

Blistered Tomato, Avocado,
and Crab Tartine with Capers

My Favorite Tomato Sandwich

GAME PLAN

TO MAKE OVER THE WEEKEND

Watermelonade

Meatballs with Tomato
and Zucchini

Quick Tomato Sauce

Boiled Green Beans

Pasta with Garlic, Tomatoes,
Basil, and Brie

Black Raspberry Chocolate
Chip Ice Cream

Half recipe of Blistered
Cherry Tomatoes (page 76)

BANG IT OUT, AND GET OUTSIDE

You're looking at around 3 1/2 hours in the kitchen
this weekend.

• Anytime Saturday or first thing on Sunday: Make the
base for the ice cream (page 141) and chill it. Put
the canister of your ice cream maker in the freezer.

• Make the chocolate chips for the ice cream.

• Heat the oven to 425°F (220°C) and make a half recipe
of Amanda's blistered tomatoes (page 76).

• While the tomatoes are roasting, make the puree for
the watermelonade (page 133) and slice the rest of the
watermelon. Put everything in the fridge.

• Make the simple syrup for the watermelonade.
Consider doubling—it lasts for weeks in the fridge.

• Zest 2 lemons for the crab and avocado salad (page 134)
and squeeze 1 cup (240ml) of lemon juice. Put 1/2 cup
(120ml) for the watermelonade in the fridge.

• Sauté the vegetables for the meatballs (page 136)
and set them aside to cool.

• Blanch and peel the tomatoes (optional) and get the
tomato sauce (page 137) on the stove.

• Make the lemon mustard dressing and the crab salad
(page 134) and refrigerate them.

• Wash and dry the greens and herbs for the week,
trim the green beans, and store them in the fridge.

• Make the meatball mixture and shape it into balls.
Refrigerate.

• Churn the ice cream. Meanwhile, cook the meatballs
on the stove or, for a quicker option, in the oven (see
Amanda's tip on page 136). Cool and refrigerate.

• Put the ice cream in the freezer. But before you do,
put a scoop in a bowl and eat it. Slowly.

Want more time in the sunshine? Save the ice cream
for a rainy day and skip the watermelonade and tomato
sauce (buy some good fresh marinara instead). This will
save you about 1 1/2 hours.

GROCERY LIST

PRODUCE

Avocados, 2 large

Bibb lettuce, 1 small head

Black raspberries, 5 cups (625g)

Celery, 4 stalks

Garlic, 6 cloves

Green beans, 3 pounds (1.4kg)

Lemons, 6

Peaches, for dessert

Scallions, 5

Shallot, 2 to get 6 tablespoons (60g) minced

Beefsteak tomatoes, 7 medium, perfectly ripe

Cherry (and/or Sun Gold!) tomatoes, 6 cups (900g) of the tiniest, sweetest you can find

Tomatoes of any kind, 3 pounds (1.4kg)

Watermelon, 1 (15-pound/6.8kg) seedless

Yellow onions, 2 small

Zucchini, 1 small-medium

HERBS

Basil leaves, 1 cup (20g) loosely packed

Tarragon, 1 teaspoon chopped

PANTRY

Capers, 1 teaspoon

Curly pasta (such as cavatappi), 1 pound (450g)

Dijon mustard, 2 tablespoons

Dry bread crumbs, ⅓ cup (35g)

Extra-virgin olive oil, 2¾ cups (650ml)

Honey, 2 teaspoons

Spaghetti, 1 pound (450g)

BAKING AISLE

Semisweet chocolate, 8 ounces (225g)

Brown sugar, for sprinkling

Sugar, 1½ cups plus 2 tablespoons (325g)

Pure vanilla extract, 1 teaspoon

DAIRY AND EGGS

Unsalted butter, 7 tablespoons (100g)

Eggs, 7

Good Brie, 12 ounces (340g)

Heavy cream, 2½ cups (590ml)

Mayonnaise, ¼ cup (60ml), plus more to have on hand

Milk, 1½ cups (355ml)

Mozzarella, for lunch

Parmesan, ¾ cup (75g) grated from a wedge, plus more for serving

Sour cream, ¾ cup plus 1 tablespoon (195ml)

MEAT AND SEAFOOD

Fresh crabmeat, 2 pounds (900g)

Ground beef (85% lean), 1 pound (450g)

Ground veal, 1 pound (450g)

BAKED GOODS

Dense whole-grain bread, for lunch

English muffins, 4

Kaiser rolls, 4

Watermelonade

At my bridal shower, the caterer served beautiful glasses of pink lemonade mixed with fresh watermelon puree. I've been making it every summer since. Only attempt this if you have excellent watermelon, or you'll end up with a wan impostor.

Puree into Pops The recipe will leave you with 6 cups (1.4L) of extra watermelon puree, which you can use to make more watermelonade later in the week. You can also use it to make refreshing ice pops. If you don't have ice pop molds, just use little paper cups with wooden sticks.

A Boozier Version I'm not going to tell you it would be a bad idea to add a little vodka to the watermelonade, or to sub in prosecco for the water. If you're feeling pure, swap in sparkling water for some fizz.

Amanda's Take "There is such a thing as a perfect summer drink, and this is it."

MAKES 10 DRINKS, WITH EXTRA WATERMELON PUREE

½ cup (100g) sugar

1 (15-pound/6.8kg) seedless watermelon

½ cup (120ml) freshly squeezed lemon juice

1 Bring the sugar and ½ cup (120ml) water to a boil in a small saucepan, stirring to dissolve. As soon as it boils, turn off the heat and set aside to cool. Keep in an airtight container in the fridge for up to 10 days.

2 Peel and cube half of the watermelon (you should have about 16 cups/2.4kg); slice the rest for eating. Working in batches, puree the cubed watermelon in a blender, then strain through a fine-mesh sieve. You should have about 8 cups (1.9L) strained watermelon puree. Keep in an airtight container in the fridge for up to 5 days.

3 **The day of:** Stir together 3 cups (710ml) cold water, 2 cups (475ml) of the watermelon puree, the sugar syrup, and lemon juice. Pour it into tumblers over ice. If you have any leftover watermelonade (I never do), it will keep in the fridge for a day or two.

Crab and Avocado Salad

I was spoiled early in life by great Maine seafood. I like lobster just fine, but I'd choose a crab roll any day—especially Maine-style: peekytoe crab on a buttered and toasted roll, bound with just enough mayonnaise to keep the crab from spilling down your front. This is a Maine crab roll turned into a salad, with sliced avocado and a lemon mustard dressing.

SERVES 4, WITH EXTRA CRAB AND DRESSING

LEMON MUSTARD DRESSING

¾ cup (180ml) extra-virgin olive oil

½ cup (120ml) freshly squeezed lemon juice

6 tablespoons (60g) minced shallot

2 tablespoons Dijon mustard

2 teaspoons honey

2 teaspoons kosher salt

SALAD

2 pounds (900g) fresh cooked crabmeat, picked over for shells

5 scallions, white and light green parts, finely chopped

4 small, tender celery stalks, finely chopped

¼ cup (60ml) mayonnaise

5 tablespoons (75ml) sour cream

Finely grated zest of 2 lemons

Kosher salt and freshly ground black pepper

1 head Bibb lettuce, leaves separated

1 teaspoon chopped fresh tarragon

1 large avocado

1 To make the dressing, combine the olive oil, lemon juice, shallot, mustard, honey, and salt in a jar with a tight-fitting lid. Screw on the lid and shake vigorously until emulsified. Keep the dressing in the fridge for up to 1 week. You'll have about 1¼ cups (300ml).

2 Combine the crabmeat, scallions, celery, mayonnaise, sour cream, lemon zest, and a few pinches of salt and pepper in a bowl. Gently toss the ingredients with your fingers until just combined (leave a few larger lumps of crabmeat). Taste and adjust the seasoning. Keep in the fridge for up to 3 days.

3 **The day of:** To assemble the salad, arrange a bed of lettuce on a serving platter. Measure out ⅓ cup (80ml) of the dressing, saving the rest for green beans later this week. Whisk in the tarragon and drizzle about two-thirds of the dressing over the lettuce. Heap 2 cups (250g) of the crab in the center of the lettuce and refrigerate the rest for crab toasties (see below). Slice the avocado thinly and arrange around the edges of the salad. Drizzle the avocado with a little more dressing and grind some pepper over everything before serving.

Crab Toasties

This is my family's favorite way to use up leftover crab salad. It comes together in 10 minutes and works any time of day. Turn it into brunch by adding a **poached egg.**

For 4 people, halve, lightly toast, and **butter 4 English muffins.** Heat the broiler. Arrange the muffin halves on a baking sheet. Top each with **a slice of ripe tomato** sprinkled with kosher salt, **about ¼ cup (30g) of crab salad,** and **a tablespoon of grated Parmesan** (or any sharp cheese). Broil the toasties for a few minutes, until golden brown. Serve right away.

Lunch: Blistered Tomato, Avocado, and Crab Tartine with Capers

Swipe **a thick slice of dense whole-grain bread** with **mayonnaise.** Coarsely chop **a teaspoon of capers** and scatter them over the mayonnaise. Add some **blistered tomatoes** (page 76) and **a few slices of avocado.** Heap some **crab salad** on top and grind pepper over everything. If you're taking the sandwich with you, add another slice of bread and wrap it tightly in aluminum foil.

Meatballs with Tomato and Zucchini

My friend Maria Becce grew up in an Italian-American household and knows her meatballs. For meatballs that are tender and juicy enough to eat on their own, without sauce, she taught me to soften onion, garlic, tomato, and zucchini in olive oil, and then fold them into the ground meat before cooking. Although they don't need it, these meatballs are also great with tomato sauce. I've included my favorite here in case you don't have a back-pocket recipe.

Beyond Summer If you're making these at other times of the year, use canned chopped tomatoes instead of fresh; omit the zucchini and add another ½ cup (120g) tomatoes to make up the difference.

Amanda's Tip for Less Mess "I'm a baked–meatball proponent. If you're okay sacrificing a little browning for a cleaner stovetop, heat your oven to 400°F (200°C). Place the meatballs 2 inches (5cm) apart on a roasting pan or baking sheet and bake until cooked through, turning once."

Spice It Up Add a teaspoon or two of merguez spice mixture (page 16) to the meat for a little more pizzazz. For a party, make mini spiced meatballs and serve them with seasoned labneh or Greek yogurt for dipping.

SERVES 4 FOR 2 DINNERS

¼ cup (60ml) extra-virgin olive oil, plus more for frying

1 small yellow onion, finely chopped

Kosher salt and freshly ground black pepper

1 cup (150g) peeled (see page 137) chopped tomato

½ cup (60g) diced zucchini

1 clove garlic, minced

1 pound (450g) ground beef (85% lean)

1 pound (450g) ground veal

½ cup (50g) grated Parmesan

⅓ cup (35g) dry bread crumbs

1 egg, lightly beaten

1 Warm the olive oil in a skillet over medium heat. Add the onion and a large pinch of salt and cook, stirring frequently, until the onion starts to soften, 3 to 5 minutes. Add the tomatoes, zucchini, garlic, and a few more pinches of salt. Cook until the vegetables have collapsed and most of the juices have cooked off, 8 to 10 minutes. Let cool.

2 Combine the beef and veal in a large bowl. Add the Parmesan, bread crumbs, egg, the cooled vegetables, and some salt and pepper and gently work everything together using the tips of your fingers or two forks. Do not overmix. The mixture will be quite soft. Fry a small piece of the mixture, taste, and adjust the seasoning.

3 Shape the meat into 1½-inch (4cm) balls. Cover and refrigerate them for at least 15 minutes and up to 24 hours.

4 Heat ¼ inch (6mm) olive oil in a large skillet with high sides over medium heat. Working in batches, add the meatballs, being careful not to crowd them. Cook on all sides until browned, then cover the pan and lower the heat to finish cooking, 6 to 8 minutes total. The meatballs may lose their shape and collapse a little as they cook—this is okay! Transfer them to paper towels to drain. Cook the remaining meatballs, adding more oil as needed. Refrigerate the cooked meatballs for up to 5 days.

5 **The day of:** Put half of the meatballs in a covered dish and warm in a 300°F (150°C) oven for about 20 minutes or in a pot of your favorite sauce.

Meatball Sandwiches with Fresh Mozzarella and Basil

I grew up eating meatloaf sandwiches, and there's not much standing between meatballs and meatloaf other than appearance. For a hearty sandwich, warm some **meatballs in tomato sauce** (opposite). Spread a little sauce on both sides of split **kaiser rolls.** Slice the meatballs thickly and layer them on the rolls with **thin slices of fresh mozzarella** and **fresh basil leaves.**

Quick Tomato Sauce

It wouldn't be a Food52 cookbook without a mention of Marcella Hazan's tomato sauce. Everyone at Food52 is obsessed with this humble little recipe, which yields spectacular results. Butter is the key: It softens any rough edges, mellowing the acidity of the tomatoes and giving the sauce a silky texture.

MAKES ENOUGH SAUCE FOR 1 POUND (480G) OF PASTA, PLUS EXTRA

3 pounds (1.4kg) fresh tomatoes or canned peeled whole tomatoes

1 small yellow onion, halved

7 tablespoons (100g) unsalted butter

2 teaspoons kosher salt

¼ cup (10g) loosely packed basil leaves

1 Peel the tomatoes if they're fresh (see right). Chop them coarsely and put them in a large saucepan with the onion, butter, salt, and basil. Bring to a boil over medium-high heat, and then simmer gently for 30 to 45 minutes, stirring occasionally.

2 Taste and adjust the seasoning, and remove the onion if you like (I usually leave it in and just hack it up a little with a sharp knife). Use the sauce right away or refrigerate for up to 5 days. It freezes nicely too—I've kept it for 6 months with no problems.

Peeling Tomatoes Yes, peeling tomatoes is a chore, but at times like these it's worth it. A sauce without tomato skins is simply better than one with them. To peel ripe tomatoes, core the stem end with the tip of a sharp knife and cut a shallow X in the skin of the opposite end. Lower the tomatoes, a few at a time, into boiling water. After 10 seconds, remove them with a slotted spoon and plunge them into an ice bath. Once the tomatoes are cool, the skins should slip off easily.

Amanda's Cheat "Merrill is a better person than I am—I never peel tomatoes. Never ever! Not even for sauce for my favorite people in the world. Please keep this between us."

Boiled Green Beans

Bring a large pot of generously salted water to a boil and have a bowl of ice water ready. Snap the stem ends off **3 pounds (1.4kg) green beans.** Add half of the green beans to the boiling water and cook for a few minutes, until bright green and just tender. Scoop out the beans with a slotted spoon and plunge them into the ice water. Lay them on a kitchen towel to dry and repeat with the remaining beans. Store the cooked beans in paper towel–lined zipper plastic bags in the fridge for up to 3 days.

Pasta with Garlic, Tomatoes, Basil, and Brie

My mother was a devotee of *The Silver Palate Cookbook* when I was growing up, and I still return to many of the dishes she made from it, like this pasta. You combine chopped tomatoes (only when they're in season, please!), olive oil, garlic, and basil in a bowl and leave it alone for several hours. When it's time to eat, you boil pasta, cube a hunk of Brie, and toss both with the magical sauce that has materialized while you were off being productive. The Brie is a brilliant curve ball; it melts into the puddle of tomatoes and olive oil, rendering it creamy and complex.

Brie Is Back Since its fall from grace in the mid-'90s (after years of being assaulted by chalky, leaden impostors at every turn, could you really blame us?), I've felt a little sorry for Brie. So I'm glad it's making a comeback. I recommend keeping the rind on the cheese when you make this pasta for a gentle hit of Brie's hallmark bitterness.

Amanda's Mother-In-Law "This pasta was the first dish my mother-in-law ever cooked for me—a sign that I'd love Tad's family. I felt similarly connected to Merrill when I learned that she, too, makes this dish!"

SERVES 4, PLUS LEFTOVERS

4 perfectly ripe tomatoes, coarsely chopped

½ cup (20g) loosely packed fresh basil leaves, coarsely chopped

2 cloves garlic, finely chopped

½ cup plus 2 tablespoons (150ml) extra-virgin olive oil

Kosher salt and freshly ground black pepper

12 ounces (340g) good Brie

1 pound (450g) curly pasta (I like cavatappi)

1 In the morning, combine the tomatoes, basil, and garlic in a large serving bowl. Pour in the olive oil and season well with salt and pepper. Gently stir everything together and cover the bowl. Let sit at room temperature for at least 2 hours and up to 12 hours.

2 About 45 minutes before you plan to eat, put the Brie in the freezer for 20 minutes to firm up, which will make it easier to cut. Cut into ½-inch (1.3cm) cubes and add to the bowl with the tomatoes.

3 Bring a large pot of generously salted water to a boil. Add the pasta and cook until just al dente. Strain the pasta and tip it into the bowl. Fold everything together until the Brie starts to melt and the pasta is slicked with cheesy tomato goodness. You will probably see a fair amount of liquid in the bottom of the bowl—those are tomato juices, so that's a good thing. Serve the pasta immediately. Keep leftovers in an airtight container in the fridge for up to 3 days.

Lunch: My Favorite Tomato Sandwich

When tomato season is in full swing, I have a tomato sandwich for lunch two or three times a week. It was not until I posted this recipe on Food52 a few years ago that I realized people have very strong opinions about tomato sandwiches! Their mayonnaise preferences alone could fill pages. Play around with any or all of the components below to create your perfect sandwich (see a photo of mine on page 134).

Toast **2 slices of dense whole grain bread**. Let them cool in the toaster (to keep them crisp) while you cut **1 perfectly ripe beefsteak tomato** (use a serrated knife, please!) into ⅛-inch (3mm) slices. Slather one side of each piece of toast with **mayonnaise** and layer as many tomato slices as you can onto one piece of toast, sprinkling kosher salt liberally as you go. Add a few grinds of pepper and top with the second piece of toast. You'd be smart to eat this over a sink to catch the juices.

Black Raspberry Chocolate Chip Ice Cream

If I had to pick one ice cream flavor for the rest of my life, it would be black raspberry. Of course, there's the shocking magenta hue. But what I love most is the perfume of the berries—lush and jammy and faintly floral, it's a flavor that takes me back to childhood. I've added chocolate chips to this recipe, using Alice Medrich's genius method. She melts and rehardens chocolate before breaking it up into small pieces, which destroys the chocolate's temper and lowers its melting point; this way, the chips stay hard in ice cream but melt more readily on your tongue.

MAKES 1 QUART (950ML)

2½ cups (590ml) heavy cream

1½ cups (355ml) milk

1 cup plus 2 tablespoons (225g) sugar

Kosher salt

6 egg yolks

1 teaspoon pure vanilla extract

5 cups (625g) fresh black raspberries (see tip for substitutions)

8 ounces (225g) semisweet chocolate, coarsely chopped

1 Combine the cream, milk, sugar, and a pinch of salt in a heavy pot. Cook over low heat until it just starts to bubble around the edges, about 5 minutes. Do not let it boil.

2 Meanwhile, beat the yolks in a small heatproof bowl. Temper them by slowly whisking in about a third of the hot cream, then pour the tempered eggs into the pot with the rest of the cream and whisk to combine.

3 Cook the custard over medium-low heat, stirring constantly, until it coats the back of a wooden spoon, about 5 minutes. Do not let it boil. Strain the custard through a fine-mesh sieve and stir in the vanilla.

4 Puree the raspberries in a blender, then strain through a fine-mesh sieve to remove the seeds. Stir the puree into the custard. Cover and refrigerate until completely chilled, at least 3 hours and preferably overnight.

5 To make the chocolate chips, line a baking sheet with parchment paper. Place the chocolate in a stainless steel bowl and set over a pan of barely simmering water. Melt the chocolate, stirring often, about 5 minutes. Pour the melted chocolate onto the baking sheet and spread it into a thin, even layer. Put the baking sheet in the freezer and freeze the chocolate until firm, at least 30 minutes. Chop the chocolate into bits or shards, put them in a plastic freezer bag, and return them to the freezer for up to a month.

6 Freeze the chilled custard in an ice cream maker, adding the chocolate chips just before the ice cream is fully frozen. Transfer the ice cream to an airtight container and put in the freezer to harden completely. **The day of:** Soften the ice cream for a few minutes at room temperature before serving.

Swaps Substitute regular raspberries or blackberries (or a mix) if you can't find black raspberries, which can be elusive. I like semisweet chocolate, but Alice's chip method works with any type of chocolate.

What to Do with All Those Egg Whites Another lesson I learned from my mother: Never toss extra egg whites! They'll keep in the fridge for a week or so and much longer in the freezer (make sure to label them, as they look a lot like chicken stock—you don't want to end up with egg-drop soup by mistake). Once you have a half dozen egg whites, whip up some meringues (page 126); with a dozen, you can make an angel food cake.

Merrill's Fall

applesauce cake

Mon.
baked pasta w/ ragu
salad
cake

Tues.
chicken
polenta
zucchini - roasted?
applesauce w/ yogurt or fool

Wed.
polenta w/ ragu
veg
cake

Thur.
chicken w/ rice
salad
pantry dessert

Fri.
Mum's chick salad
fool or applesauce w/ yogurt or cream

THE WEEK AHEAD

DINNER TWO

Rosy Chicken

Oven-Roasted Polenta

Roasted Zucchini with Chile and Mint

Greek yogurt with Roasted Applesauce

TO DO TODAY Make the zucchini. Reheat the polenta and the chicken. Top yogurt with spoonfuls of applesauce for dessert.

DINNER THREE

Sausage Ragù

Oven-Roasted Polenta

Roasted Zucchini with Chile and Mint

Applesauce Cake with Caramel Icing

TO DO TODAY Bring the zucchini to room temperature. Reheat the polenta and the sausage ragù. Serve the ragù over the polenta and pass Parmesan at the table.

THE RECIPES

DINNER FOUR

Rosy Chicken

Simple Baked Rice

Green salad with The Best Red Wine Vinaigrette

Chocolate and prune plums

TO DO TODAY Make the rice and reheat the chicken. Dress the salad. Pass some good chocolate and fresh prune plums (or pears) for dessert.

HOW THEY COME TOGETHER

DINNER ONE

Baked Pasta with Sausage Ragù

Green salad with The Best Red Wine Vinaigrette

Applesauce Cake with Caramel Icing

TO DO TODAY Set out the vinaigrette to come to room temperature. Assemble and bake the pasta. Dress the salad right before you sit down to eat, adding chopped basil or chives if you have extra.

DINNER FIVE

Warm Chicken Salad

Apple Fool

TO DO TODAY Whip the cream for the apple fool and refrigerate. Make the chicken salad. Assemble the fool right before dessert.

BROWN BAG LUNCHES

Baked Sweet Potato with Sausage Ragù

Roasted Zucchini with Chile and Mint with Greek yogurt and pita

GAME PLAN

TO MAKE OVER THE WEEKEND

Rosy Chicken

Baked Pasta with
Sausage Ragù

Oven-Roasted Polenta
(page 232)

Roasted Applesauce

Applesauce Cake with
Caramel Icing

PUT ON YOUR APRON—WE'RE MAKING SAUCE

You'll be hunkered down in the kitchen for about 3 hours
this weekend.

- Heat the oven to 375°F (190°C). Peel and cut up the
  apples for the applesauce (page 156). Roast them.

- Get the sausage ragù (page 155) on the stove. Grate
  the cheeses for the baked pasta (page 155) and
  refrigerate.

- When the applesauce is out of the oven, turn it
  down to 350°F (175°C). Get the polenta roasting
  (page 232). You're using a slightly higher temperature
  than Amanda's recipe calls for, so make sure to check
  it frequently and add more water as necessary.

- Butter and flour the pan for the cake (page 156).

- Puree enough roasted apples to make 1½ cups (355ml)
  of applesauce for the cake (page 156). Freeze 1½ cups
  (355ml) of apples for the future (for the brown sugar
  pound cake on page 173, for example) and refrigerate
  the rest for later this week.

- Make the batter for the cake and put it in the oven.

- While the cake bakes, wash and dry your salad greens
  for the week and put them in the fridge. Scrub the
  potatoes and put them on to boil (page 152).

- Make the vinaigrette (page 31). Prepare the rosy
  chicken (page 148) and chicken thighs for the warm
  chicken salad (page 152).

- When the cake is done, put the rosy chicken and
  the chicken thighs in the oven.

- Take a little break—you're nearly there!

- When the cake is cool, make the icing and pour
  it over the top.

- Put everything in the fridge and go ask your partner/
  child/next-door neighbor for a foot rub.

To scale back. Skip the baked pasta and polenta; serve
the ragù over pasta one night and over baked sweet
potatoes another (page 155). Use good store-bought
applesauce for the cake, and skip the icing (the cake
will still be good). These shortcuts will save you about
1½ hours.

GROCERY LIST

PRODUCE

Apples (such as Golden Delicious, Macoun, or Honeycrisp), 6 pounds (2.7kg)

Baby white potatoes, 1 pound (450g)

Garlic, 9 large cloves

Prune plums (or pears), for dessert

Red leaf or Bibb lettuce, 6 cups (120g)

Salad greens, enough for a side salad in 2 meals

Sweet potatoes, 4 for lunch

Cherry tomatoes, 2 cups (300g)

Fresh or canned chopped tomatoes, 8 cups (1.4kg fresh/ 2.5kg canned)

Tomatoes, 2 large

Yellow onions, 2 large

Zucchini and/or summer squash, 9

HERBS

Basil leaves, 16

Chives, 1 tablespoon chopped

Mint leaves, 1/2 cup (10g) loosely packed

Thyme, 3 sprigs

SPICES

Ground allspice, 1/4 teaspoon

Ground cinnamon, 2 teaspoons, plus more to have on hand

Ground ginger, 1 teaspoon

Red pepper flakes, 1/2 teaspoon plus a pinch

PANTRY

Chicken stock, 1 1/2 cups (355ml)

Coarsely ground polenta, 2 cups (320g)

Extra-virgin olive oil, 2 1/2 cups (590ml), plus more to have on hand

Long-grain white rice, 1 cup (185g)

Red wine vinegar, 6 tablespoons (90ml)

Sherry vinegar, 6 tablespoons (90ml)

Short pasta (such as penne or small shells), 1 pound (450g)

Vegetable oil, 2/3 cup (160ml)

BAKING AISLE

All-purpose flour, 2 cups (250g)

Baking soda, 1 1/2 teaspoons

Good chocolates, for dessert

Confectioners' sugar, 3/4 to 1 cup (90 to 125g) sifted

Dark brown sugar, 1/2 cup (110g) firmly packed

Light brown sugar, 1/2 cup (110g) firmly packed

Sugar, 1 cup plus 2 teaspoons (200g)

Pure vanilla extract, 1 teaspoon

DAIRY AND EGGS

Unsalted butter, 3/4 cup (170g), plus more to have on hand

Eggs, 2

Fresh ricotta, 1/4 cup (60g)

Greek yogurt, 3 cups (710ml)

Heavy cream, 1 1/3 cups (315ml), plus more for whipped cream

Mozzarella, 1 cup (110g) grated

Parmesan, 1/2 cup (50g) grated from a wedge

MEAT AND SEAFOOD

Bone-in, skin-on chicken thighs or legs, 6 pounds (2.7kg)

Your favorite sausage (chicken or pork, sweet or hot), 2 pounds (900g)

BOOZE AND SUCH

Dry, fruity rosé, 2/3 cup (160ml)

BAKED GOODS

Pita, for lunch

Rosy Chicken

This dish was inspired by a recipe from Jamie Oliver for slow-roasted chicken legs with garlic, tomatoes, and chopped chiles. After devouring his version, I considered the thought that it might be even better with a sauce to spoon over rice or drag hunks of bread through. A rummage in the fridge unearthed a half-empty bottle of rosé from the night before, so I added a slosh or two. The garlic and tomatoes melted into the wine in the oven, and voilà, I had a fragrant pink sauce for my chicken.

Wine Trade If you don't have rosé, use a dry, fruity white wine instead. No one will know the difference. And if you open a bottle to make the dish, why not serve the rest of it with dinner?

A Rosé Dessert from Amanda "A good use of leftover rosé is to simmer it with sugar (4 parts rosé to 3 parts sugar) to make a syrup. Poach peaches or pears in the rosé syrup with a handful of fresh basil (which you already have on hand for the sausage ragù)."

SERVES 4 FOR 2 DINNERS

4 pounds (1.8kg) bone-in, skin-on chicken thighs or legs

Kosher salt and freshly ground black pepper

3 tablespoons extra-virgin olive oil

6 large cloves garlic, finely chopped

2 large tomatoes (about 12 ounces), chopped

2 cups (300g) cherry tomatoes

3 thyme sprigs

½ teaspoon red pepper flakes

10 fresh basil leaves, chopped

⅔ cup (160ml) dry, fruity rosé

Rice (page 83), Oven-Roasted Polenta (page 232), or crusty bread for serving

1 Heat the oven to 375°F (190°C). Pat the chicken dry with paper towels and season with salt and pepper.

2 Put 1 tablespoon of olive oil, the garlic, and the chopped tomatoes in a baking dish large enough to hold all of the chicken in one layer. Arrange the chicken, skin side up, on top. Scatter the cherry tomatoes over the chicken, tucking them into the crevices wherever they'll fit.

3 Add the thyme sprigs to the dish and sprinkle the pepper flakes and basil evenly over the chicken, followed by more salt and pepper. Pour the rosé gently into the crevices, being careful not to splash the chicken. Drizzle the remaining 2 tablespoons olive oil over everything.

4 Bake the chicken, uncovered, until the skin is crisp and the tomatoes have slackened and started to caramelize, about 1 hour.

5 If the sauce seems thin, transfer the chicken to a plate and turn up the heat for a few minutes; let the sauce boil until it thickens and becomes glossy. Discard the thyme sprigs, taste, and adjust the seasoning.

6 Return the chicken to the sauce and let cool. Cover and refrigerate in the pan for up to 5 days.

7 **The day of:** Reheat the chicken in the pan in a 250°F (120°C) oven for about 20 minutes. Serve with rice, polenta, or crusty bread.

Roasted Zucchini with Chile and Mint

This recipe was born of two different sources. The first is a dish I used to order frequently at one of my favorite restaurants, Lunetta, before it closed (sniff). The second is a method for roasting zucchini from one of Christopher Hirsheimer and Melissa Hamilton's envy-inducing daily e-mails, Canal House Cooks Lunch. In order to coax maximum flavor into the zucchini (like eggplant, it's basically a sponge), I drizzle on a mint and chile dressing before roasting, and then splash on some more once the zucchini is cooked.

Our Favorite Kind of Recipe This is one of those magical dishes that can be eaten at any temperature. And the iterations are endless. Here are some more recipes that can bend and flex the same way.

- Jonathan's Roasted Asparagus (page 15)
- Frittata with Peas, Spring Greens, and Ricotta (page 31)
- Chicken Fingers (page 45)
- Blistered Cherry Tomatoes (page 76)
- Olive Oil–Braised Peppers (page 103)
- Roasted Mushrooms (from the Farro Salad with Roasted Mushrooms and Parmesan on page 119)
- Grilled Shrimp with Arugula and Garlic Scape Pesto (page 123)
- Roasted Applesauce (page 156)
- Spicy Roasted Cauliflower (page 169)
- Braised Fennel (page 185)
- Roasted Brussels Sprouts (page 196)

SERVES 4 AS A SIDE FOR 2 DINNERS, PLUS LEFTOVERS

CHILE-MINT DRESSING
½ cup (120ml) extra-virgin olive oil

5 tablespoons (75ml) sherry vinegar

⅛ teaspoon sugar

Pinch of red pepper flakes

Kosher salt and freshly ground black pepper

½ cup (10g) loosely packed fresh mint leaves

ZUCCHINI
9 small zucchini and/or summer squash (all the same size)

1 Heat the oven to 350°F (175°C). Combine the olive oil, vinegar, sugar, pepper flakes, salt, and pepper in a jar with a tight-fitting lid. Screw on the lid and shake vigorously. Coarsely chop the mint, add it to the dressing, and shake again. Taste and adjust the seasoning.

2 Trim the ends off the zucchini and halve them lengthwise. Arrange them cut side up in a large, shallow baking dish (or two if you don't have one big enough to fit them in a single layer). Sprinkle lightly with salt and drizzle half of the dressing over the zucchini. Roast until they're just tender when you pierce them with a sharp knife, about 40 minutes.

3 Heat the broiler and position the rack about 5 inches (13cm) from the flame. Broil the zucchini until browned, 3 to 5 minutes, watching carefully and rotating the dish if necessary to make sure the zucchini browns evenly. Let it cool for a few minutes and then spoon some more dressing over the top. Refrigerate the rest of the dressing for salads later this week, up to 5 days. Serve the zucchini immediately and refrigerate the leftovers in a container for up to 4 days.

4 **The day of:** Bring the zucchini to room temperature before serving, or eat it cold.

Warm Chicken Salad

The second night of roast chicken is often a disappointment. The skin is no longer as crisp, the meat not quite as juicy. My father lives for a cold chicken sandwich on white bread with butter, but I just can't get jazzed about it. My mother has an excellent remedy for the leftover roast chicken problem: She warms the meat in a pan with a simple vinaigrette and tosses in some cut-up cooked potatoes if she has them. She spoons it all over a bed of soft lettuces, which wilt just slightly when they're hit with the warm chicken juices and vinaigrette. This salad is so good, you might even roast some chicken just to make it, as I've done for this menu.

SERVES 4

2 pounds (900g) chicken thighs, bone in and skin on (or 3 cups/405g leftover roast chicken)

Kosher salt and freshly ground black pepper

3 tablespoons red wine vinegar

½ cup (120ml) extra-virgin olive oil

6 cups (120g) red leaf or Bibb lettuce, torn into large bite-size pieces

1 cup (225g) boiled potatoes (right), cut into chunks or slices

1 tablespoon chopped fresh chives

1 Heat the oven to 375°F (190°C). Pat the chicken dry and season well with salt and pepper. Lay the chicken, skin side up, on a rimmed baking sheet and bake for 1 hour, until the chicken is tender and the skin is crisp and brown. Cool slightly and store in the fridge for up to 5 days.

2 **The day of:** In a small bowl, whisk the vinegar with ½ teaspoon salt and a few grinds of pepper. Slowly drizzle in the olive oil, whisking constantly. Taste and adjust the seasoning.

3 Arrange a bed of lettuce on a platter. Remove the cooked chicken from the bones and shred into bite-size pieces (including the skin).

4 Put half of the vinaigrette in a large heavy nonreactive pan over medium heat. When it's hot, add the chicken and potatoes. Cook, turning gently with a spatula from time to time, until the chicken and potatoes are warmed through, 3 to 5 minutes.

5 Drizzle a few spoonfuls of the remaining vinaigrette over the lettuce and then pile the chicken and potatoes on top. Sprinkle the chives over everything and serve immediately, with the rest of the vinaigrette on the side.

Salad Days We eat a lot of salad, so there are a lot of salad dressings in this book—one for any mood that strikes you. Here they are, all in one place.

- Lemon Dressing (page 14)
- The Best Red Wine Vinaigrette (page 31)
- Roberta's Roasted Garlic Dressing (page 42)
- Preserved Lemon Dressing (page 61)
- Lemon Mustard Dressing (page 134)
- Chile-Mint Dressing (page 151)
- Onion Confit Vinaigrette (page 166)
- Simple Lemon Dressing (page 185)
- Creamy Mustard Vinaigrette (page 198)
- Anchovy Dressing (page 219)
- Lime Dressing (page 258)

Boiled Potatoes

Here's a great recipe to outsource to the less experienced cooks in your house. Rinse **1 pound (450g) of baby white potatoes.** Put them in a large saucepan, cover with 2 inches (5cm) of water, and generously season the water with salt. Bring to a boil over medium-high heat, then reduce the heat and simmer until just tender, 12 to 15 minutes. Drain and store in the fridge for up to a week.

Baked Pasta with Sausage Ragù

I went to college in Providence, Rhode Island, and Al Forno's baked pasta is the best I've come across. I've leaned on their technique many times, adding everything from butternut squash to mushrooms to asparagus. My kids' favorite version has sausage, three kinds of cheese, and enough heavy cream to make Julia Child blush. The crisp, burnished top is perfection.

Reheating Leftovers I'd be lying if I told you that after you reheat this pasta it will have the same structural integrity. If that bothers you, assemble half the recipe and save the rest of the ingredients for another night. If you're okay with slightly mushy, less saucy baked pasta, make the whole recipe, cover the leftovers in foil right in the pan, and reheat (covered) in a 350°F (175°C) oven for about 20 minutes.

SERVES 4 FOR 2 DINNERS, WITH
PLENTY OF EXTRA RAGÙ

SAUSAGE RAGÙ

2 tablespoons extra-virgin olive oil

2 pounds (900g) your favorite sausage (chicken or pork, sweet or hot), removed from the casings

1 large yellow onion, diced

Kosher salt

2 fat cloves garlic, finely chopped

8 cups (1.4kg/2.5kg) fresh or canned chopped tomatoes (preferably Pomi)

6 fresh basil leaves

BAKED PASTA

Soft butter, for the baking dish

1 cup (240ml) heavy cream

1 cup (110g) grated mozzarella

½ cup (50g) grated Parmesan

¼ cup (60g) fresh ricotta

½ teaspoon kosher salt

1 pound (450g) short pasta (such as penne or small shells)

2 tablespoons cold unsalted butter, cut into cubes

1 To make the ragù, warm the olive oil in a large heavy saucepan over medium-high heat. Brown the sausage, breaking it up as it cooks, about 5 minutes.

2 Clear a spot in the middle of the pan and add the onion and a couple pinches of salt. Cook until softened, about 5 minutes. Add the garlic and cook for 1 minute.

3 Stir in the tomatoes and basil and simmer until the sauce thickens and the flavors meld, at least 45 minutes. (Add a little water if the sauce looks dry.) Taste and adjust the seasoning and discard the basil. Store in the fridge for up to 5 days.

4 **The day of:** Heat the oven to 500°F (260°C). Butter a shallow 2-quart (1.9L) baking dish and bring a large pot of salted water to a boil.

5 In a large bowl, combine the 4 cups (950ml) ragù with the heavy cream, mozzarella, Parmesan, ricotta, and salt.

6 Cook the pasta for 3 minutes, then drain and run it under cold water to stop the cooking. Add the pasta to the bowl, tossing gently to combine.

7 Spread the pasta evenly into the baking dish. Scatter the cubed butter over the top.

8 Bake until bubbly and brown, about 10 minutes. Cool slightly before serving. Reserve half for later in the week—right in the baking dish, or transfer to a container.

Lunch: Baked Sweet Potato with Sausage Ragù

For a hearty lunch or dinner, reheat leftover **ragù** and a **baked sweet potato** (page 32) in the microwave. Split the potato in half, scuff up its middle with a fork, and season with salt and pepper. Mound the ragù onto the potato, drizzle with **extra-virgin olive oil,** and eat!

Applesauce Cake with Caramel Icing

Whether they admit it, all cooks have one recipe they're most proud of. This is mine. It's a simple cake, but because of the caramel glaze, it's pretty enough for guests. If you're missing allspice, don't fret. Add a pinch of ground cloves or press on without it.

SERVES 4 FOR 2 TO 3 DESSERTS

CAKE

2 cups (250g) all-purpose flour

1½ teaspoons baking soda

1 teaspoon kosher salt

¼ teaspoon freshly ground black pepper

2 teaspoons ground cinnamon

1 teaspoon ground ginger

¼ teaspoon ground allspice

2 eggs

1 cup (200g) sugar

½ cup (110g) firmly packed dark brown sugar

1½ cups (405g) roasted applesauce (right) or good store-bought unsweetened applesauce

⅔ cup (160ml) vegetable oil

1 teaspoon pure vanilla extract

ICING

¼ cup (60g) butter, cut into cubes

½ cup (110g) firmly packed light brown sugar

⅓ cup (80ml) heavy cream, plus more as needed

¼ teaspoon kosher salt

¾ to 1 cup (90 to 125g) sifted confectioners' sugar

1 To make the cake, heat the oven to 350°F (175°C). Butter and flour a 12-cup (3L) Bundt pan. Sift together the flour, baking soda, salt, pepper, cinnamon, ginger, and allspice into a bowl. Using another bowl and a handheld electric mixer—or a stand mixer fitted with the paddle attachment—beat the eggs and sugars until light, about 3 minutes. Add the applesauce, oil, and vanilla and beat until smooth.

2 Fold in the dry ingredients until just combined. Pour the batter into the Bundt pan and bake for about 45 minutes, until a cake tester inserted into the center comes out clean. Transfer the pan to a rack and let cool for 10 minutes. Invert the cake onto the rack and let cool completely, about 2 hours, before you make the glaze.

3 Put a piece of aluminum foil or parchment paper under the rack to catch any drips. To make the icing, in a saucepan, combine the butter, brown sugar, cream, and salt and cook over medium heat. Bring to a full rolling boil, stirring constantly. Boil for 1 minute exactly and turn off the heat.

4 Let the glaze cool in the pan for a minute, then gradually whisk in the confectioners' sugar until you have a thick but pourable glaze (you may not need all of the sugar). If the mixture seems too thick, add a splash of cream. Pour the glaze quickly over the cake, covering as much surface area as possible. Let the glaze set for at least 10 minutes before storing in an airtight container for up to 5 days.

Roasted Applesauce

Applesauce is applesauce, right? Judy Rodgers, the Zuni Café chef known for her impeccable palate and lack of fussiness, knew better. To make her delicious roasted applesauce, peel, core, and coarsely chop about **10 large apples** (I like Golden Delicious, Macoun, or Honeycrisp)—you want **6 pounds (2.7kg) chopped apples.** Toss with a pinch of kosher salt and **1½ teaspoons sugar.** Spread the apples on rimmed baking sheets and cover with aluminum foil. Bake at 375°F (190°C) until soft, 30 to 40 minutes. Uncover and raise the heat to 500°F (260°C) to brown the apples for a few minutes. Mash them with the back of a fork until you have a chunky applesauce (about 5 cups/700g). Puree enough to make 1½ cups (405g) for the applesauce cake, freeze 1½ cups (210g) for the future (page 173), and store the rest in the fridge for up to a week.

Stretch Your Fruit Use this same technique for other fruits, such as pears, peaches, or plums. Spoon it over cake or Greek yogurt, or on top of ricotta toasts (page 20), without the garlic!

Apple Fool

For a charmingly old-fashioned dessert, whip **heavy cream** with **a bit of sugar.** Fold in an equal amount of **cold applesauce** and a little **ground cinnamon** and serve.

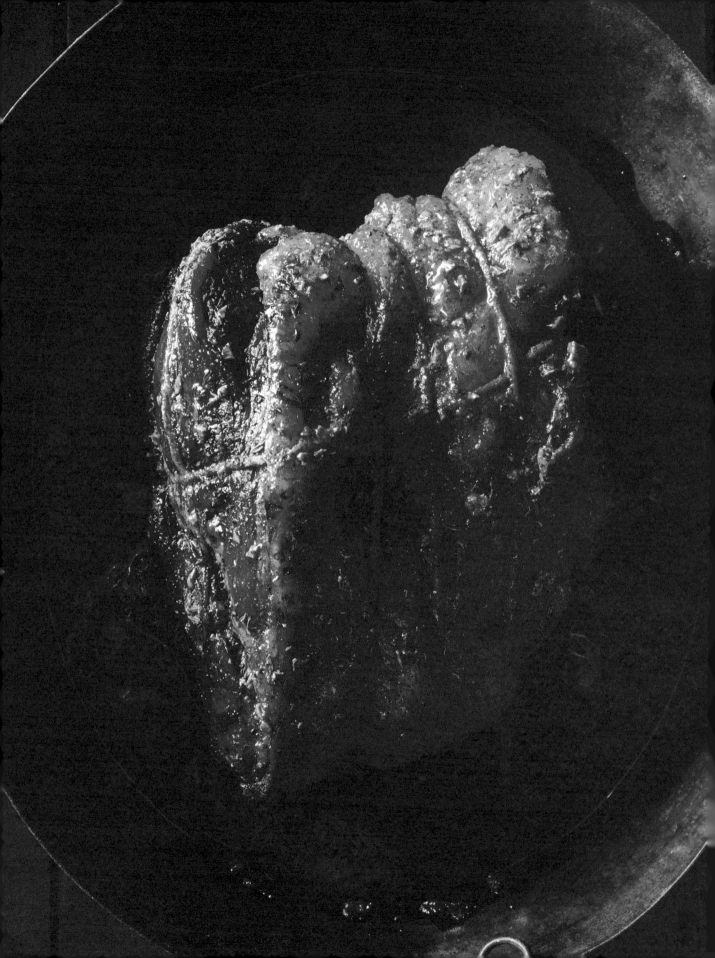

THE WEEK AHEAD

THE RECIPES

HOW THEY COME TOGETHER

DINNER ONE

Barley Salad with Persimmon, Onion Confit,
and Sheep's Milk Cheese

Braised Chickpeas with Celery

Spicy Roasted Cauliflower

Brown Sugar Pound Cake with Crème Fraîche
Whipped Cream and Roasted Applesauce
from the freezer

TO DO TODAY In the morning, move the applesauce from
the freezer to the fridge. Bring the salad, chickpeas, and
cauliflower to room temperature before serving. Warm
half of the applesauce in the microwave and serve with
cake and whipped cream.

DINNER TWO

Overnight Roast Pork

Spicy Roasted Cauliflower

Escarole with Onion Confit Vinaigrette

Affogato

TO DO TODAY Set out the onion confit oil to come to
room temperature. Warm the pork and the cauliflower.
Make the vinaigrette, then coarsely chop the escarole
and dress it lightly. For the affogato, pour espresso
over your favorite ice cream.

DINNER THREE

Broccoli, Lemon, and Parmesan Soup

Thinly sliced prosciutto

Crusty bread and good salted butter

Toasted Brown Sugar Pound Cake
with ice cream

TO DO TODAY Heat the soup and squeeze in some
lemon juice. Slice the bread. Toast slices of pound
cake and top with ice cream for dessert.

DINNER FOUR

Overnight Roast Pork

Barley Salad with Persimmon, Onion Confit,
and Sheep's Milk Cheese

Apples with cheese and honey

TO DO TODAY Warm the pork and bring the barley
salad to room temperature. Slice some apples and
serve with cheese and honey for dessert.

DINNER FIVE

Bucatini with Cauliflower, Pecorino,
Chile, and Bread Crumbs

Greek yogurt with Roasted Applesauce
and honey

TO DO TODAY Make the pasta. Spoon applesauce
and honey over yogurt for dessert.

BROWN BAG LUNCHES

Broccoli, Lemon, and Parmesan Soup,
with cheese and crackers

Roast pork with barbecue sauce and
pickles on brioche rolls

Escarole, Roasted Cauliflower, and Chickpeas
with Onion Confit Vinaigrette

GAME PLAN

TO MAKE OVER THE WEEKEND

Broccoli, Lemon, and
Parmesan Soup

Overnight Roast Pork

Barley Salad with
Persimmon, Onion Confit,
and Sheep's Milk Cheese

Spicy Roasted Cauliflower

Braised Chickpeas with
Celery

Brown Sugar Pound
Cake with Crème Fraîche
Whipped Cream

READY TO GIVE YOUR OVEN A WORKOUT?

This weekend you'll be in the kitchen for about 3½ hours of active cooking time—welcome back, slow cooking!

- The night before, soak the barley for the salad (page 166). If you're using dried chickpeas, get them soaking as well. Or use the quick-soak method (see page 264) the next day.

- Cut 1 cup (225g) unsalted butter for the pound cake (page 173) into chunks and set out to soften.

- Drain the barley and set it on to boil. Start the quick soak for the chickpeas if you didn't soak them yesterday.

- Heat the oven to 450°F (230°C) and get the cauliflower roasting (page 169).

- Start sautéing the garlic for the soup (page 162). Cut the broccoli for the soup into florets and trim, peel, and chop the stems. Add the broccoli to the pot, cover, and let it do its thing for an hour or so.

- Start the onion confit for the barley salad (page 166).

- When the cauliflower is done, lower the temperature to 350°F (175°C). Make the pound cake (page 173) and put it in the oven.

- Toast the almonds for the barley salad (page 166) alongside the cake.

- Start braising the chickpeas and put a pot of water on to boil for the persimmons (page 166).

- Drain and cool the barley. Blanch and peel the persimmons. Cool the onion confit.

- Add the chicken stock to the broccoli soup (page 162); simmer for a few minutes, then remove from the heat.

- Make the crème fraîche whipped cream for the pound cake (page 173) and refrigerate.

- Puree the broccoli soup (page 162) and add the Parmesan and lemon juice. Let the soup cool.

- Wash and spin dry the escarole and put it in the fridge.

- Strain the onion confit and assemble the barley salad.

- Put everything in the fridge, clean up, and take a break until it's time to cook the pork.

- An hour or two before bed, set the pork butt (page 165) out at room temperature. Tie it with twine and salt it all over. Stir together the paste for the pork and keep it covered at room temperature.

- About 30 minutes before bed, heat the oven to 475°F (245°C). Rub the pork with the paste and put it in the oven. After 15 minutes, cover it, turn down the temperature to 200°F (95°C) and head for bed. Zzzzzz . . .

To steal some time back. Skip the broccoli soup and pound cake, use canned chickpeas, and make a batch of plain barley instead of the full salad. Toss some of the barley with the chickpeas and cauliflower one night for a main course (maybe add some soft-boiled eggs), and serve the rest as a side for the pork for another dinner. Supplement with takeout one night this week. The truncated plan will take you about 1½ hours.

GROCERY LIST

PRODUCE

Apples, for dessert

Arugula, 3 ounces (85g)

Broccoli, 4 pounds (1.8kg)

Cauliflower, 4½ pounds (2kg) (about 2 large heads)

Celery, 12 ounces (340g)

Escarole, for side salad and lunch

Fuyu persimmons, 2

Garlic, 13 large cloves

Lemons, 2

Limes, 3

Yellow onions, 4 large

HERBS

Bay leaf, 1

Flat-leaf parsley, 1½ cups (30g) chopped and loosely packed

Thyme, 1 sprig plus 1½ teaspoons of leaves

SPICES

Cayenne, 1¼ teaspoons

Garlic powder, 1 teaspoon

Ground chipotle, ⅛ to ¼ teaspoon

Ground ginger, ½ teaspoon

Red pepper flakes, a large pinch

Sweet smoked paprika, 1 teaspoon

PANTRY

Barbecue sauce, for lunch

Bucatini (or spaghetti), 1 pound (450g)

Chickpeas, 5 cups (830g) cooked or 3 (15-ounce/425g) cans

Dijon mustard, 1 tablespoon plus 1 teaspoon

Espresso, for dessert

Extra-virgin olive oil, 2¼ cups plus 2 tablespoons (530ml), plus more to have on hand

Homemade or low-sodium chicken stock, 8 cups (1.9L)

Honey, for dessert

Hulled barley, 1¾ cups (320g)

Maple syrup, ¼ cup plus 1 teaspoon (60ml)

Pickles, for lunch

Red wine vinegar, ¼ cup (60ml)

Flaky salt

Sherry vinegar, ½ cup (120ml)

Wheat crackers, for lunch

BAKING AISLE

All-purpose flour, 1¾ cups (220g), plus more to have on hand

Almonds, 1½ cups (210g)

Baking powder, ½ teaspoon

Light brown sugar, 1⅔ cups (335g) firmly packed

Pure vanilla extract, 1½ teaspoons

DAIRY AND EGGS

Good salted butter

Unsalted butter, 1 cup (225g)

Crème fraîche, ⅓ cup (80ml)

Eggs, 4

Heavy cream, ⅔ cup (160ml)

Parmesan, 1½ cups (150g) grated from a wedge

Pecorino, ¼ cup (25g) grated from a wedge, plus more for serving

Sheep (or goat) Gouda or another hard cheese like Pecorino or Manchego, 6 ounces (170g)

Your favorite cheese, for dessert

MEAT AND SEAFOOD

Boneless pork butt, 1 (5-pound/2.3kg)

BOOZE AND SUCH

Dry white wine, ½ cup (120ml)

FREEZER

Your favorite ice cream, for 2 desserts

BAKED GOODS

Brioche rolls, for lunch

Crusty bread, 2 loaves

Broccoli, Lemon, and Parmesan Soup

Kristen Miglore, our creative director, first introduced me to Roy Finamore's Broccoli Cooked Forever and its magical transformation of a boring old crucifer into something lush and melting and complex. We got so hooked on the stuff that I started using it as a base for soup. I usually puree half of the soup, keeping the rest chunky, and I add enough lemon juice so that you can really taste it. Plenty of Parmesan makes the soup rich and savory. Don't forget some good, crusty bread to wipe your bowl clean!

To Puree or Not to Puree If I'm in a rush, I sometimes skip pureeing. If I want to be fancy, I puree all of the soup and dollop a little crème fraîche on top.

SERVES 4 FOR 2 DINNERS

½ cup (120ml) extra-virgin olive oil

6 fat cloves garlic, smashed

4 pounds (1.8kg) broccoli, cut into florets and stems trimmed, peeled, and chopped

Kosher salt and freshly ground black pepper

8 cups (1.9L) homemade or low-sodium chicken stock

1½ cups (150g) grated Parmesan

Juice from 1 or 2 lemons

Crusty bread, for serving

1 Combine the olive oil and garlic in a 6- to 8-quart (5.7 to 7.5L) Dutch oven and sauté over very low heat for 3 to 5 minutes, stirring occasionally, until the garlic softens and starts to turn golden.

2 Add the broccoli to the pot, season with salt and pepper, and stir to coat with the oil. Cover, turn the heat as low as it will go, and cook for about an hour, gently stirring from time to time, until the broccoli yields when you press it with the back of a wooden spoon. The garlic and broccoli will probably brown a little—don't worry, this is a good thing.

3 Add the chicken stock and simmer for 5 minutes. Turn off the heat and let the soup cool a bit.

4 Puree half of the soup using a blender or food processor. Pour the pureed soup back into the pot and add the Parmesan and lemon juice to taste. Taste and adjust the seasoning. Cool slightly, transfer to lidded containers, and refrigerate for up to 5 days.

5 **The day of:** Reheat gently on the stove over low heat, adding another squeeze of lemon juice. Serve with plenty of crusty bread.

Overnight Roast Pork

This roast pork came about by accident. I found a beautiful pork butt at the farmers' market on a Sunday morning and set my sights on pork tacos (page 263). I didn't realize until I got home that the roast was frozen solid. After thirty hours in the fridge, it had finally thawed, but by then it was Monday night and I didn't have time to make the taco filling before bed. I'd heard that you can cook a pork roast overnight, and a quick Google search told me that Jamie Oliver is a believer. If he's on board, that's good enough for me. I made a quick paste of garlic, brown sugar, mustard, thyme, and spices and slathered the pork with it. I gave it a quick blast in a scorching oven to get some caramelization going, then turned the oven down as low as it would go, and went upstairs to bed. The next morning, we woke in a cloud of garlic, sugar, and pork aroma—like bacon on steroids. The surface of the roast was burnished and crisp, and when I went at it with two forks, the meat virtually fell apart. Every accident should be this happy.

Buying Pork Pork has changed a lot over the years. Commercial pork is leaner than it used to be, making it less flavorful and prone to dryness. I typically don't buy it a lot, except for the occasional sausage. Instead, I seek out local pork from small farms whenever possible. It may be a bit more expensive, but the taste is far superior. When you're buying pork shoulder, look for a piece of meat with good marbling and a generous fat cap. You'll taste the difference.

How Amanda Riffs "I make this pork shoulder as often as possible, and when I do, I sometimes change up the seasoning. I capitalize the spices and lowercase the sweetness by adding a tablespoon of smoked paprika in place of the chipotle and a large pinch of red pepper flakes, and omitting the maple syrup and brown sugar."

SERVES 4 FOR 2 DINNERS, WITH LOTS OF LEFTOVERS

1 (5-pound/2.3kg) boneless pork butt (see buying tips)

Kosher salt and freshly ground black pepper

⅓ cup (75g) firmly packed light brown sugar

3 tablespoons maple syrup

1 tablespoon Dijon mustard

1½ teaspoons chopped fresh thyme leaves

3 large cloves garlic, minced

⅛ to ¼ teaspoon ground chipotle (or use chili powder in a pinch)

1 Tie the pork with twine in several places so that it's nice and compact. Place it on a plate or small baking sheet and season liberally with salt. Let it sit at room temperature for about an hour.

2 Combine the brown sugar, maple syrup, mustard, thyme, garlic, and ground chipotle in a small bowl. Add a couple pinches of salt and several grinds of pepper. Set aside.

3 Heat the oven to 475°F (245°C). Smear the sugar, mustard, and garlic mixture all over the pork, concentrating a good amount on the top of the roast, where the fat is. Nestle the pork (fat side up) into a roasting pan or cast iron baking dish just big enough to hold it. Put it in the oven for 10 to 15 minutes, until you start to smell garlic and sugar. Remove the pork from the oven and cover the pan tightly with foil. Return the pork to the oven and turn the heat down to 200°F (95°C).

4 Leave the pork in the oven overnight to cook for at least 8 hours and up to 10 hours. When you wake up, your house will smell amazing and the pork will be tender. Cover the roast with foil and keep it in the fridge for up to 5 days.

5 **The day of:** Slice or shred what you think you'll need, put it in a covered baking dish, and reheat in a 200°F to 250°F (95°C to 120°C) oven.

Barley Salad with Persimmon, Onion Confit, and Sheep's Milk Cheese

This dish comes from Food52's test kitchen chef, Josh Cohen (you can see the finished dish on page 171). It's what we serve for lunch to our most important visitors because we all love it so much. Josh says, "For me, the confit onions, almonds, and cheese remain a constant presence in this dish. But the arugula and persimmon can easily change: asparagus and hard-boiled eggs in the spring, or zucchini, corn, and basil in the summer." The onion confit—and onion-scented oil it produces—are what put this salad over the top. I've got some suggestions below for how to make the most of any leftover oil. If you can't find persimmons, you can use ripe pears, or try a cup of pomegranate arils.

SERVES 4 FOR 2 DINNERS, WITH EXTRA ONION OIL

SALAD

1 ¾ cups (320g) hulled barley

2 Fuyu persimmons

1 cup (140g) chopped toasted almonds

1 cup diced sheep (or goat) Gouda or another hard cheese like Pecorino or Manchego, about 6 ounces (170g)

¼ cup (60ml) red wine vinegar

3 ounces (85g) arugula

1 cup (20g) loosely packed fresh flat-leaf parsley leaves, coarsely chopped

Kosher salt and freshly ground black pepper

ONION CONFIT

3 large yellow onions, diced

½ cup (120ml) extra-virgin olive oil

Kosher salt and freshly ground black pepper

1 Soak the barley in plenty of cold water overnight.

2 Drain the barley and put it in a large saucepan. Add enough water to cover it by 3 to 4 inches (7.5 to 10cm) and add enough salt to make the water taste like saltwater. Bring to a boil, lower the heat, and simmer until tender, about 90 minutes.

3 Meanwhile, make the onion confit: Combine the onions and olive oil in a heavy pot and set over medium heat. Season with salt and pepper and cook, stirring often, until the onions soften and turn translucent, about 5 minutes. Lower the heat so that the onions are gently simmering and continue to cook them until they're soft, sweet, and caramelized, about 45 minutes. Turn off the heat and let them cool.

4 While the onions cook, blanch and peel the persimmons, as you would tomatoes (see page 137). Cut them into bite-size pieces.

5 Drain the barley and spread it out on a rimmed baking sheet to cool. Once it's cool, put it into a large mixing bowl.

6 Set a fine-mesh strainer over a bowl and pour the onion mixture into the strainer, catching the oil in the bowl. Add the onions to the barley, along with ¼ cup (60ml) of the oil. Stir to combine. If the salad seems dry, you can add more oil at the end.

7 Add the persimmons, almonds, cheese, and vinegar to the barley and stir to combine. Taste and adjust the seasoning. Add the arugula and parsley and stir to combine. Store in the fridge for up to 3 days. Keep the rest of the oil in the fridge for up to 10 days and use it to fry an egg or make salad dressing (see below).

8 **The day of:** Remove the salad from the refrigerator at least 30 minutes before serving and let it come to room temperature.

Onion Confit Vinaigrette

Use extra onion oil from the barley salad to flavor this simple fall vinaigrette: Combine **6 tablespoons (90ml) sherry vinegar, 4 teaspoons maple syrup, 1 teaspoon Dijon mustard, 2 teaspoons kosher salt, ½ cup (120ml) extra-virgin olive oil, 2 tablespoons onion oil,** and some freshly ground pepper in a jar with a tight-fitting lid. Screw on the lid and shake vigorously until emulsified. Taste and adjust the seasoning. Keep in the fridge for up to 10 days. Makes 1 cup (240ml).

Spicy Roasted Cauliflower

In the fall and winter, roasting becomes my default cooking method—especially for vegetables. I can cook multiple things at once, and I don't have to pay attention the way I do with things bubbling away on the stove. Broccoli and cauliflower are my workhorses because they happily absorb any flavors I throw at them. I switch up the marinade often so no one gets bored (try thyme, lemon juice, cumin, and pumpkin seed oil in place of 1 tablespoon of the olive oil in the recipe below), and I always add something acidic for brightness. You can apply the same basic rules to carrots, parsnips, potatoes, winter squash, what have you. (See finished dish on page 171.)

SERVES 4 AS A SIDE FOR 2 DINNERS, PLUS LEFTOVERS

½ cup (120ml) extra-virgin olive oil

2 tablespoons sherry vinegar

1 teaspoon sweet smoked paprika

1 teaspoon garlic powder

Kosher salt and freshly ground black pepper

½ to 1 teaspoon cayenne, depending on your heat preference

4½ pounds (2kg) cauliflower (about 2 large heads), cut into florets

3 limes, halved

1 Heat the oven to 450°F (230°C). In a very large bowl, whisk together the olive oil, vinegar, paprika, garlic powder, 1 teaspoon salt, and cayenne. Add the cauliflower and a few grinds of pepper, toss to coat, and spread on a rimmed baking sheet. (You may need to do this in batches.) Repeat with the second half of the ingredients.

2 Roast the cauliflower, turning once with a spatula, until tender and charred around the edges, about 30 minutes. Squeeze the limes over the cauliflower and toss. Taste and adjust the seasoning. Let cool and store in the fridge for up to 5 days.

3 **The day of:** Reheat the cauliflower on a baking sheet in a 300°F (150°C) oven for about 10 minutes, or serve at room temperature.

Bucatini with Cauliflower, Pecorino, Chile, and Bread Crumbs

For a quick weeknight dinner for 4, heat the oven to 425°F (220°C). In a food processor, combine **1 cup (110g) bread chunks** and **1 tablespoon extra-virgin olive oil** and pulse into coarse crumbs. Spread on a rimmed baking sheet and bake until golden, 5 to 7 minutes. Bring a large pot of generously salted water to a boil and cook **1 pound (450g) bucatini (or spaghetti)** until al dente. Meanwhile, gently heat **2 tablespoons extra-virgin olive oil** in a large skillet, add **2 finely chopped cloves of garlic,** and cook until fragrant. Add 1½ **cups (260g) coarsely chopped spicy roasted cauliflower** and **a large pinch of red pepper flakes** and cook until heated through. Reserve ⅔ **cup (160ml) of the pasta water,** then drain the pasta and tip it into the pan with the cauliflower. Add ¼ **cup (25g) grated Pecorino** and a splash of the pasta water and toss to combine, adding more water as necessary to create a thin, glossy sauce. Toss with **2 tablespoons chopped fresh flat-leaf parsley** and sprinkle the bread crumbs and more Pecorino over the pasta.

> **Amanda's Thinking Ahead** "I recommend making extra bread crumbs. Once you've had bread crumbs on pasta, you'll find yourself reaching for them every time you cook pasta. They add an addictive wispy crunch."

Lunch: Escarole, Roasted Cauliflower, and Chickpeas with Onion Confit Vinaigrette

Coarsely chop **escarole** and pack it up with some **spicy roasted cauliflower, drained braised chickpeas** (page 170), and **chopped almonds.** Pack some **onion confit vinaigrette** (page 166) and some **good wheaty crackers.** Toss the salad with the dressing right before you eat.

Braised Chickpeas with Celery

My family is a bunch of card-carrying meat eaters. Sometimes, though, we need a breather. But even when I'm not cooking meat, I don't have to let go of my favorite cooking method: the braise. Legumes take to braising like a bear to honey, swelling to plumpness as they absorb the flavorful liquid surrounding them and leaving just enough behind for a brothy sauce. I find chickpeas and celery to be a particularly happy flavor duo, especially when you introduce a little white wine to the mix. Most of the ingredients here are de rigueur, but I've sneaked in some ground ginger for a bit of zip.

Cooking Your Own Chickpeas Canned chickpeas are perfectly fine (as long as you rinse them well), but if you have the time, cooking your own is worth the effort—the flavor is just plain better. Cover dried chickpeas with plenty of cold water and let them soak overnight, or use the quick-soak method on page 264. Drain the chickpeas and put them in a large pot with 4 cups (950ml) water and ¼ teaspoon kosher salt for each cup of soaked chickpeas. (If you like, add some fresh herbs or a smashed clove of garlic.) Simmer for an hour or more, depending on how tender you want them. If you're cooking the chickpeas further, like in the braised chickpeas, you might want to pull them off the heat sooner; if you're using them for hummus or tossing them straight into a salad, make sure they're very tender. Drained and cooled, cooked chickpeas will keep in the fridge for up to 5 days. Or freeze them for up to 6 months: Dry the chickpeas thoroughly on a kitchen towel, then spread them on a parchment paper–lined baking sheet in a single layer; freeze until hard, then transfer to a freezer-friendly zipper plastic bag or container and return to the freezer. If you freeze them this way, the chickpeas won't stick together and you can dip into the freezer for only what you need. Note: 1 cup (200g) dried chickpeas makes about 2⅓ cups (385g) cooked.

SERVES 4 AS A SIDE FOR 2 DINNERS, PLUS LEFTOVERS

3 tablespoons extra-virgin olive oil

1 yellow onion, diced

12 ounces (340g) celery, diced

2 cloves garlic, peeled and smashed

¼ teaspoon cayenne

½ teaspoon ground ginger

1 thyme sprig

1 bay leaf

½ cup (120ml) dry white wine (or rosé, if you have some open)

5 cups (830g) cooked chickpeas (see tip) or 3 (15-ounce/425g) cans chickpeas, rinsed and drained

Kosher salt and freshly ground black pepper

1 Warm the olive oil in a large heavy skillet over medium heat. Add the onion, celery, and garlic and cook until the onion starts to soften, about 4 minutes (if the vegetables begin to brown, lower the heat). Add the cayenne, ginger, thyme, and bay leaf, and cook for 1 minute. Add the wine and cook until the liquid is reduced by half.

2 Add the chickpeas and 1½ cups (355ml) water and season with salt and pepper. Bring to a boil, then lower the heat, cover, and simmer until the vegetables are tender, 10 to 15 minutes. If the mixture looks dry at any point, add a bit more water. Taste and adjust the seasoning, then discard the thyme and bay leaf. Cool and store the chickpeas in their cooking liquid in the fridge for up to 5 days.

3 **The day of:** Warm the chickpeas gently on the stovetop or in the microwave. Serve as a side or as a main dish over rice (page 83) or polenta (page 232).

Brown Sugar Pound Cake with Crème Fraîche Whipped Cream

When I saw a recipe for brown sugar pound cake on the back of the Domino sugar box, I knew I had to make it right away. So I did, serving it with roasted peaches (this was in early August) and tangy crème fraîche whipped cream. The cake is denser than a standard pound cake with deep caramel notes. It plays nicely with most fruit, so use whatever is ripe and roast it (see the roasted applesauce on page 156) or serve it fresh.

Toast It Up By day 3 or 4, any pound cake you haven't eaten will benefit from a little TLC. Amanda has a brilliant recipe for toasted cake with ice cream on page 191. Or for something a little less sweet, toast a thin slice of pound cake and spread it with salted butter. With a cup of tea, it's the perfect pick-me-up.

SERVES 4 FOR 2 DINNERS

POUND CAKE
1 ¾ cups (220g) all-purpose flour, plus more for the pan

½ teaspoon baking powder

½ teaspoon kosher salt

1 cup (225g) unsalted butter, at room temperature

1 cup (220g) firmly packed light brown sugar

4 eggs

1 teaspoon pure vanilla extract

CRÈME FRAÎCHE WHIPPED CREAM
⅔ cup (160ml) heavy cream

⅓ cup (80ml) crème fraîche

½ teaspoon pure vanilla extract

Fresh or roasted fruit, for serving

1 To make the pound cake, heat the oven to 350°F (175°C) and butter and flour a standard loaf pan.

2 In a bowl, whisk together the flour, baking powder, and salt.

3 In the bowl of a stand mixer fitted with a paddle attachment or using a handheld electric mixer and a large bowl, beat the butter and brown sugar until fluffy, 3 to 5 minutes. Beat in the eggs one at a time until combined, followed by the vanilla. Don't dismay if the batter starts to curdle. All will be well shortly.

4 Gradually add the dry ingredients and beat just until combined.

5 Scrape the batter into the loaf pan. Bake until a toothpick inserted in the center of the cake comes out clean, 50 to 60 minutes. Cool the cake in the pan on a rack, then turn it out onto the rack to cool completely. It will keep in an airtight container for up to 5 days—although I doubt it will last that long.

6 To make the whipped cream, beat the cream, crème fraîche, and vanilla to very soft peaks. Store in the fridge for up to 2 days.

7 **The day of:** Whisk the cream briefly to return it to soft peaks. Slice the pound cake and serve each slice with a cap of whipped cream and fresh or roasted fruit.

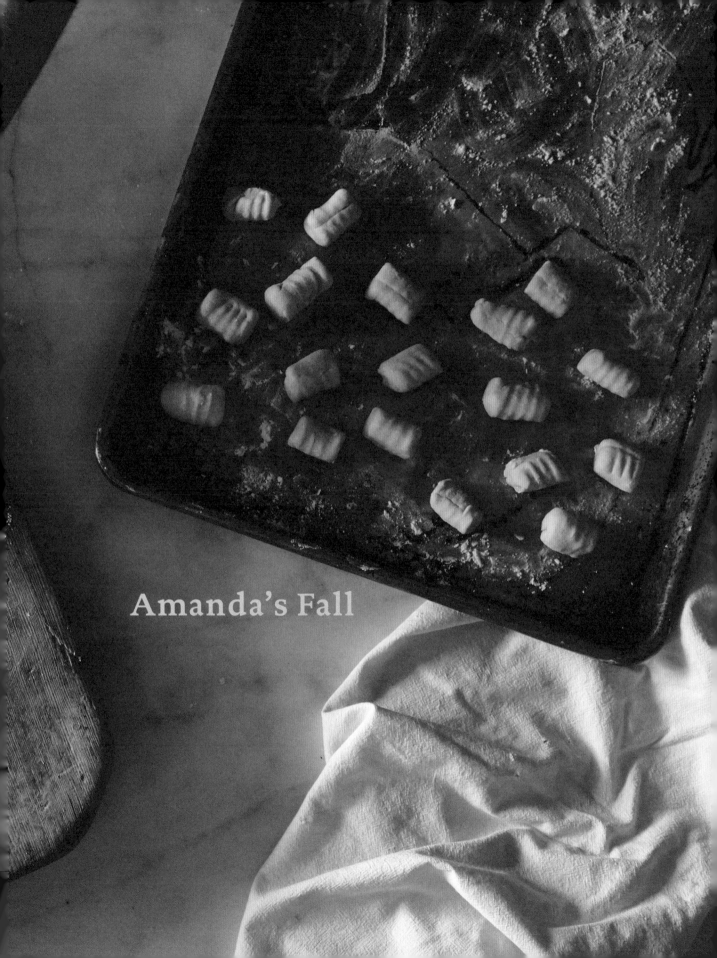

Amanda's Fall

THE WEEK AHEAD

THE RECIPES

HOW THEY COME TOGETHER

DINNER ONE

Beef Short Ribs in Red Wine

Country bread

Braised Fennel

Chocolate Olive Oil Cake

TO DO TODAY Reheat the short ribs and set
out the fennel to bring to room temperature.

DINNER TWO

Pan-Roasted Chicken

Butternut Squash Puree

Arugula with Simple Lemon Dressing

Chocolate Olive Oil Cake

TO DO TODAY Reheat the chicken and the
butternut squash. Dress the arugula.

DINNER THREE

Cream of Roasted Tomato Soup

My Mom's Grilled Cheese with Bacon

Plums and Frothy Cinnamon Cream

TO DO TODAY Warm the soup and stir in the cream.
Make the grilled cheese sandwiches. Before dinner, get
the plums in the oven and make the cinnamon cream.

DINNER FOUR

Chicken Salad with Fennel and Smoked Almonds

Country bread

Mint Ice Cream with Toasted Cake and
Whipped Cream

TO DO TODAY Put together the salad. Toast the cake
crumbs and whip the cream for the dessert. After eating
the salad, have everyone assemble their own dessert.

DINNER FIVE

Beef Short Ribs in Red Wine

Penne rigate

Arugula with Simple Lemon Dressing

Butter cookie and salted caramel sandwiches

TO DO TODAY Spread 8 butter cookies with salted caramel
sauce and top with 8 more cookies. Chill in the fridge. Easy!
Cook 1 pound (450g) penne rigate. Warm up the remaining
beef short ribs. Dress the arugula. Serve the penne topped
with the short ribs and some grated cheese.

BROWN BAG LUNCHES

Chicken Salad Sandwich on Brioche

Fennel Salad and Soppressata

Egg Salad with crackers

GAME PLAN

TO MAKE OVER THE WEEKEND

Cream of Roasted Tomato Soup

Egg Salad

Pan-Roasted Chicken

Chicken Salad with Fennel and Smoked Almonds

Beef Short Ribs in Red Wine

Butternut Squash Puree

Braised Fennel

Chocolate Olive Oil Cake

GET IN, GET OUT!

Should take 3 hours, give or take a few minutes.

- In the morning, season the chicken thighs (page 184) and put them uncovered in the fridge.

- When you're ready to cook, heat your oven to 350°F (175°C). Make the cake batter (page 191) and bake the cake.

- While the cake bakes, get the short ribs started by chopping the vegetables, browning the short ribs, and so on, until the braise is happily simmering away (page 187). If you're time-crunched, don't brown the short ribs.

- When the cake is done, increase the oven heat to 375°F (190°C). Prep the tomatoes and roast them for soup (page 181), then mash in a saucepan and store them in the fridge (in the saucepan, if possible, so reheating is easier).

- Make the butternut squash puree (page 188).

- When the tomatoes are out of the oven, increase the oven temperature to 400°F (200°C) for the chicken (page 184). Brown the chicken, then transfer to the oven to finish cooking. It's done when the juices run clear. Remove from the oven, let cool, and store in the fridge.

- Braise the fennel (page 185), then let cool and store in the fridge.

- Hard-boil 6 eggs, then make the egg salad (page 182).

- Bonus points if you make the lemon dressing for the chicken salad (page 185); otherwise make it the day of.

- You're almost there! Check on the short ribs. When they're tender, turn off the heat and let them cool. Store, covered, in the fridge, ideally in the pot you've cooked them in.

- Now get back to making your Halloween costume. Or put your feet up.

Can't do the whole menu? Here's how to cool your jets. Skip the short ribs altogether and grill lamb shoulder chops on the first night and serve cured meats, salad, and cheese on the second. You can always trim dessert from the menu because good ice cream is just a freezer aisle away. Think of the time you'll save if you don't make the cake (but it is really good, just sayin'). Together these changes will save you an hour if not more.

GROCERY LIST

PRODUCE

Baby arugula or baby kale,
14 ounces (400g)

Beefsteak tomatoes, 4 pounds
(1.8kg, about 8)

Butternut squash, 2 medium

Carrots, 4

Celery, 2 stalks for lunch

Fennel bulbs, 3 large with fronds

Garlic, 8 cloves

Lemon, 1

Meyer lemons, 2

Plums, 8

Radishes, 1 bunch for lunch

Yellow onions, 3

HERBS

Dill, flat-leaf parsley, what have
you, for lunch salad

Handful of sage, rosemary, and/or
thyme sprigs

SPICES

Ground cinnamon, ½ teaspoon

PANTRY

Agave syrup, 1 teaspoon

Aged sherry vinegar or other
vinegar you like

Canned chopped tomatoes
(preferably Pomi), 3 cups (720g)

Capers, for lunch

Crackers, for lunch

Extra-virgin olive oil, about
3 cups (710ml), plus more to
have on hand

Grainy mustard, 1 tablespoon,
plus more for lunches

Mayo, for lunch

Penne rigate, 1 pound (450g)

Peppadews or other pickled hot
pepper, 4

Pickled vegetables (beans,
carrots, cauliflower, or
cucumbers), 1 jar for lunch

Pitted olives, for lunch

Salted caramel sauce, for dessert

Tabasco or Cholula hot sauce,
for lunch

BAKING AISLE

All-purpose flour, 2 cups (250g)

Baking powder, ½ teaspoon

Baking soda, ½ teaspoon

Bittersweet chocolate,
6 ounces (170g)

Light brown sugar, ¾ cup (150g)

Raw sugar, 1 teaspoon

Sugar, 1 ¾ cups (350g), plus more
to have on hand

Smoked almonds, ½ cup (70g)

Unsweetened cocoa powder,
¾ cup (60g)

Pure vanilla extract, a few drops

DAIRY AND EGGS

Salted butter, a few tablespoons

Unsalted butter, 6 tablespoons
(85g)

Eggs, 9

Gruyère, 4 cups (460g) grated
from a wedge

Parmesan, 1 cup (100g) grated
from a wedge

Heavy cream, 2 cups plus
1 tablespoon (475ml)

Milk, 1½ cups (355ml)

MEAT AND SEAFOOD

Bacon, 4 slices

Bone-in, skin-on chicken
thighs, 12

Bone-in short ribs, 6 pounds
(2.7kg)

Pancetta, 5 ounces (140g)

Soppressata, thinly sliced
for lunch

BOOZE AND SUCH

Bourbon, ¼ cup (60ml)

Orange juice, ¼ cup (60ml)

Red wine, 2 (750ml) bottles

FREEZER

Mint ice cream, for dessert

BAKED GOODS

Brioche, for lunch

Good butter cookies, 16

Good country bread, 2 loaves

Cream of Roasted Tomato Soup

I like a recipe that allows me to feel like I'm cheating the system. Traditional tomato soup makes me think of peeling tomatoes and long simmering (long suffering?). It can turn out well, but lacks the depth of flavor you get in a tomato that's been exposed to direct heat.

There's always another way, and with some tinkering, I found it: I slice and roast beefsteak tomatoes smothered with garlic and olive oil. By the time they're roasted, the soup is pretty much done. To finish it, simply mash the tomatoes with some cream and adjust the seasoning. The soup is heavily textured—call it rustic!—and genuinely all about the deep flavor of tomatoes.

SERVES 4

4 pounds (1.8kg) beefsteak tomatoes (about 8), cored and halved

4 cloves garlic, lightly crushed and left in their skins

Extra-virgin olive oil, for sprinkling

Salt and coarsely ground black pepper

6 tablespoons (90ml) heavy cream

Pinch of sugar (optional)

1 Heat the oven to 375°F (190°C) and line a rimmed baking sheet or large casserole dish with aluminum foil. Lay the tomatoes cut side down. Wedge the garlic cloves wherever they'll fit. Sprinkle with olive oil and season with salt. Roast until the tomatoes are soft and caramelized, about 1 hour. Remove from the oven and let cool.

2 Pull the skins off the tomatoes and discard them. Squeeze the garlic cloves from their skins. Begin mashing the tomatoes with a potato masher until they're pulpy, but not chunky; you can do this directly on the baking sheet. (If you prefer to use a food processor, go ahead—just make sure you leave it pulpy.) Let cool, transfer to a container, and store in the fridge for up to 5 days.

3 **The day of:** Warm the soup over medium heat. When the mixture is hot but not boiling, stir in the cream. Season with salt and add a pinch of sugar, if needed. Ladle into bowls and season with pepper.

My Mom's Grilled Cheese with Bacon

My mother, an excellent cook, likes to dispense her cooking wisdom in a slow, carefully timed trickle of detail. For years, I made her oven-fried chicken and wondered why mine was never as crisp. Because she hadn't yet told me about the critical step of soaking the chicken in salted ice water for a few hours before cooking it.

With grilled cheese, I felt I'd learned a pretty good version on my own—buttering the outside of the bread and grating cheese for the inside, so the exterior gets supercrisp and toasty and the center is a glorious goo. Merrill and I even did a video on this grilled cheese. My mom watched the video and said, "Looked good, but you forgot the bacon." She always laid a piece of bacon across the outside of the sandwich so it would be embedded in the grilled cheese like a fossil and the bacon fat would scent the bread. Mom, 1. Me, 0.

SERVES 4

About 6 tablespoons (85g) unsalted butter, at room temperature

8 large slices country bread

4 slices bacon, halved crosswise

4 cups (460g) grated Gruyère

1 cup (100g) grated Parmesan

1 Lightly butter one side of each slice of bread. Lay a half slice of bacon across the middle (lengthwise) of each buttered side.

2 Place a large cast-iron skillet over medium heat. (If you can squeeze all the sandwiches into one pan, bravo; otherwise cook them in batches or in two pans side by side.) Lay 2 slices of bread, butter-and-bacon side down, in the pan. Sprinkle one-half of each of the cheeses on top, then top with 2 slices of bread, butter-and-bacon side up. Press down on the sandwiches with a spatula. Cook until the bacon renders and the sandwich warms through, 5 minutes or so. When the bacon and bread are nicely browned, turn and toast the other side for about 5 minutes more. Transfer the sandwiches to plates (you can keep them warm in a 200°F/95°C oven as well) and cook the second batch.

Egg Salad

Whenever I buy eggs for something on my weekly menu (here, it's for the cake), I'll make a point to hard-boil a handful of them (actually, 6 in this case) for egg salad. I start in cold water and count 6 minutes once the water simmers. I keep my salad simple, mashing the **egg** with **mayonnaise, mustard, a little Tabasco or Cholula, capers, shaved fennel, radishes,** and **herbs (dill, parsley, fennel fronds,** what have you). I pack egg salad sandwiches or egg salad and **crackers** for lunches. And if I'm having a tough week and didn't get to all of my cooking, egg salad works for dinner too.

Merrill's Mom's Egg Salad "I'm about to tell you to do something a little crazy. If you're the kind of person who enjoys cottage cheese and egg salad separately, it may be time to try them together. When my sister and I were small, my mother would fold equal amounts of egg salad and cottage cheese together, and then pile the pale yellow mixture onto toast for our dinner. It was a little tangy and very delicious."

Pan-Roasted Chicken

This is more technique than recipe and is a great one to have in your back pocket, because it works as both a make-ahead recipe (the chicken reheats well and can be sliced and added to salads) and a last-minute save. Pan-roasting chicken produces brown, crisp skin and juicy insides in a single pot in very little time. (See finished dish on page 189.)

It's easiest if you use all chicken thighs, as they'll cook at the same pace, but if you believe it's better to buy all the parts of a bird, then just plan to remove the pieces from the pan as they finish cooking.

How Merrill Uses Leftover Chicken Most weeks—except perhaps during the height of summer—I roast a whole chicken or bake a pan of chicken thighs (page 148). I recently adopted Amanda's pan-roasting method, and I've been won over by the deep browning of the chicken skin and the aromatics, which you only get if you dedicate a few extra minutes to monitoring the chicken on the stovetop before you slide it into the oven. Here are some recipes that call for leftover chicken, or where it would make a nice addition or substitution.

• Sliced Chicken, Avocado, and Lemon Salad (page 42)
• Grain Salad with Asparagus, Baby Turnips, Feta, and Preserved Lemon Dressing (page 61)
• Jasmine Rice Salad with Blistered Tomatoes, Tuna, Olives, and Capers (page 76)
• Thai Steak Salad (page 80)
• Grilled Squid Salad with Lemon, Capers, and Couscous (page 96)
• Tuna Salad with Peppers and Smoked Paprika Mayonnaise (page 103)
• Warm Chicken Salad (page 152)
• Chicken Salad with Fennel and Smoked Almonds (opposite)
• All-in-One Lamb Salad with Horseradish, Watercress, and Celery (page 198)
• Turbo Jook with Baby Mustard Greens (page 213)

SERVES 4, PLUS LEFTOVERS FOR THE CHICKEN SALAD

12 bone-in, skin-on chicken thighs

Salt and freshly ground black pepper

Extra-virgin olive oil, for cooking

4 cloves garlic, skins left on and smashed

Handful of sage, rosemary, and/or thyme sprigs

1 In the morning, place the chicken thighs on a plate or small baking sheet and season with salt and pepper. Place, uncovered, in the fridge.

2 When you're ready to cook, heat the oven to 400°F (200°C) and set out the chicken. Place two large cast-iron pans (you can do this in batches in one pan but two makes it faster) over high heat. When the pans are hot, add enough oil to thickly coat the base of the pan. Add the chicken thighs, skin side down, in the pan. Let them cook, undisturbed, until the skin is well browned and easily releases from the pan, about 7 to 10 minutes. Turn the pieces and cook the other side until well browned, about 5 minutes longer. Adjust the heat so the chicken doesn't burn.

3 Tuck the garlic and herbs around and under the chicken pieces, and transfer the pans to the oven to finish cooking, 10 to 15 minutes—the chicken is done when the internal temperature is 160°F (71°C). Let cool and store in containers in the fridge for up to 5 days.

4 **The day of:** Place 8 of the chicken thighs in a skillet and loosely tent with a piece of aluminum foil. Reheat in a 300°F (150°C) oven for 15 to 20 minutes.

A Million Variations, and Here Are Three You can make this chicken any time of year. Pair it with green sauce (page 198), ramp butter (page 20), or romesco (page 107).

Chicken Salad with Fennel and Smoked Almonds

I like a chicken salad that's as much greens as chicken and other components. I added some of the leftover braised fennel, along with smoked almonds and some Peppadews to add a little life to the party. But this salad could be taken in a bunch of directions. Add a couple of handfuls of black or Le Puy lentils. Leave out the Peppadews and add grapefruit or blood orange segments. You could even swap the smoked almonds for bacon. Merrill has a great take on chicken salad as well (page 152)—hers is warmed in a vinaigrette.

SERVES 4

SIMPLE LEMON DRESSING

6 tablespoons (90ml) extra-virgin olive oil

Zest and juice of 1 lemon (Meyer if you have an extra)

1 tablespoon grainy mustard

1 teaspoon agave nectar

Salt and freshly ground black pepper

SALAD

4 large handfuls (7 ounces) baby arugula or baby kale

2 cups (280g) leftover chicken (opposite), pulled from the bones into small pieces

1 cup (160g) coarsely chopped braised fennel (right)

4 Peppadews or other pickled hot pepper, thinly sliced

½ cup (70g) smoked almonds, chopped

1 To make the dressing, combine the olive oil, lemon zest and juice, mustard, and agave in a jar with a tight-fitting lid. Season with salt and pepper. Screw on the lid and shake vigorously until emulsified. Store in the fridge for up to 10 days.

2 **The day of:** Arrange a bed of arugula on a large, deep serving platter. Top with the chicken, fennel, Peppadews, and almonds. Sprinkle half the dressing on top and mix the salad at the table. Save the remaining dressing for arugula salads through the week.

Braised Fennel

This is a handy technique for cooking firmer vegetables—it works well with young carrots and artichokes as well. Trim **3 large fennel bulbs** (removing the outer layer if it's tough) and slice into ¾-inch (2cm) wedges. Chop the fennel fronds and set aside. Put the fennel wedges in a large saucepan. Pour in ⅓ **cup (80ml) extra-virgin olive oil** and season with salt. Cook, covered, over medium-high heat, stirring occasionally, until the fennel is lightly browned and tender, about 25 minutes. Top with **chopped fennel fronds.** Let cool, then store in the fridge for up to a week. Reserve some of the braised fennel for lunch (see below) and for the chicken salad (left). When serving, remove from the fridge and let come to room temperature 20 minutes in advance. Sprinkle with **aged sherry vinegar.**

Lunch: Chicken Salad Sandwich on Brioche

Leftover **chicken salad** makes a great sandwich. Spread slices of **brioche** with **mayo** and pile on the salad.

Lunch: Fennel Salad and Soppressata

Combine some **salad greens, pitted olives,** and **braised fennel** and toss in **leftover lemon dressing.** Pack it alongside **sliced soppressata** and either **good crackers** or a **slab of bread.**

Beef Short Ribs in Red Wine

This recipe grew out of one from Mario Batali's *Simple Italian Food*, in which he braises brisket and Barolo—two expensive ingredients that I've throttled down to short ribs and whatever red wine you have on hand. His recipe also calls for celery, which I don't love in mirepoix (sorry France!), so I've added a bunch more carrots. This braise is best prepared one or two days in advance, which makes serving it for dinners even easier because all you have to do is heat it up. For this menu, I suggest serving it with country bread and penne rigate, but it's also great with roasted potatoes (page 50), mashed potatoes and parsnips (page 251), farro (page 216), or polenta (page 232). If you're up to it, take the country bread one step further: Toast it then brush it with olive oil.

Flavor Brightener If you'd like to liven up the short ribs, make a gremolata—a mix of finely grated lemon zest, chopped fresh parsley, and a smashed and chopped garlic clove—and sprinkle on top.

6 tablespoons (90ml) extra-virgin olive oil

6 pounds (2.7kg) bone-in short ribs

Salt and freshly ground black pepper

3 yellow onions, chopped

4 carrots, peeled and chopped into ¼-inch (6mm) dice

5 ounces (140g) pancetta, cut into ¼-inch (6mm) dice

5 cups (1.2L) red wine

3 cups (720g) canned chopped tomatoes (preferably Pomi)

1 Warm the olive oil in your largest Dutch oven over high heat until nearly smoking. Season the short ribs liberally with salt and pepper. Working in batches, add the short ribs to the pan and sear until well browned on all sides, about 3 minutes per side. Adjust the heat so the short ribs brown but don't burn. Transfer to a plate as you sear the remaining short ribs and add more oil as needed. Pour off any excess fat, leaving a small amount in the pot for the vegetables.

2 Add the onions, carrots, and pancetta to the pot, turn down the heat to medium-high and cook until the vegetables are light brown and starting to soften, about 8 minutes. Season with salt and pepper.

3 Return the short ribs to the pot and add the wine and tomatoes. Bring to a boil, then lower the heat and simmer until the meat is very tender, 2½ to 3 hours. Let cool in the pot, then cover and transfer to the fridge to store for up to 5 days.

4 **The day of:** Skim the layer of chilled fat off the top of the short ribs. Reheat the short ribs over medium heat in the covered pot you cooked and stored them in, adding a splash of water and stirring now and then, about 15 minutes.

Butternut Squash Puree

Unlike most purees, which involve cooking a vegetable in liquid, pulverizing it in a food processor or blender, and then adding cream and butter—this recipe rebels against such conventions. I wanted a puree that I could make in a single pan. I also wanted to focus on concentrating the flavor of the squash instead of thinning it out with cream. I'd like to tell you that I spent months perfecting it; I did not. Lazy, one weekend, I threw a bunch of butternut squash cubes into a pan with lots of olive oil. I covered the pot and simmered the butternut squash in this bath of oil until it was good and soft. Then I mashed it right in the pan and swirled in a few tablespoons of cream. It worked. Without further ado . . .

Merrill Doubles Down "This puree is now a staple in our house at Thanksgiving, and I usually double the recipe so that we're sure to have lots of leftovers (it's especially popular with our toddler, Henry). I find it just as luxurious without the cream, so if you don't have any on hand, don't let that stop you from making it."

SERVES 4, PLUS LEFTOVERS

12 cups (1.7kg) peeled and cubed butternut squash (from about 2 medium squash, cut into ½-inch/1.3cm cubes)

½ cup (120ml) olive oil

Salt

3 tablespoons heavy cream, plus more as needed

1 Pile the squash into a large heavy saucepan or Dutch oven. Add the olive oil and season with salt. Cover the pan and place it over medium-high heat. You want the squash to rapidly sauté and steam in the oil, though you should still give it an occasional stir. Continue to cook until the squash is very tender, about 15 minutes. Adjust the heat as needed to make sure the squash doesn't burn. Turn off the heat.

2 With a potato masher, crush the squash until it's a very smooth mash with no large chunks. Return the puree to medium heat and pour in the cream so that it just pools on top. Cook until the puree bubbles, then stir the cream in. Taste and adjust the seasoning, adding more salt or cream as needed. Store in the fridge for up to 5 days.

3 **The day of:** Reheat the squash in a saucepan over medium heat, stirring often, for 8 to 10 minutes (or in the microwave).

Chocolate Olive Oil Cake

I never tire of cake's magical transformation from pudding-like batter to soaring, airy tower. But I also bake cakes because just a single batch creates a homemade dessert that carries you through the week. That effort-to-reward ratio passes muster for most busy cooks. Sometimes when I don't get to the cake on the weekend, I'll make it on Monday or Tuesday night. You feel pretty savvy when you come home from work, dinner is done, and you've got time to bake.

This cake was inspired by one of my favorites— the orange-scented olive oil cake from Maialino, a restaurant off Manhattan's Gramercy Park. In the Maialino cake, the orange and olive oil are fragrant and chatty. My chocolate version took about fifty-seven tries to get right, and here it is for you—chocolate and olive oil, happily cavorting, uninhibited by any demands for sophistication.

MAKES A 9-INCH (23CM) ROUND CAKE

2 cups (250g) all-purpose flour	1⅓ cups (315ml) extra-virgin olive oil
1 cup (200g) sugar	1½ cups (355ml) whole milk
¾ cup (150g) light brown sugar	3 large eggs
1½ teaspoons kosher salt	¼ cup (60ml) orange juice
½ teaspoon baking soda	6 ounces (170g) bittersweet chocolate, melted
½ teaspoon baking powder	

1 Heat the oven to 350°F (175°C). Oil, butter, or spray a 9-inch (23cm) cake pan that is at least 2 inches (5cm) deep and line the bottom with parchment paper.

2 In a bowl, whisk the flour, sugars, salt, baking soda, and baking powder. In another bowl, whisk the olive oil, milk, eggs, and orange juice. Add the dry ingredients; whisk until just combined. Scrape the melted chocolate into the batter and fold together.

3 Pour the batter into the prepared pan and bake for 1 hour, until the top is domed and a cake tester comes out almost clean. Transfer the cake to a rack and let cool for 30 minutes.

4 Run a knife around the edge of the pan, invert the cake onto the rack, and let cool completely, 2 hours.

Mint Ice Cream with Toasted Cake and Whipped Cream

If there's any cake left, your family is more disciplined than mine. And you'll also have a good dessert option: Heat your oven to 350°F (175°C). Break the remaining **cake** into hazelnut-size pieces on a baking sheet. Bake until the cake is toasted, 10 to 12 minutes. Meanwhile, whip **½ cup (120ml) heavy cream**—no sugar is needed. In 4 tumblers, layer **mint ice cream,** cake, and whipped cream, twice. Eat with long spoons.

Plums and Frothy Cinnamon Cream

Before you sit down to dinner, slice **8 plums** and place them in a small baking dish with a pat or two or three of **salted butter.** Bake in a 300°F (150°C) oven while you eat dinner. The plums are ready when they're warm and juicy and beginning to brown on the edges, about 30 minutes. Also before dinner, combine **1 cup (240ml) heavy cream** with **½ teaspoon ground cinnamon, a few drops of pure vanilla extract,** and **1 teaspoon raw sugar** in a jar with a tight-fitting lid. Screw on the lid and shake vigorously until blended and very thick and frothy, then put the jar in the fridge; shake once more before serving. Serve the plums doused in frothy cream.

THE WEEK AHEAD

THE RECIPES

HOW THEY COME TOGETHER

DINNER ONE

Lamb Blade Chops with Green Sauce

Stuck-Pot Rice

Roasted Brussels Sprouts

Chewy Vanilla Spice Cookies with Chocolate Chunks (Vegan, Too!)

TO DO TODAY Broil or grill the lamb chops. Reheat the rice. Let the brussels sprouts come to room temperature. Bake off a batch of the cookies.

DINNER TWO

Gnocchi with Creamed Kale

Sliced pears with sheep's milk cheese

TO DO TODAY Cook the gnocchi. Warm the kale. Top the gnocchi with the kale and Parmesan. Set out the cheese before you sit down to dinner.

DINNER THREE

All-in-One Lamb Salad with Horseradish, Watercress, and Celery

Wheat or rye country bread

Chewy Vanilla Spice Cookies with Chocolate Chunks (Vegan, Too!)

TO DO TODAY Put together the salad. Slice some country bread. Bake off the remaining cookies.

DINNER FOUR

Gnocchi with Brown Butter, Sage, Shaved Brussels Sprouts, and Pine Nuts

Coffee Ice Cream with Toasted Marshmallows

TO DO TODAY Shave the brussels sprouts and toast the pine nuts, then assemble the sauce. Cook the gnocchi. Toast the marshmallows just before scooping the ice cream.

DINNER FIVE

Stuck-Pot Rice, Creamed Kale, and Fried Egg

Banana, kefir, and maple shakes

TO DO TODAY Reheat the rice and kale. Fry the eggs. After dinner, make the shakes: In a blender, combine 2 cups (475ml) kefir (a tangy yogurt-like drink), 2 large scoops coffee ice cream, 2 ripe bananas, a handful of ice, and 3 tablespoons maple syrup. Blend on high until smooth and frothy.

BROWN BAG LUNCHES

Lamb Sandwich with Kale and Green Sauce

Shaved Brussels Sprouts Salad with Pine Nuts and Raisins, plus your favorite cheese and crackers

GAME PLAN

TO MAKE OVER THE WEEKEND

Green Sauce	Stuck-Pot Rice
Roasted Brussels Sprouts	Chewy Vanilla Spice Cookies with Chocolate Chunks (Vegan, Too!)
Creamed Kale	
Ricotta Gnocchi	

BRING IT, KALE.

Plan on a 3-hour investment in a week of great dinners.

- The night before or in the morning, mix together the cookie dough (page 204), then store covered in the fridge.

- When you're ready to cook, heat the oven to 400°F (200°C). While it warms up, blend up the green sauce (page 198) and store it in the fridge. You're going to need your food processor again, so either rinse it out or just live with a little green sauce in your creamed kale.

- Parboil the rice (page 203), then drain it. Start the second stage of cooking the rice, this time in oil (this is the part when it sticks to the pot!). Once it's done, store in the fridge.

- Meanwhile, trim half of the brussels sprouts (page 196) and get them ready to go in the oven. Clean and prep the kale and broccoli rabe for the creamed kale (page 199).

- Roast the trimmed sprouts (page 196), then let them cool, and store in the fridge.

- Work on the creamed kale (page 199), browning the pancetta and cooking the kale and rabe. When you have a free moment, mix the gnocchi dough (page 200). It's a bit of a balancing act but will build character.

- Take a minute to puree the kale and rabe. Store the creamed kale in two containers, half of it in each one.

- Roll and cut the gnocchi, then freeze them (page 200).

- Lots of dishes to wash today. Fingers crossed you have someone who can help!

The life-changing magic of trimming back your menu.
The best way to save time this week is to swap out the gnocchi for a dried pasta like penne rigate or orecchiette. If you need to cut back even more, then make baked rice (page 83) rather than stuck-pot rice. You'll still have a week of lovely food! And this will save you nearly an hour.

GROCERY LIST

PRODUCE

Broccoli rabe, 1 pound (450g)

Brussels sprouts, 2 ¾ pounds (1.3kg) small

Celery stalks, 2

Garlic, 1 large clove

Horseradish, for grating

Lacinato kale, 1 bunch, plus more for lunch

Lemons, 4

Ripe bananas, 2

Ripe Bosc pears, 4 for dessert

Romaine, 3 cups (60g) torn

Watercress, 3 cups (60g)

HERBS

Basil, 1 ½ cups (45g) packed

Flat-leaf parsley, 3 cups (60g) packed

Sage leaves, 8

SPICES

Ground chile (such as piment d'Espelette), ¼ rounded teaspoon

Ground cinnamon (preferably Saigon), 1 teaspoon

Nutmeg, 1 whole

Red pepper flakes, generous pinch

PANTRY

Anchovy fillets, 3

Basmati rice, 2 ½ cups (460g)

Capers, 1 tablespoon

Crackers, for lunch

Dijon mustard, 1 tablespoon

Grainy mustard, 1 tablespoon

Maple syrup, 3 tablespoons

Marshmallows, 8

Mayonnaise, for lunch

Canola oil, ½ cup plus 1 tablespoon (135ml)

Extra-virgin olive oil, about 2 cups (475ml), plus more to have on hand

Peanut, grapeseed, or corn oil, 5 tablespoons (75ml)

Golden raisins, for lunch

Potato chips, for lunch

Red wine vinegar, 3 tablespoons

Flaky salt

BAKING AISLE

All-purpose flour, 6 cups (750g), plus more to have on hand

Baking powder, 1 teaspoon

Baking soda, ¾ teaspoon

Dark chocolate, 8 ounces (225g)

Pine nuts, ¼ cup (35g)

Salted pistachios, ¼ cup (30g)

Dark brown sugar, ½ cup (110g) firmly packed

Sugar, ½ cup (100g)

Vanilla bean, 1

DAIRY AND EGGS

A small wedge of your favorite cheese, for lunch

Unsalted butter, ½ cup (110g)

Buttermilk, 3 tablespoons

Crème fraîche, ⅓ cup (80ml)

Eggs, 6 to 10

Fresh whole-milk ricotta, 2 pounds (900g)

Heavy cream, ¼ cup plus 1 tablespoon (75ml)

Kefir, 2 cups (475ml)

Parmesan, ½ cup (50g) grated from a wedge, plus more for serving

Pecorino, for serving

Plain yogurt (preferably whole milk), ⅓ cup (80ml)

Sheep's milk cheese, for dessert

MEAT AND SEAFOOD

Lamb blade chops, 8, about ¾ inch (2cm) thick

Pancetta, 4 ounces (115g)

FREEZER

Coffee ice cream, for dessert

BAKED GOODS

Ciabatta or kaiser rolls, 4 for lunch

Wheat or rye country bread

Lamb Blade Chops

Lamb blade chops are what I turn to when I need a quick main dish that's not superexpensive or taxing to handle. They're less prim than a regular lamb chop, which is why they're also cheaper. You can marinate them with yogurt, spices, and herbs, and sometimes I do. But mostly, I prepare them simply—they have beautiful flavor and can easily fit in with other dishes. Here, I top them with green sauce and serve stuck-pot rice (page 203) on the side. You should cook all the lamb chops at once and save the leftovers for the salad (page 198) and lunches.

SERVES 4, PLUS LEFTOVERS FOR THE SALAD AND SANDWICHES

8 lamb blade chops, ¾ inch (2cm) thick	Green sauce, for topping (page 198)
Salt and freshly ground black pepper	1 lemon, cut into wedges (optional)

1 About 30 minutes before serving, season all the lamb chops with salt and pepper and let them sit at room temperature. Heat your grill or broiler. If you're grilling, heat the coals until very hot so you get a good char, then grill about 2 minutes per side for medium-rare. If you're broiling, place the chops in a cast-iron skillet and broil the chops 4 inches (10cm) from the flame, about 2 minutes per side for medium-rare (internal temperature of 130°F to 135°F/54°C to 57°C).

2 Top 4 of the chops with a spoonful of green sauce and serve with a lemon wedge. Let the remaining chops cool, then put in a container and store in the fridge for up to 5 days.

Roasted Brussels Sprouts

Heat the oven to 400°F (200°C). Spread out **2 pounds (900g) small trimmed brussels sprouts** on a baking sheet and drizzle the sprouts with enough **extra-virgin olive oil** to lightly coat them (like a salad dressing). Season the sprouts with salt. Shake the baking sheet to roll the sprouts and evenly coat them with the oil and salt.

Roast until browned and just tender, 10 to 15 minutes. If they're very small, just a few minutes will do—taste one to see! Let cool, then store in the fridge for up to 4 days. Roasted brussels sprouts don't rewarm well, so I prefer letting them come to room temperature before serving.

I use this same roasting method with cauliflower, delicata squash, radishes, carrots, and Romanesco cauliflower. The cooking times will vary depending on the vegetable, as well as on how you cut it. Don't get too caught up with these details. If you're in the kitchen already, just check the oven every few minutes, and you can't go wrong. I like to use small brussels sprouts because they're sweeter, but larger ones work, too. For any sprouts bigger than a large grape, cut them in half lengthwise.

Lunch: Shaved Brussels Sprouts Salad with Pine Nuts and Raisins

If you have leftover **raw brussels sprouts,** shave them and toss them with some **pine nuts, golden raisins,** and **vinaigrette** (page 198). Put this into a container and pack **a wedge of good cheese** and **a few crackers.**

All-in-One Lamb Salad with Horseradish, Watercress, and Celery

A great way to transform leftover lamb into a second meal is to make a big, peppery chopped salad with it. Put together a bowlful of chopped romaine and watercress. Add a handful or two of sliced celery. Cube the lamb and add it to the bowl. Dress the salad with a creamy vinaigrette, then blanket it all with freshly grated horseradish. (If you can't find fresh horseradish, buy jarred horseradish and mix 1 tablespoon into the dressing—add more if you like.)

Not a Cold Lamb Fan? Dress the greens, reheat the lamb, and lay it on top of the salad.

SERVES 4

3 cups (60g) torn romaine

3 cups (60g) watercress (or mizuna or arugula)

2 celery stalks, thinly sliced

Cubed leftover lamb (page 196), about 1½ to 2 cups

⅓ cup (80ml) creamy mustard vinaigrette (recipe follows)

Fresh horseradish, peeled

1 In a large bowl, fold together the romaine, watercress, celery, and lamb. Add the dressing. Toss well and add more dressing as needed. Taste and adjust the seasoning. Grate horseradish over the salad.

Creamy Mustard Vinaigrette

Combine ⅓ cup (80ml) extra-virgin olive oil, 3 tablespoons red wine vinegar, 3 tablespoons buttermilk, 1 tablespoon Dijon mustard, 1 tablespoon grainy mustard, 1 tablespoon heavy cream, ¼ teaspoon salt, and ¼ teaspoon freshly ground black pepper in a jar with a tight-fitting lid. Screw on the lid and shake vigorously until smooth and emulsified. Taste and adjust the seasoning. Store in the fridge for up to 2 weeks. (Makes 1 cup/240ml.)

Green Sauce

In a food processor or blender, combine **3 cups (60g) packed flat-leaf parsley leaves, 1½ cups (45g) packed basil leaves, 3 anchovy fillets, 1 tablespoon capers, 1 large clove garlic, a pinch or two of piment d'Espelette or crushed red pepper flakes,** and a pinch of salt. Pulse the mixture until the leaves are broken down. With the machine running, add oil in a slow, steady stream. If you like a dense green sauce, **¾ cup (175ml) extra-virgin olive oil** will do; if you want it to be looser, add up to 1 cup (140ml) oil.

Squeeze the **juice from a lemon half** into the sauce. Taste and add more lemon, salt, or piment d'Espelette—I like the sauce to have a spark of heat but not be hot. Store in the fridge for up to 5 days.

Lunch: Lamb Sandwich with Kale and Green Sauce

Toasted ciabatta roll (or kaiser roll) + **mayonnaise** + **green sauce** + **thinly sliced leftover lamb** + **lacinato kale,** torn into large pieces. Pack with **pickled vegetables** or **potato chips** on the side.

Creamed Kale

Kale's hearty disposition works well for creamed greens, as it produces a sturdy, minerally side dish and topping. No offense to creamed spinach—I still like you—but kale has more complex, adult flavors. Sometimes I make this recipe with kale alone (doubling the amount), but I also like it with a bitter green like broccoli rabe. Together they're a fearsome pair—you will get healthy and you will like it! And I vouch for them—you *will* like it. (See finished dish on page 197, as well as pages 200 and 203.)

Merrill's Love Affair with Creamed Greens "This is one of my favorite recipes from Amanda's arsenal, and I use the same technique with other greens like spinach and chard. For a last-minute dinner, I scramble some eggs and stir in a little creamed greens at the end. Or I cook 1 pound (450g) of pasta and heat 1½ cups (335g) creamed greens, then fold them together with a splash of olive oil, some pasta water, grated Pecorino, and freshly ground black pepper."

MAKES 4 CUPS (900G), ENOUGH FOR 2 DINNERS

1-pound (450g) bunch broccoli rabe, trimmed

1 bunch lacinato kale, stemmed

4 ounces (115g) pancetta, cut into ¼-inch (6mm) dice

¼ cup (60ml) extra-virgin olive oil

Salt

¼ cup (60ml) heavy cream

Generous pinch of red pepper flakes

Juice of ½ lemon

⅓ cup (80ml) crème fraîche

1 Rinse the broccoli rabe and kale in plenty of water, then drain, letting the excess water cling to the leaves.

2 Spread the pancetta in a sauté pan and cook over medium heat until the fat renders and the pancetta is crisp; you may need to lower the heat as you go. Transfer the pancetta to a paper towel–lined plate to drain.

3 Pile the still-wet-from-rinsing broccoli rabe and kale into a large pot. Pour the oil over the greens and season with salt. Place over high heat and cook until the greens begin to wilt, moving them from the bottom of the pot to the top using tongs. When the greens are fully wilted and most of the liquid has cooked off (if it hasn't, pour off all but ¼ cup/60ml), add the cream and red pepper flakes and cook for 1 minute more.

4 Transfer the greens to a food processor, adding about half of the creamy liquid from the pot. Puree the greens until broken down but still coarse, adding more liquid as needed; reserve any extra liquid. Add the lemon juice and crème fraîche and puree until smoother but still a little coarse. Taste and adjust the seasoning, then stir in the pancetta, if using. Store in a container in the fridge for up to 5 days.

5 **The day of:** Reheat the greens with a splash of water in a small saucepan over medium-low heat. Use as directed, with gnocchi (below) or stuck-pot rice (page 203).

Gnocchi with Creamed Kale

Bring a large stockpot of generously salted water to a boil. Meanwhile, warm **half of the creamed kale** with a splash of water in a small saucepan set over medium-low heat. Add **half of the frozen gnocchi** (page 200) to the boiling water and gently stir once with a wooden spoon to create movement and prevent the gnocchi from sticking to the bottom of the pot. As the gnocchi rise to the top (a sign they are done cooking), about 5 minutes later, scoop them out with a slotted spoon. Shake off the excess water, reserving some of the pasta water for later use. Place the gnocchi into wide, shallow serving bowls, and alternate adding the gnocchi and the creamed kale into the bowls to eliminate the need to stir the gnocchi with the sauce, which runs the risk of damaging or smashing the pasta. Sprinkle with the reserved pasta water, if needed. Generously grate **Parmesan** over the top and serve.

Ricotta Gnocchi

People think of gnocchi as a project, but in fact it's much simpler to make gnocchi dough than it is to make cookie dough. There's no creaming of butter, very little measuring, and gnocchi can be cooked all at once—gnocchi should get a gold star, no? I've doubled this batch so that it can get you through two dinners. Sometimes I'll make a quadruple batch just so I can freeze a bunch—it's also a good excuse for helpers. When they grow up, they can say, "In our day, we had to cut our own gnocchi and ride scooters to school."

This recipe comes from Christina DiLaura, who was one of our earliest Food52 team members and also launched our online shop. Christina comes from a family of serious Italian cooks, and this is a family classic. I understand why—the ricotta makes the gnocchi tender, almost feathery—and it's a recipe that once you've made it a few times, it's a snap to remember.

SERVES 4 FOR 2 DINNERS

2 pounds (900g) fresh whole-milk ricotta

2 eggs

2 tablespoons extra-virgin olive oil

½ cup (50g) grated Parmesan, plus more for serving

¼ teaspoon freshly grated nutmeg

4 cups (500g) all-purpose flour, sifted, plus more for rolling the dough

1 In a large bowl, stir together the ricotta, eggs, and oil until thoroughly combined. Stir in the Parmesan and sprinkle with nutmeg. Add the flour a little at a time and continue to stir thoroughly until the dough comes together.

2 Dump the dough onto a generously floured surface and use your hands to bring it together into a smooth ball. Add more flour as needed until the dough is smooth and no longer sticks to your hands.

3 Cut off slices of dough as if you were slicing a loaf of bread. With your hands flat and your fingers stretched out, roll each slice into a rope that's as thick as your thumb. Be sure to roll from the center out to the ends of the rope.

4 Line one rope parallel to another and cut both of them into 1 inch (2.5cm) pieces. Roll each piece off the back of a fork to make imprints that will help hold the sauce.

5 Transfer the gnocchi pieces to a lightly floured or nonstick baking sheet so they don't stick together and put the sheet in the freezer while making the rest of the gnocchi. If you plan to save any gnocchi for future use, let them freeze completely on the baking sheet before storing in a freezer-friendly zipper plastic bag to prevent them from sticking together. Freeze for up to 8 weeks.

Gnocchi with Brown Butter, Sage, Shaved Brussels Sprouts, and Pine Nuts

Bring a large stockpot of generously salted water to a boil. Meanwhile, melt **½ cup (110g) butter** with **a handful of sage leaves (8, if we're being exact)** and **¼ cup (35g) pine nuts** in a wide skillet over medium heat. Cook until the butter begins to brown lightly, 5 to 7 minutes, then fold in **12 ounces (340g) brussels sprouts**, trimmed and very thinly sliced, and turn off the heat.

Add **half of the gnocchi** to the boiling water and gently stir once with a wooden spoon to create movement and prevent the gnocchi from sticking to the bottom of the pot. As the gnocchi rise to the top (a sign they are done cooking), about 5 minutes later, scoop them out with a slotted spoon, shaking off excess water, and immediately add to the butter.

Spoon into wide, shallow bowls and top with **pine nuts** and **grated Pecorino.** Season with pepper.

Stuck-Pot Rice

Stuck-pot rice requires a few more steps than steamed rice, none of which you'll regret, because you end up with a pot of crisp, toasty grains. You parboil rice, then cook it a second time in an oiled pan, creating a crackly rice shell that you break apart into the core of tender rice. This pared-down recipe, which I learned from Mark Bittman, goes with almost anything, but you can perk it up with any number of spices—try star anise, cinnamon, and coriander, or cumin, turmeric, and garlic. It's best to cook this in a heavy pot. I make it in a small enameled cast-iron Dutch oven. A seasoned cast-iron or heavy stainless steel pot would also work well.

SERVES 4 FOR 2 DINNERS

Salt and freshly ground black pepper

2½ cups (460g) basmati rice, rinsed

⅓ cup (80ml) plain yogurt (preferably whole milk)

5 tablespoons (75ml) peanut, grapeseed, or corn oil

2 tablespoons freshly squeezed lemon juice

1 Bring a large pot of salted water to a boil. Stir in the rice, return to a boil, and lower the heat so the water is at a lively simmer. Cook for 5 minutes, then drain and season with salt.

2 In a large bowl, whisk together the yogurt, 3 tablespoons of the oil, and the lemon juice. Season with salt and pepper and whisk until smooth. Add the parboiled rice and fold together until the yogurt mixture lightly but evenly coats the rice.

3 Put the remaining 2 tablespoons of oil in a large heavy pot with a tight-fitting lid and place over medium-high heat. Carefully swirl the oil around so it comes a few inches up the sides of the pot. Add the rice mixture, pressing it down in the pot and up the sides with the back of a spoon.

4 Wrap a kitchen towel around the lid so it completely covers the underside of the lid; gather the corners on top so they do not fall anywhere near the stove's flame. Place the lid on the pot, sealing it tightly.

5 When the rice is fragrant, about 3 to 5 minutes, turn the heat to low. Cook, undisturbed, for about 30 minutes; the rice should smell toasty but not burnt. Turn off the heat and let sit 5 minutes more.

6 Remove the lid and kitchen towel, and using a wooden spoon, scrape the toasted rice from the sides and base of the pan, breaking it up and mixing it into the rest of the rice as you do. Season with salt and pepper. Let cool and store in the fridge for up to a week.

7 **The day of:** Reheat in a covered dish in a 300°F (150°C) oven for about 15 minutes or in the microwave.

Stuck-Pot Rice, Creamed Kale, and Fried Egg

Reheat the **rice** in a covered dish in a 300°F (150°C) oven for about 15 minutes. Warm **half of the creamed kale** (page 199) with a splash of water in a small saucepan over medium-low heat. Fry up **a bunch of eggs,** 1 or 2 per person. In large, shallow bowls, layer the rice followed by the kale and top with the fried eggs. Sprinkle with grated **Pecorino cheese,** freshly ground black pepper, and **your best olive oil.**

Chewy Vanilla Spice Cookies with Chocolate Chunks (Vegan, Too!)

Merrill and I had a cookie bake-off in 2015 where each of us was tasked with creating a holiday cookie that incorporated vanilla. I wanted a cookie that merged the benefits of a chewy chocolate chip cookie with the fragrance of a holiday spice cookie. I began by using a chocolate chip cookie base that's made with vegetable oil rather than butter—inspired by Ovenly's vegan chocolate chip cookie. I infused this base with vanilla by grinding up a whole vanilla bean with the sugar; I increased the chocolate (because I wanted to win) and chopped it so there would be a mix of shavings and chunks; and I gave it a little holiday oomph with cinnamon and ground chile.

Merrill went in another direction, blending chocolate and almond flour into her dough and larding it with plump dried cherries. We handed out twenty-eight thousand of them around the city from our Holiday Cookie Truck. The public voted on social media. And vote they did. If you'd like to bake the winning cookie, turn to page 252, but if you're more of an underdog type, then settle in here.

MAKES 20 COOKIES

2 cups (250g) all-purpose flour

1 teaspoon baking powder

¾ teaspoon baking soda

½ teaspoon salt

1 teaspoon ground cinnamon (preferably Saigon)

¼ rounded teaspoon ground chile (preferably piment d'Espelette)

6 ounces (170g) dark chocolate, chopped into ¼-inch (6mm) chunks; reserve any shavings

1 vanilla bean, cut crosswise into 6 pieces

½ cup (100g) sugar

½ cup (110g) firmly packed dark brown sugar

½ cup plus 1 tablespoon (135ml) canola oil

¼ cup plus 1 tablespoon (75ml) water

Flaky sea salt, such as Maldon, for sprinkling

1 In a large bowl, whisk together the flour, baking powder, baking soda, salt, cinnamon, and chile. Fold the chocolate chunks (and all the shavings on your cutting board) into the flour mixture. Look at that—you've barely started the recipe and you're already done with half of the ingredients!

2 In a blender, combine the vanilla bean and sugar and blend until the vanilla is reduced to flecks in the sugar. In a separate large bowl, whisk the vanilla sugar and brown sugar with the canola oil and water until you have a smoothish liquid.

3 Sprinkle the dry ingredients onto the sugar mixture and fold together with a rubber spatula until just combined.

4 Cover the bowl with plastic wrap. Refrigerate the dough for at least 12 hours and up to 24 hours. As Ovenly says, do not skip this step!

5 **The day of:** Heat the oven to 350°F (175°C). Line a rimmed baking sheet with parchment paper. Scoop the dough into 2-inch (5cm) mounds, placing them on the prepared baking sheet and flattening them slightly with your hands. If your chocolate chunks are big, you may also need to press the dough together with your fingers. Sprinkle the dough with flaky salt and slide the baking sheets into the freezer for 10 minutes.

6 Bake for 6 minutes, then rotate the baking sheet 180 degrees and continue baking until the edges are beginning to toast, about 6 minutes more. Let cool on the baking sheet for 5 minutes, then transfer to a rack to cool completely. You can bake off the rest of the dough now, or do it in a single batch when you want to serve them. Store the cookies in an airtight container for up to a week.

Merrill on Spice "If you consort with spiceaphobes, just leave out the chile; there's still plenty of zip from the Saigon cinnamon. And they make great ice cream sandwiches—try them with cinnamon ice cream to double down on the spice."

Amanda's Winter

this weekend:
turbo jook
oxtail stew
farro
anchovy
dressing
coconut dream bars

choc

THE WEEK AHEAD

THE RECIPES

HOW THEY COME TOGETHER

DINNER ONE

Turbo Jook with Baby Mustard Greens
Coconut Dream Bars

TO DO TODAY Reheat half of the jook, roast the
sausage (see page 213), and put out the jook toppings.

DINNER TWO

Oxtail Stew

Farro

Brussels Sprouts Salad with Anchovy Dressing

Chocolate Ice Cream with Hot Honey and
Maraschino Cherries

TO DO TODAY Reheat half of the stew and half
of the farro. Prep the brussels sprouts and dress
the salad. Scoop and top the ice cream for dessert.

DINNER THREE

Jook with a Fried Egg on Top

Mango ice cream from the store

TO DO TODAY Gently reheat the jook. While it warms,
fry some eggs and get the toppings ready.

DINNER FOUR

Farro with Mustard Greens, Almonds, Currants,
and Shaved Cheese

Coconut Dream Bars

TO DO TODAY Put together and dress the farro.

DINNER FIVE

Oxtail Hash over Toast

Mustard greens salad

Chocolate Ginger Ice Cream Sandwich

TO DO TODAY Make the ice cream sandwiches
and chill before dinner. Cook the hash with the
leftover oxtails. Dress some mustard greens
with olive oil and lemon juice.

BROWN BAG LUNCHES

Farro and Brussels Sprouts Salad

Mustard Greens Salad with a Ham and
Butter Sandwich

Brussels Sprouts Salad with Anchovy Dressing
and Hard-Boiled Egg plus Greek Yogurt

GAME PLAN

TO MAKE OVER THE WEEKEND

Turbo Jook with Baby
Mustard Greens

Oxtail Stew

Farro

Brussels Sprouts Salad
with Anchovy Dressing

Coconut Dream Bars

TODAY'S THEME: LOW AND SLOW

You'll need about 2 to 2½ hours to get it all done.

• Heat your oven to 350°F (175°C) and get started on
the coconut bars (page 220), pressing the dough into
the pan.

• While you bake the bars' shortbread base, prepare the
coconut topping. Spread the topping over the base and
bake for a second time.

• Dessert is done! On to chopping the vegetables and
browning the meat for the oxtail stew (page 214).

• While the oxtails simmer, cook the farro (page 216)—
saving 2 cups (320g) for the oxtail stew, 2 cups (320g)
for the farro salad later in the week, and the rest for
a lunch salad.

• Now it's time for the turbo jook (page 213), aka
savory rice porridge. Simmer the rice, pork bones,
and aromatics—you'll be all set to put together
the toppings later in the week.

• While the jook simmers, make the anchovy dressing
(page 219) and store in the fridge. Then wash and spin
dry all greens and leafy herbs.

• The oxtail will still be cooking, but you'll be done
with all your prep work. Go do something fun—or
do nothing!—until the oxtail is tender.

A slimmed-down strategy for a busy weekend. Make
a simple green salad with a vinaigrette instead of the
brussels sprouts salad and save the coconut dream bars
for another day; buy coconut ice cream instead. This
slimmer plan should take 1½ hours of active prep time.

GROCERY LIST

PRODUCE

Brussels sprouts, 1 pound (450g)

Carrots, 2

Celery, 8 inner stalks

Garlic, 1 clove

Ginger, 1 large nub about
the size of a wine cork

Horseradish root, 1 hunk

Lemons, 4

Limes, 2

Scallions, 4

Yellow onions, 3 small

Young mustard greens, baby kale,
or spinach, 2 large bunches

HERBS

Cilantro, 1 bunch for garnish

Flat-leaf parsley, 1 handful
chopped

Marjoram or thyme, 4 sprigs, or
1½ teaspoons dried marjoram

SPICES

Ground cinnamon, ½ teaspoon

Ground cloves, ½ teaspoon

Piment d'Espelette or other
ground chile, large pinch

PANTRY

Anchovy fillets, 3

Extra-virgin olive oil, ¾ cup
(175ml), plus more to have
on hand

Green olives, ½ cup (80g)
chopped

Farro, 2½ cups (450g)

Fish sauce, for garnish

Grainy mustard, 2 teaspoons

Jasmine or basmati rice,
2 cups (370g)

Mike's Hot Honey, for dessert

Peeled whole Italian tomatoes,
2 (28-ounce/794g) cans

Sesame oil, for garnish

Soy sauce, for garnish

Sriracha or Cholula hot sauce,
for garnish

Tomato paste, 3 tablespoons

BAKING AISLE

All-purpose flour, 1¼ cups (155g)

Almonds, ½ cup (70g) chopped

Baking powder, ½ teaspoon

Currants, ¼ cup (40g)

Italian Maraschino cherries,
for dessert

Light brown sugar, 1 cup (220g)
firmly packed

Unsweetened coconut flakes,
1½ cups (120g)

Pure vanilla extract, 1 teaspoon

Walnuts, 1 cup (120g) chopped

DAIRY AND EGGS

Unsalted butter, ½ cup (110g),
plus more to have on hand

Eggs, 7

Greek yogurt, for lunch

Heavy cream, 3 tablespoons

Shaved Pecorino (preferably from
a wedge), about ⅔ cup (70g), plus
more for serving

MEAT AND SEAFOOD

Cured ham (such as speck,
prosciutto, or salami), thinly sliced

Italian or other pork sausages,
1 pound (450g)

Oxtails, 6 pounds (2.7kg)
(trimmed weight)

Pancetta, 6 ounces (170g)

Raw pork or chicken bones,
2 pounds (900g)

BOOZE AND SUCH

White wine, 1 (750ml) bottle

FREEZER

Chocolate ice cream, for
2 desserts

Mango ice cream, for dessert

BAKED GOODS

Airy country bread or white
sandwich bread, 4 thick slices

Baguette or wheat sandwich
bread, for lunch

Chewy ginger cookies (ideally
from a good bakery), 8

Turbo Jook with Baby Mustard Greens

This recipe for jook—a Chinese word for rice porridge—comes from Vanessa Vichit-Vadakan, who was one of Food52's earliest community members. I made her Boosted Jook a few times, and then one Sunday I asked my husband, Tad, if he could get the jook going. After it had been simmering for a while, I asked about the large white lump in the middle of the rice. "It's ginger," he replied. I fished out the lump with tongs and smelled it. Not ginger, but horseradish! No harm done: We added ginger, too, and have been making it with both ever since. With its supercharged aromatics, Tad has renamed the dish Turbo Jook.

I love this dish because you can make it on Sunday and it'll hold up in the fridge throughout the week, so if your schedule goes awry, it will still be good on Friday. I find jook to be a particularly restorative dish after a tough day at work. It's a breakfast for dinner that happens to be dinner. And our kids love it because they can pick and choose their toppings. We often include pickled onions (page 86); store-bought kimchi would also be good.

MAKES ENOUGH FOR 2 DINNERS FOR 4 PEOPLE

JOOK

12 cups (2.8L) water, plus more as needed

2 pounds (900g) raw pork or chicken bones

2 cups (370g) jasmine or basmati rice

1 large nub peeled ginger, about the size of a wine cork

2 (1-inch/2.5cm) slices peeled horseradish root

1 teaspoon kosher salt

TOPPINGS

Thinly sliced scallions, white and green parts

Fresh cilantro leaves

Mustard greens, arugula, or spinach, coarsely chopped

Minced roasted Italian or other pork sausage (see right)

Sesame oil

Fish sauce

Soy sauce

Sriracha or Cholula

Lime wedges

1 To make the jook, combine all of the ingredients in a large pot. Bring to a boil, then lower to a simmer and cook, uncovered, for 1 to 1½ hours. Be sure to stir occasionally and add more water as needed. You want the jook to be porridgelike.

2 The jook is ready when the rice is cooked to the point of nearly falling apart; the final consistency is up to you. Add a little water if you prefer a more brothy jook or cook it a little longer if you like a thicker porridge.

3 Remove and discard the bones, horseradish, and ginger. Let cool and store in the fridge for up to 5 days.

4 **The day of:** Gently reheat half of the jook over medium heat for 10 minutes (or in the microwave), adding water if needed. Let everyone add the toppings at the table.

How to Roast Sausage Heat your oven to 350°F (175°C). Prick the sausages with a fork, lay them in a small baking dish, and roast, turning once, until lightly browned and cooked through, about 15 minutes.

Merrill's Dirty Secret "Whenever I overcook rice (what? never!), I secretly rejoice because I know I can turn it into jook just by adding more water and cooking it longer. I like to top my jook with roast pork (page 165), which I shred and combine with chopped greens."

Two Variations

Jook with a Fried Egg on Top: The second night we have jook, the sausage is usually eaten up so I fry an **egg,** sunny-side up, for each person and lay it on top of the **jook** before adding the rest of the **toppings.** Then it becomes Turbo Jook Bimbap, a loving and delicious abomination of true bibimbap.

Turbo Jook with Brussels Sprouts and Oxtails: Top the jook with **brussels sprouts salad** (page 219), **leftover oxtail meat** (page 214), and all the usual **toppings.**

Oxtail Stew

Some people are squeamish about oxtails, the bony and richly flavored meaty tail of cattle. I say let them be—that's more for us! I think of it as the poor man's short ribs. When cooked slowly, oxtail meat nearly falls off the bones and can be pulled apart with a fork. And the bones and gelatin in the tail make for a beautiful silky sauce. Because oxtail isn't super common, call ahead to your butcher or grocery store to see if they have it or can order it for you. If you can't find oxtails, use short ribs and in step 5, add just enough water to cover the meat.

No More Dirty Dishes Braised oxtail is better after resting for 2 days, so plan to serve this later in the week. I cook it in an enameled cast-iron Dutch oven, and once cool, I store it in this pan in the fridge. I'm not into transferring everything to containers, just to have to put them back in a pan to reheat.

Oxtail Riches With the leftover oxtail stew, pull the meat off the bones and save it for the hash (page 216). It's also great on jook (page 213, bottom), and in tacos, or in any of the lunch salads (pages 217 and 219).

SERVES 8, WITH LEFTOVERS

6 ounces (170g) pancetta, cut into ¼-inch (6mm) dice

2 carrots, peeled and finely chopped

2 small yellow onions, finely chopped

8 inner celery stalks, 2 finely chopped, 6 cut into 3-inch (7.5cm) segments

3 tablespoons extra-virgin olive oil, plus more as needed

6 pounds oxtails (trimmed weight), cut into 3-inch (7.5cm) pieces

Sea salt or kosher salt and freshly ground black pepper

3 tablespoons tomato paste

1 (750ml) bottle white wine

4 marjoram or thyme sprigs, or 1½ teaspoons dried marjoram

½ teaspoon ground cloves

½ teaspoon ground cinnamon

2 (28-ounce/794g) cans peeled whole Italian tomatoes

1 Heat the oven to 325°F (165°C). In a large Dutch oven or deep pot, combine the pancetta, carrots, onions, and chopped celery and enough oil to cover the bottom of the pot, about 3 tablespoons.

2 Place the pan over medium heat and cook until the pancetta begins to brown, about 15 minutes. Meanwhile, season the oxtails on all sides with salt and pepper. Transfer the pancetta and vegetables to a plate. Pour off all but a tablespoon or two of fat.

3 Increase the heat to medium-high. Add the oxtails to the pot, and brown well on all sides, about 4 minutes per side; you'll need to do this in batches. Remove the oxtails and set aside in a bowl.

4 Return the pancetta and vegetables to the pot. Stir in the tomato paste and cook until it caramelizes, about 2 minutes. Pour in the wine and boil for 3 minutes. Add the marjoram, cloves, and cinnamon, followed by the tomatoes and their juices, carefully squishing them between your fingers as they fall into the pot.

5 Return the oxtails to the pot. The liquid should come about one-third of the way up the ingredients. If not, add water. Bring the liquid to a boil, then cover the pot and place in the oven. Braise, turning the oxtails now and then, until just tender, 2 to 3 hours.

6 Add the remaining celery and braise until the oxtails are very tender, 30 to 60 minutes more.

7 Remove the pot from the oven and season the stew with salt and pepper. Discard the marjoram sprigs. Let the stew cool in the pot and store in the fridge for up to a week.

8 **The day of:** Skim the layer of chilled fat off the top of the oxtails. Reheat half of the oxtails over medium heat in the covered pot you cooked and stored them in (reserve the rest in a container for the hash on page 216 and other uses). Serve on a large platter or in shallow bowls, making sure everyone gets a bit of the pulpy sauce and celery.

Oxtail Hash over Toast

The most common way to use up oxtail leftovers is to pull the meat from the bones, warm it in the sauce, and serve it over pasta. Since you would likely figure this out on your own, I'm suggesting another, less obvious, approach: making oxtail hash. All you do is simmer chopped bits of oxtail in some of its sauce and finish with a little cream before spooning it over toast. You can add spices and herbs if you like. Serve with hot sauce if that's your thing! It's a bit breakfast-for-dinner, and at the end of the week, this suits me just fine.

SERVES 4

1 tablespoon extra-virgin olive oil

½ small yellow onion, chopped

2 cups (460g) chopped cooked oxtail meat (page 214)

½ cup (120ml) oxtail sauce (page 214)

4 thick slices airy country bread or white sandwich bread

3 tablespoons heavy cream

1   Warm the olive oil in a sauté pan over medium heat. Add the onion and cook until softened and lightly browned on the edges, 8 to 10 minutes. Add the oxtail meat and sauce and cook until warmed through, 5 to 7 minutes. This would be a good time to put your bread in the toaster. When the oxtail is warmed through, pour in the cream and simmer for a minute or two. Spoon the oxtail hash over the toasts. Feel like a 19th-century pubgoer.

Farro

Bring a large pot of generously salted water to a boil. Add **2 ½ cups (450g) farro** and cook until just tender, about 30 minutes. Drain the farro and return it to the pot. Pour in just enough **extra-virgin olive oil** to lightly coat the farro. Put half of the farro in a container and store in the fridge—it can be reheated in the microwave to serve with the oxtails (page 214). Use the remaining half to make the farro with mustard greens, almonds, currants, and shaved cheese (opposite).

Farro with Mustard Greens, Almonds, Currants, and Shaved Cheese

Whenever I cook a grain to go with a main course, I always make extra to stretch into lunches or a dinner salad. Farro is such an amiable grain—it pairs well with nuts, absorbs the blow of briny elements like capers or olives, and comes more alive with a grated hard cheese. I added some sweetness here with currants (but you could use golden raisins), and peppery greens for levity and kick.

Make a Grain Salad: Rinse and Repeat When I'm not able to assemble a full week's menu, I'll make enough of this farro salad over the weekend to last me a few nights, and then pair it with something I can easily pull off after work, like pan-roasted chicken (page 184) or a grilled steak (page 120).

SERVES 4

2 cups (320g) cooked farro tossed with oil (opposite)

Salt and freshly ground black pepper

½ cup (70g) chopped almonds (toasted if you're feeling ambitious)

¼ cup (80g) chopped green olives

¼ cup (40g) currants

4 cups (80g) torn young mustard greens, arugula, or other spicy green

⅓ cup (80ml) anchovy dressing (page 219)

1 lemon, halved (optional)

⅓ cup (30g) shaved Pecorino or any other hard salty cheese, for garnish

1 In a large bowl, season the farro with salt and pepper. Fold in the almonds, olives, and currants. Add the mustard greens and dressing and toss until the salad is evenly dressed. Add a squeeze of lemon juice. Shave a bunch of Pecorino over all.

Lunch: Mustard Greens Salad with Ham and Butter Sandwich

Make a ham and butter sandwich with any **cured ham,** be it speck, prosciutto, or salami. A sturdy **baguette** is best, but wheat sandwich bread works too. Pair it with **spicy greens, radishes,** or **sliced young turnips,** lightly dressed with **olive oil** and **lemon juice.**

Brussels Sprouts Salad with Anchovy Dressing

Summer salads get a lot of love for their sweetness and breezy demeanor, but I like the flintiness and incorrigibility of winter greens. You have to work with them, be assertive, and show that you are up to the challenge. Winter greens will yield—just dress them with anchovy, a lashing of garlic and chile, and a stream of lemon juice. They'll even do you a favor and last for a few days. This brussels sprouts salad is best dressed at least 15 minutes before serving and will hold up in the fridge for two or three days—and that's why I sneak it into lunches in this menu.

You can prep the brussels sprouts in a food processor or with a mandoline, but slicing is best and makes me less nervous than a mandoline. The brussels sprouts and greens can be prepped and kept in zipper plastic bags or a container for up to 3 days.

Brussels sprouts haters at home? It happens. This salad is also great with shaved celery root, or fold the dressing into roasted beets, cauliflower, or broccoli.

SERVES 4, PLUS LEFTOVERS AND DRESSING FOR OTHER MEALS

ANCHOVY DRESSING

3 anchovy fillets

1 clove garlic

Salt

Juice of 1 lemon, plus more as needed

2 teaspoons grainy mustard

Large pinch of piment d'Espelette or other ground chile

½ cup (120ml) extra-virgin olive oil

SALAD

1 pound (450g) brussels sprouts, trimmed and very thinly sliced (you want 4 ½ cups/450g)

2 handfuls of mustard greens, baby kale, or spinach, stemmed and torn into bite-size pieces (about 4 cups/80g)

¼ cup (25g) shaved Pecorino

1 In a mortar and pestle, mash together the anchovies, garlic, and a pinch of salt until you have a pulp. If your mortar is large enough, make the rest of the dressing in it; otherwise transfer to a bowl. Whisk in the lemon juice, mustard, and piment d'Espelette, followed by the olive oil. Store the dressing in the fridge for up to a week.

2 **The day of:** Combine the brussels sprouts and mustard greens in a large bowl, pour in one-quarter of the dressing, and toss together until evenly coated. Add more dressing as you like and a squeeze of lemon juice to freshen things up, reserving the rest for the farro with mustard greens salad (page 217). Pile the dressed salad into a serving bowl and top with the Pecorino. This salad is best dressed at least 15 minutes before serving, though it will keep for a couple of days.

Lunch: Farro and Brussels Sprouts Salad

Take cues from Merrill's farro salad with roasted mushrooms and Parmesan (page 119) and fold any leftover **brussels sprouts salad** into **farro** (page 216) that you've set aside. Add a handful of **chopped fresh flat-leaf parsley** and/or **a teaspoon of fresh chopped thyme** if you have them. Then shave **a nice mound of Pecorino** over the salad and mix it in, too. Season the salad with salt and lots of coarsely ground pepper, adding more **oil** or **lemon juice** as needed. If you've got **pickled peppers** or **preserved lemon** in the fridge, add some to take the salad in a new direction.

Lunch: Brussels Sprouts Salad with Anchovy Dressing and Hard-Boiled Egg plus Greek Yogurt

Hard-boil the **egg** while you're getting breakfast ready, then assemble and pack the **salad** and top with the halved egg. Tuck the **yogurt** into your lunch bag, too. A sophisticated lunch is yours with only 5 additional minutes of prep.

Coconut Dream Bars

I've long searched for a coconut bar that wasn't too gooey or sweet. Such bars are rarefied and elusive. Then one fell right into my lap on Food52, thanks to former editor and now prodigious baking contributor Posie Harwood. Her bars are footed with a layer of shortbread and topped with a deliciously shaggy coconut roof. To make the shortbread layer thin and crackerlike, I make these bars in a larger pan.

My mother used to make a similar dessert called Magic Cookie Bars, which involved lots of coconut, chocolate chips, and evaporated milk—a delicious, 1970s sugar bomb. As a nod to this fond memory, I sometimes add 1 cup (170g) of chopped chocolate to the topping.

MAKES 18 SMALL BARS

SHORTBREAD LAYER

1 cup (125g) all-purpose flour

½ cup (110g) unsalted butter, at room temperature

½ cup (110g) firmly packed light brown sugar

COCONUT LAYER

2 eggs

½ cup (110g) firmly packed light brown sugar

¼ cup (30g) all-purpose flour

½ teaspoon baking powder

¼ teaspoon salt

1½ cups (120g) unsweetened coconut flakes

1 cup (120g) chopped walnuts

1 teaspoon pure vanilla extract

1 Heat your oven to 350°F (175°C) and butter a 9½ by 12½–inch (24 by 31cm) rectangular baking pan. Line the pan with a parchment paper sling and liberally butter the parchment. (A parchment paper sling stretches across the base and up the opposite sides of the pan, leaving an inch/2.5cm or two excess on both sides so you can later use these ends to lift the bars out of the pan.)

2 To make the shortbread, mash together by hand the flour, butter, and brown sugar in a bowl. Press the dough evenly into the base of the pan. Prick the dough in several places with a fork. Bake until the shortbread is cooked through and golden, about 15 minutes.

3 To make the coconut layer, place the eggs in the bowl of a stand mixer fitted with a whisk attachment and beat on high speed until very pale and fluffy, about 5 minutes. Add the brown sugar and beat until light and thick, several minutes more.

4 In a separate bowl, whisk together the flour, baking powder, and salt. Add the dry ingredients to the eggs, along with the coconut, walnuts, and vanilla. Stir until thoroughly blended.

5 Pour the coconut mixture over the shortbread crust. Bake until lightly golden brown around the edges, about 20 minutes. Let cool, then remove the bars from the pan using the parchment sling, and cut into squares. Store in an airtight container.

Chocolate Ginger Ice Cream Sandwich

All you need are **8 chewy ginger cookies** (from a bakery, if possible) and **your favorite chocolate ice cream.** Put a scoop of softened ice cream on a cookie and top with another cookie, pressing down to push the ice cream to the edges. Rinse and repeat! Then wrap in waxed paper and put in the freezer for at least 1 hour to firm up before serving. If you have time to assemble these over the weekend, make a big batch for the week.

Chocolate Ice Cream with Hot Honey and Maraschino Cherries

If you haven't tried **Mike's Hot Honey,** infused with chiles, this is your moment—first you get the sweet, and it's quickly followed by a tingling and fiery heat. You'll soon be looking for ways to use it. Will this rice cracker do? Yes. How about my morning yogurt? Absolutely. And this is how I came to drizzle it over **chocolate ice cream.** I like this combination with a **few spoonfuls of good Maraschino cherries** from Italy tossed in (with their syrup). If you can't find them, soak some dried cherries in brandy for a day or two, and they'll do a fine job.

THE WEEK AHEAD

THE RECIPES

HOW THEY COME TOGETHER

DINNER ONE

Baby turnips and radishes with salt
Oven-Roasted Polenta
Bolognese
Almond biscotti from the store

TO DO TODAY Set out the radishes and turnips on a platter with a small dish of softened butter and a tiny bowl of salt. Reheat half of the bolognese and half of the polenta.

DINNER TWO

Luciana's Porchetta
Sour Cream Mashed Potatoes
Blood Orange Salad
Chocolate Rosemary Pudding

TO DO TODAY Reheat enough thinly sliced porchetta and potatoes for 4 people. Assemble the blood orange salad (using half of the ingredients). Set out the chocolate pudding before dinner.

DINNER THREE

Crisped Potatoes
Bolognese
Chocolate Rosemary Pudding

TO DO TODAY Crisp the potatoes while you reheat the bolognese. Spoon the bolognese over the potatoes and top with grated cheese. Set out the chocolate pudding so it warms up by dessert time.

DINNER FOUR

Blood Orange Salad
Luciana's Porchetta
Country bread
Salted caramel ice cream

TO DO TODAY Make the blood orange salad with the remaining ingredients. Slice the porchetta and serve it at room temperature on a platter, with bread passed at the table.

DINNER FIVE

Oven-Roasted Polenta with Garlicky Greens and fried or poached eggs
Cheeses with Medjool dates, prunes, and almonds

TO DO TODAY Reheat the remaining polenta and greens and spoon into 4 shallow bowls. Top with eggs fried sunny-side up or poached and grated Pecorino cheese. Arrange cheeses (I like a mix of soft cow's milk cheeses with hard sheep's milk cheeses) and accoutrements on a plate before sitting down to eat.

BROWN BAG LUNCHES

Porchetta, Pickled Onion, and Garlicky Greens Sandwich
Spinach Salad with Pancetta, Wheat Croutons, and Egg
Avocado and Blood Orange Salad

GAME PLAN

TO MAKE OVER THE WEEKEND

Luciana's Porchetta

Sour Cream Mashed Potatoes
(using Merrill's recipe on
page 251 but using all baby
Yukon gold potatoes)

Crisped Potatoes

Bolognese

Oven-Roasted Polenta

Garlicky Greens

Chocolate Rosemary
Pudding

IT'S ITALY IN THE KITCHEN TODAY

Get ready for 2½ hours of quiet time in the kitchen—
some dishes will take longer to finish cooking, but they'll
do that on their own and you'll already be cleaned up.

- On Saturday, make the spice and herb rub for the
  porchetta (page 228), coat the pork shoulder with it,
  and let it sit, uncovered, in the fridge overnight. (If you
  really want to get ahead, make the pudding now, too.)

- On Sunday, set out the pork for 30 to 60 minutes to
  come to room temperature. Heat the oven to 325°F
  (165°C). Roast the porchetta.

- While the pork is in the oven, start the bolognese sauce
  (page 231).

- While the bolognese begins its first of several simmers,
  whisk together the polenta (page 232) and put it in the
  oven with the porchetta.

- Boil the potatoes (page 251). Meanwhile, wilt the
  spinach (page 235).

- Wash and trim the radishes and turnips, keeping the
  tops on if they're in good shape.

- When the potatoes are just tender, remove half of
  them from the pan; let them cool and store in the
  fridge for making the crisped potatoes (page 231).
  Keep cooking the remaining potatoes until very tender,
  then drain and mash them, reserving 1 cup of the
  cooking water. Follow the instructions for mashing
  (page 251) but using half the amount of sour cream,
  butter, and olive oil.

- Make the chocolate rosemary pudding (page 236).

- Once the bolognese finishes its last stage of
  simmering, let it cool, then pack it up and put it in the
  fridge. Do the same with the porchetta when it's done.

- Pour a glass of wine and make a toast to the week ahead.

Need to pare down the menu? Take the bolognese
and pudding off the menu. In place of the bolognese,
pan-roast chicken thighs (page 184) and make a simple
pan sauce for serving the chicken with the polenta. Also,
instead of mashing half of the potatoes, mash them all.
These changes should bring your weekend prep time
down to 1½ hours.

GROCERY LIST

PRODUCE

Avocado, 1

Baby radishes, 1 bunch

Baby turnips, 1 bunch

Baby Yukon gold potatoes,
4 pounds (1.8kg)

Blood oranges, 7

Carrot, 1 cup (130g) chopped,
from about 3 carrots

Clementines or mandarins, 4

Garlic, 4 large cloves

Lemon, 1

Orange, 1

Red onion, 1

Spinach, 1¼ pounds (570g), plus
more for lunch

Yellow onion, 1

HERBS

Cilantro leaves, small handful

Rosemary, 1 bunch

SPICES

Bay leaves, 2

Black peppercorns, 1 tablespoon

Coriander seeds, 2 teaspoons

Fennel seeds, 2 teaspoons

Nutmeg, 1 whole

Piment d'Espelette or other
ground chile (such as cayenne or
Aleppo pepper), for garnish

Red pepper flakes, 1½ teaspoons

PANTRY

Almond milk, 4½ cups (1.1L)

Canned peeled whole Italian
tomatoes, 2½ cups (600g)

Cider vinegar, 1½ cups (355ml)

Coarsely ground polenta,
2 cups (320g)

Extra-virgin olive oil, ¾ cup
(175ml)

Green olives, 20 pitted and torn
into quarters, plus more chopped
for lunch

Mayonnaise, for lunch

Red wine vinegar, 1½ cups plus
8 teaspoons (395ml)

Flaky salt

Vegetable oil, 1 tablespoon

BAKING AISLE

Almond extract, ½ teaspoon

Almonds, for dessert

Almond milk, 4½ cups (1.1L)

Bittersweet chocolate,
10 ounces (285g)

Cocoa, ¼ cup (20g)

Cornstarch, ¼ cup (30g)

Medjool dates, for dessert

Prunes, for dessert

Sugar, ½ cup plus 4 tablespoons
(150g)

DAIRY AND EGGS

Unsalted butter, 1 cup (225g)

Buttermilk, 2 tablespoons

Cheese, 3 wedges (a mix of soft
cow's milk cheeses with hard
sheep's milk cheeses), enough
to serve 4

Crumbled blue cheese, for lunch

Eggs, 7

Heavy cream, for serving

Milk, 1¼ cups (300ml)

Parmesan, for serving

Sour cream, heaping ¾ cup
(175ml)

MEAT AND SEAFOOD

Ground beef, 1 pound (450g)

Ground pork, 8 ounces (225g)

Pancetta, 8 thin slices

Pork shoulder, 4 pounds (1.8kg)
butterflied (ask your butcher to
do this)

BOOZE AND SUCH

Dry white wine, 1 cup (240ml)

FREEZER

Salted caramel ice cream,
for dessert

BAKED GOODS

Almond biscotti

Country bread

Whole wheat rolls, 8 for lunch
and croutons

Blood Orange Salad

This salad is best prepared the day you're serving it, so if you're serving it two nights as I suggest you do, then halve the ingredients when you make it. But if you want to save time, you can make the full batch at once and save the leftovers for the second day; no one will suffer.

I make this salad as often as possible during blood orange and clementine season. You can mix and match the toppings—any vinegar, briny caper or olive, and chile will do. It's also a dinner party staple that guests rave about, so much so that I always think, "Thanks, but how about my labor-intensive tart! Was it good, too?"

Mix It Up You can use this salad as a base recipe for all sorts of citrus. I sometimes mix blood oranges with satsumas. Pink grapefruit and blood oranges are lovely together. And when I can get my hands on kumquats, I like to slice them paper thin and toss them in for texture and shape.

ENOUGH FOR 2 SALADS, EACH SERVING 4

6 blood oranges

4 clementines or mandarins

About ½ small red onion

8 teaspoons good red wine vinegar

4 tablespoons (60ml) best-quality olive oil

20 green olives, pitted and torn into quarters

Piment d'Espelette or other ground chile (such as cayenne or Aleppo pepper), for sprinkling

Flaky salt

1 Halve this if making 1 salad. Cut the peel and pith from the oranges and clementines, making sure to remove all of the outer membrane without losing too much of the flesh. Cut the oranges and clementines crosswise into ⅛-inch (3mm) slices. Slice the onion thinly across the equator so that you can see through the slices; use a mandoline if needed. You will need about 8 slices.

2 Divide the citrus among 4 plates, overlapping the slices. Scatter a few slices of onion over the top. Sprinkle about 1 teaspoon vinegar and 1½ teaspoons of the olive oil over each plate; don't measure, just splash! Divide the olives among the plates and sprinkle each plate with a generous pinch of piment d'Espelette. Season with salt. Admire all the colors, then serve!

Lunch: Avocado and Blood Orange Salad

Combine **1 sliced avocado, supremes from 1 blood orange,** and **a small handful of cilantro leaves** in a bowl. Rub a few thin slices of **red onion** with a pinch of salt and let sit for 5 minutes. Fold the onion into the salad. Dress with **extra-virgin olive oil** and **vinegar.**

Luciana's Porchetta

This is a recipe I've been making since 2010, our proof-of-concept year for Food52. We started with weekly contests, and cooks from all over began sharing their excellent recipes. This one came from Ali Waks-Adams, who was a chef in Philadelphia at the time. There's so much to love about porchetta: (1) It's made with pork shoulder, an inexpensive cut, (2) it requires almost no labor in the kitchen, just some time in your oven, and (3) it produces a roast that's robustly flavored and goes with almost anything.

Ali's version is brilliant: She has you toast the spices, then combines them with fresh rosemary, garlic, and finely grated orange zest. By the time the roast emerges from the oven, your entire house smells like an Italian trattoria.

It's important to buy great pork, preferably heritage, and if you can get it with the skin on, do. Either way, use pancetta to lay over the top of the pork; it will protect the roast from drying out and makes delicious pancetta chips for the spinach salad (page 235).

Luciana's Porchetta Meets Merrill's Overnight Roast Pork You can also make this recipe using the overnight technique in Merrill's overnight roast pork (page 165). Prepare the porchetta up through step 5, then roast it according to Merrill's instructions. The resulting pork will have more of a tender, braised texture. And you can still make the sauce as directed in the recipe here.

SERVES 8, WITH LEFTOVERS FOR LUNCHES

1 tablespoon coarse salt

1 tablespoon black peppercorns

2 teaspoons fennel seeds

2 teaspoons coriander seeds

½ teaspoon red pepper flakes

2 teaspoons chopped rosemary

2 teaspoons finely grated orange zest

3 large cloves garlic, smashed and chopped

2 tablespoons extra-virgin olive oil

4 pounds (1.8kg) butterflied pork shoulder (ask your butcher to do this)

2 bay leaves

8 thin slices pancetta

½ cup (120ml) good red wine vinegar

1 The day before roasting, toast the salt, peppercorns, fennel seeds, coriander seeds, and red pepper flakes in a skillet over medium heat until fragrant, about 3 minutes. Let cool, then coarsely crush the spices in a mortar and pestle or a blender.

2 In a bowl or dish large enough to fit the pork, stir together the ground spices with the rosemary, orange zest, and garlic. Add the olive oil and stir into a paste.

3 Add the pork and slather the spice mixture all over it; wedge the bay leaves in and around the pork. Place the pork, uncovered, in the fridge overnight.

4 The next day, heat your oven to 325°F (165°C) and bring the pork to room temperature, 30 to 60 minutes.

5 Roll the pork and tie it with butcher's twine at 1-inch (2.5cm) intervals. Stick the bay leaves under the twine in the middle of the roast. Lay the pancetta in overlapping rows across the top of the pork, like fish scales.

6 Place the porchetta in a roasting pan and roast, rotating the pan halfway through cooking, until the internal temperature reaches 155°F (68°C), 1½ to 2 hours. Remove from the oven and let sit until the temperature rises to 160°F (71°C). Transfer the porchetta to a cutting board to rest while you make the pan sauce.

7 Set the roasting pan over medium heat and deglaze the pan with the vinegar, scraping up any browned bits. Don't let the sauce reduce too much, just enough to tone down the sharpness (it should be like a porky vinaigrette). Refrigerate the pork and sauce in separate containers and save the pancetta chips.

8 **The day of:** Heat the oven to 300°F (150°C). Thinly slice the porchetta and arrange in a baking dish along with some of the pancetta. Spoon some of the gravy on top.

Bolognese

I like a bolognese that's heavy on the carrots, and you'll notice there's no celery. I don't love cooked celery, except with oxtails (page 214)! This version from Marcella Hazan is a great one to make a double batch of and freeze the extra in 4-person portions. This way you can thaw it and sneak it into your weekly menus and get a free pass for another weekend.

Saucing Target I'm serving the bolognese in this menu with polenta one night and potatoes a second, but if you'd like to make it with pasta, I recommend 1 pound (450g) of penne rigate for each 4-person portion of sauce.

SERVES 4 FOR 2 DINNERS

1 tablespoon vegetable oil	1¼ cups (300ml) milk
3 tablespoons butter	¼ teaspoon freshly grated nutmeg
⅔ cup (105g) chopped yellow onion	1 cup (240ml) dry white wine
1 cup (130g) chopped carrot	2½ cups (600g) canned peeled whole Italian tomatoes, broken up with your hands, with their juice
8 ounces (225g) ground pork	
1 pound (450g) ground beef	
Salt and freshly ground black pepper	Grated Parmesan, for serving

1 Put the oil, butter, and onion in a heavy 5-quart (4.7L) pot and turn the heat to medium-low. Cook until the onion has become translucent, then add the carrot. Cook for about 2 minutes, stirring the vegetables to coat well.

2 Add the ground pork and beef, a large pinch of salt, and a few grindings of pepper. Crumble the meat with a fork, stir well, and cook until the meat has lost its raw, red color and has browned lightly.

3 Add the milk and let it simmer gently, stirring frequently, until it has bubbled away completely, about 30 minutes. Add the tiny grating of fresh nutmeg and stir.

4 Add the wine and let it simmer until it has evaporated, another 20 to 30 minutes. Add the tomatoes and stir thoroughly to coat all of the ingredients well. When the tomatoes begin to simmer, turn the heat down so that the sauce cooks at the laziest of simmers, with just an intermittent bubble breaking through the surface.

5 Cook, uncovered, for 2 to 3 hours, stirring from time to time. While the sauce is cooking, you are likely to find that it will begin to dry out and the fat will separate from the meat. To keep it from sticking, add ½ cup (120ml) water as necessary. Cook until the sauce is the texture and concentration you like. Taste and correct for salt. Store in a container in the fridge for up to 5 days.

6 **The day of:** Gently reheat half the sauce in a covered saucepan over medium-low heat, stirring every few minutes; you can also reheat it in the microwave. Serve with grated Parmesan on the side.

Crisped Potatoes

Boil **2 pounds (900g) baby Yukon gold potatoes** until tender, then let cool. Use the palm of your hand or a meat pounder to lightly crush them into disks. Warm a large cast-iron skillet over medium-high heat. Coat the base of the pan with **olive oil** and toss in a **smashed garlic clove.** When the oil is hot, add the potatoes in a single layer (you might need to do this in batches). Let them cook, undisturbed, until very crisp and browned on the bottom (remove the garlic before it burns). Turn once and brown the other side. Season with salt and pepper.

Oven-Roasted Polenta

My life changed for the better when I learned how to roast polenta in the oven. It's a blasphemous way to cook polenta, but it works, and for me, it put polenta back on the menu. Rather than relentlessly stirring a pot on the stove (and still ending up with lumpy polenta), you stir the polenta every 15 minutes while the bubbling mass is safely contained in the oven. I like to challenge myself and see how many other things I can get done in between each stir, then I declare it my workout for the day.

A Fallback from Merrill "In the fall, I serve this polenta with braised chicken thighs (page 184) or sausage ragù (page 155). I love Amanda's brilliant reheating method, but if you're feeling nervous about lumps, you can cut squares of chilled polenta, fry them in olive oil, and then top with bolognese (page 231), greens (page 235), chicken thighs, or ragù."

SERVES 4 FOR 2 DINNERS

2 cups (320g) coarsely ground polenta

2 teaspoons salt

¼ cup unsalted butter

Grated Parmesan (optional)

1 Heat the oven to 325°F (165°C). Pour 8 cups (1.9L) water into a Dutch oven. Whisk in the polenta and salt. Place the uncovered Dutch oven into the oven and bake for 1½ to 2 hours, stirring every 15 minutes. Add more water as needed. When the polenta is soft and puddinglike, remove from the oven and let sit for a few minutes. Adjust the seasoning; stir in the butter and Parmesan.

2 **The day of:** Polenta wasn't designed to be reheated, but it can be. Scoop it into a heavy saucepan over medium heat. Add a little water to the pan and break it up with a strong wooden spoon. If it's very clumpy, I sometimes use a potato masher to smash the lumps and smooth it out.

Garlicky Greens

You may already have your own variation of this recipe. If not, it's a great basic to be able to turn to when you need a little greenery in your dinner plan. I've called for spinach here, but it also works with kale, chard, escarole, and mustard greens.

Storage Tips Use half of the spinach for dinner and save the rest for another night or lunch. Pack it into a container and store in the fridge. The spinach may give off water while in the fridge; pour this off before reheating. I find the microwave to be the best way to reheat greens.

Spinach Balls Another way to cook spinach ahead of time is to steam the spinach (or other green) without olive oil and, when it's cool, squeeze out any excess liquid by pressing handfuls of the spinach in your palms and form a spinach ball. Store the balls in a container in the fridge. To serve, cut the balls into slices, pull apart the spinach, and rewarm it in olive oil over medium-low heat.

SERVES 4

2 tablespoons extra-virgin olive oil	Salt and freshly ground black pepper
1 large clove garlic, smashed	Freshly grated nutmeg
1¼ pounds (570g) spinach or other hardy green like kale or chard	

1 Pour the oil into a large deep pot and place over medium-high heat. Add the garlic and cook until softened and lightly toasted. Pile the spinach into the pot and sprinkle with salt. Cover the pot for about 30 seconds. Lift off the lid and use tongs to stir the spinach. Once it begins wilting, remove the cover and set aside. Let the water in the bottom of the pot cook off, tossing the spinach as you go. When the spinach is wilted and most of the water is cooked off, taste and adjust the salt, then season with pepper and nutmeg.

Lunch: Spinach Salad with Pancetta, Wheat Croutons, and Egg

Combine a **couple of handfuls of baby spinach** with the **chopped pancetta chips** from the roasted porchetta (page 228), **green pitted and chopped olives,** and **pickled onions** (page 86). Whisk together about **2 tablespoons each extra-virgin olive oil and buttermilk** with **a squeeze of lemon juice,** and use this to dress the salad. Top with **wheat croutons** (made from cutting wheat bread into cubes and toasting), **crumbled blue cheese,** and a **halved hard-boiled egg.**

Lunch: Porchetta, Pickled Onion, and Garlicky Greens Sandwich

Toast **a halved whole wheat roll.** Spread with **mayo.** Layer with **thinly sliced porchetta** (page 228), **pickled onions** (page 86), and **garlicky greens.**

Chocolate Rosemary Pudding

Pudding is a lower-stress endeavor than custard, and I've always loved Dorie Greenspan's blender technique. No lumps! This is very much a dump-and-blend pudding, made with almond milk and rosemary, that's appealingly not too sweet. If you want to serve this in individual portions, you'll need ¾-cup (175ml) ramekins; otherwise, use one large bowl and spoon it into smaller bowls to serve (this is also the easier way).

SERVES 8, AKA DESSERT FOR 2 NIGHTS

4½ cups (1.1L) almond milk	10 ounces (285g) bittersweet chocolate, melted and still warm
10 tablespoons (120g) sugar	
2 rosemary sprigs	¼ cup (60g) unsalted butter, at room temperature and cut into 4 pieces
¼ cup (20g) cocoa	
¼ cup (30g) cornstarch	½ teaspoon almond extract
½ teaspoon salt	Heavy or whipped cream, for serving
2 eggs plus 4 yolks	

1 Combine 4 cups (950ml) of the almond milk, 6 tablespoons (75g) of the sugar, and the rosemary in a large saucepan and bring to a boil. While the milk is heating, sift the cocoa, cornstarch, and salt onto a sheet of waxed paper. Place the eggs and egg yolks and the remaining 4 tablespoons (50g) of sugar in the blender and mix for 1 minute. Scrape down the sides of the blender and add the remaining ½ cup (120ml) of almond milk. Process for a few seconds, add the dry ingredients to the blender, and pulse just until smooth.

2 Remove the rosemary from the milk mixture. With the blender running, add half the hot milk in a slow, steady stream, processing to blend. The mixture will be foamy, but the bubbles will disappear when the pudding is cooked. Pour the mixture into the saucepan with the remaining milk and cook over medium-low heat, stirring continuously, until the pudding thickens, about 2 minutes. (Do not let the pudding boil.) Off the heat, whisk in the chocolate, butter, and almond extract.

3 Scrape half of the pudding into the blender and pulse until smooth. Pour the pudding into four ¾-cup (175ml) ramekins or 1 large bowl. Blend the remaining half of the pudding, then pour it into four ¾-cup (175ml) ramekins or into the large bowl. Cover and store in the fridge for up to a week.

4 **The day of:** Let the pudding warm to room temperature, then serve plain or topped with heavy cream, whipped or not.

Coffee Ice Cream with Toasted Marshmallows

Place **8 marshmallows** (from a bakery or a bag, whichever you prefer) 2 inches (5cm) apart on a baking sheet and toast them under a broiler until puffy and browned, turning once, about 3 minutes. While they're nice and hot, scoop store-bought **coffee ice cream** into 4 bowls and top each serving with 2 toasted marshmallows. If you have **chocolate** and **salted pistachios** handy, you could chop them and sprinkle them over the ice cream.

Merrill's Winter

THE WEEK AHEAD

THE RECIPES

Pinwheels with Pecorino and Horseradish 244

Sherry Temple 245

Shirley Temple 245

Red Wine Beef Stew with Parsnips and Carrots 247

Creamy Butternut Squash Soup with Sherry 248

Sour Cream Mashed Potatoes and Parsnips 251

Mashed Potato and Parsnip Cakes 251

Soft Chocolate Almond Cherry Cookies 252

Peppermint Stick Ice Cream 252

The Best Red Wine Vinaigrette 31

Creamed Kale 199

HOW THEY COME TOGETHER

DINNER ONE: DINNER PARTY FOR 6

Sherry Temple

Shirley Temple

Pinwheels with Pecorino and Horseradish

Red Wine Beef Stew with Parsnips and Carrots

Sour Cream Mashed Potatoes and Parsnips

Red leaf salad with The Best Red Wine Vinaigrette

Soft Chocolate Almond Cherry Cookies

Peppermint Stick Ice Cream

TO DO TODAY An hour before your guests arrive, mix the sherry temple base and set out the vinaigrette. Slice and bake the pinwheels right before party time. Stir up sherry and shirley temples for your guests. Warm the stew and the mash and toss the salad. Serve leftover Prosecco from the sherry temples with dinner.

DINNER TWO

Pasta with Creamed Kale

Soft Chocolate Almond Cherry Cookies

TO DO TODAY Make a double batch of creamed kale and toss half with pasta, saving the rest for later in the week.

DINNER THREE

Creamy Butternut Squash Soup with Sherry

Crusty bread and good salted butter

Pears and sharp cheese (I like aged goat Gouda or cheddar) with honey

TO DO TODAY Warm the soup and slice the bread. Serve sliced pears with cheese and honey for dessert.

DINNER FOUR

Red Wine Beef Stew with Parsnips and Carrots

Creamed Kale

Mashed Potato and Parsnip Cakes

Peppermint Stick Ice Cream

TO DO TODAY Warm the stew and the kale. Make the potato cakes.

DINNER FIVE

Creamy Butternut Squash Soup with Sherry

Toast and good salted butter

Red leaf salad with The Best Red Wine Vinaigrette

Clementines and Soft Chocolate Almond Cherry Cookies

TO DO TODAY Warm the soup. Make toast using your leftover crusty bread and toss the salad.

BROWN BAG LUNCHES

Creamy Butternut Squash Soup with Sherry plus bread or crackers and cheese

Mashed Potato and Parsnip Cakes, medium-cooked egg, red leaf salad with The Best Red Wine Vinaigrette

GAME PLAN

GET READY TO PARTY

This week you'll need about 3½ hours of hands-on
cooking time—it'll be worth it, I promise.

• In the morning, move the puff pastry dough from the
freezer to the fridge for the pinwheels (page 244).
When you're ready to start cooking, set out ½ cup
plus 3 tablespoons (185g) unsalted butter to soften
for the cookies (page 252). Set out the beef for the
stew (page 247).

• Get chopping! Cut up the pancetta and vegetables for
the stew (page 247), the butternut squash and leeks
for the soup (page 248), and the parsnips and potatoes
for the mash (page 251); put the potatoes and parsnips
in a bowl of cold water to keep them from browning.

• Wash and dry the greens for the week and store them
in zipper plastic bags in the fridge.

• Heat the oven to 350°F (175°C). Brown the beef
in batches.

• While the beef is browning, get the butternut squash
soup simmering, as well as the potatoes and parsnips
for the mash. Get the stew in the oven.

• Make the dough for the cookies (page 252) and put it
in the fridge for 30 minutes.

• Mash the potatoes and parsnips and add the rest of the
ingredients. Make the red wine vinaigrette (page 31).
Put both in the fridge.

• Form the cookie dough into balls, roll in sugar, and bake
alongside the stew. Or refrigerate them in a container
and bake them later, as you need them.

• While the cookies are baking, puree the soup, transfer
to containers, and refrigerate.

• Set out the vanilla ice cream to soften for the
peppermint stick ice cream (page 252). Make the
filling for the pinwheels and roll them up; wrap
the log and put it in the fridge (or freezer).

• Once the beef is tender, remove it from the pot and
reduce the liquid. Return the beef to the pot, cool
slightly, and refrigerate the stew in the pot.

• Smash the peppermint sticks and mix them into the
ice cream; put the ice cream back in the freezer (steal
a bite for yourself first). Time to party!

Double-booked every night? Have holiday cards to write?
Crank out 1½ batches of the stew and soup, make the
mash and the vinaigrette, and skip the rest. You're sure to
get some decent holiday treats you can use to supplement.
And with a pint of vanilla on hand, you can whip up the
peppermint stick ice cream (page 252) whenever you
have 15 minutes to spare. With this shortened plan, your
active cooking time will be less than 2 hours.

GROCERY LIST

PRODUCE

Broccoli rabe, 2 pounds (900g)

Butternut squash (whole),
7 to 8 pounds (3.2 to 3.6kg)

Carrots, 4 (about 12 ounces/
340g)

Celery, 2 stalks

Clementines, for dessert

Garlic, 1 fat clove

Lacinato kale, 2 pounds (900g)

Leeks, 3

Lemons, 4

Navel oranges, 2

Parsnips, 2 pounds 9 ounces (1.2kg)

Red leaf lettuce, 3 heads

Ripe pears, for dessert

Yellow onion, 1 large

Yukon gold potatoes,
2 pounds (900g)

HERBS

Bay leaf, 1

Rosemary, 1 sprig
(or ½ teaspoon dried)

Thyme, 4 to 5 sprigs

SPICES

Nutmeg, 1 whole

PANTRY

Beef stock, 2 cups (475ml)

Canned chopped tomatoes,
1 cup (240g)

Chicken or vegetable stock,
5 to 6 cups (1.2 to 1.4L)

Extra-virgin olive oil,
about 2 cups (475ml)

Honey, for dessert

Panko or other bread crumbs,
1 cup (60g)

Penne or other pasta, 1 pound (450g)

Prepared horseradish, 2 tablespoons

Red wine vinegar, 3 tablespoons

Sherry vinegar, 1 tablespoon

BAKING AISLE

All-purpose flour, 6½ tablespoons
(50g), plus more for rolling

Almond flour, 1 heaping cup plus
2 tablespoons (125g)

Baking soda, ½ teaspoon

Bittersweet chocolate,
5 ounces (140g)

Candy canes, 12

Dried cherries, ⅔ cup (135g)

Good peppermint extract
(optional), 1 teaspoon

Light brown sugar, ⅔ cup (135g)
firmly packed

Sugar, 1 cup (200g)

Unsweetened cocoa powder,
⅓ cup (30g)

Pure vanilla extract, 1 teaspoon

DAIRY AND EGGS

Good salted butter

Unsalted butter, 1½ cups plus
2 tablespoons (370g)

Cream cheese, 3 tablespoons

Crème fraîche, ⅔ cup (160ml),
plus more to have on hand

Eggs, 2 dozen

Pecorino, ½ cup (50g) grated
from a wedge

Heavy cream, ¾ cup (175ml)

Milk, 2 cups (475ml)

Sharp cheese (such as goat Gouda
or cheddar), for dessert

Sour cream, heaping ¾ cup (175ml)

MEAT AND SEAFOOD

Beef chuck, 3 pounds (1.4kg)
cut into 1½-inch (4cm) cubes
(ask your butcher to do this)

Pancetta, 12 ounces (340g)

BOOZE AND SUCH

Dry red wine, 2 cups (475ml)

Dry sherry, about 1 cup (240ml)

Gin, ⅜ cup (90ml)

Ginger ale, for cocktails (or two
6-inch/15cm bulbs of ginger,
2 cups/400g of sugar, and club
soda to make your own! See
page 268)

Grenadine, for drinks

Maraschino cherries, for drinks

Prosecco, 1 bottle

FREEZER

Frozen puff pastry, 1 sheet

Good vanilla ice cream,
1 quart (950ml)

BAKED GOODS

Baguette, 1

Crusty bread, 1 large loaf
for dinner

Pinwheels with Pecorino and Horseradish

It's life changing when you finally have a back-pocket hors d'oeuvre to throw together at the last minute. I always keep frozen puff pastry sheets on hand so I can make some version of these crunchy, salty pinwheels on relatively short notice. (It is a miraculous day if I happen to have a log of them already made in the freezer.) They're endlessly adaptable (see tips below), and they look like you spent more time on them than you did (see for yourself on page 239).

Ready to Entertain With a log of these in the freezer, you're always ready for guests. Double-wrap the rolled, unsliced log in plastic wrap and freeze for up to 2 months. Some other fillings you might try: Dijon mustard and grated sharp cheddar, prosciutto and Parmesan, spinach and cream cheese, and finely chopped cooked mushrooms and Gruyère.

MAKES ABOUT 3 DOZEN PINWHEELS,
ENOUGH FOR 10 TO 12

1 sheet frozen puff pastry

3 tablespoons cream cheese, at room temperature

2 tablespoons prepared horseradish, drained

½ teaspoon chopped fresh thyme leaves

½ teaspoon freshly ground black pepper

Finely grated zest of 1 lemon

Flour, for rolling

½ cup (50g) grated Pecorino

1 Thaw the puff pastry in the refrigerator until you can work with it, at least 6 hours.

2 Combine the cream cheese, horseradish, thyme, pepper, and lemon zest in a small bowl.

3 Lay the puff pastry on a lightly floured surface. Roll it into a 10 by 14-inch (25 by 36cm) rectangle that's about ⅛ inch (3mm) thick.

4 Working quickly, spread the cream cheese mixture evenly over the pastry, leaving a ½-inch (1.3cm) border uncovered. Sprinkle the Pecorino evenly over the cream cheese mixture.

5 With a short side facing you, roll the pastry into a compact log. Wrap it tightly in parchment or waxed paper and put it in the fridge for at least 30 minutes, or freeze it (see tip).

6 **The day of:** If you froze the pinwheels, move the log from the freezer to the fridge first thing in the morning. About 30 minutes before serving, heat the oven to 375°F (190°C) and line 2 baking sheets with parchment paper. Using a very sharp knife, slice the log into ¼-inch (6mm) rounds and place them 1 inch (2.5cm) apart on the prepared baking sheets. Bake, rotating the sheets halfway through, until golden brown and crisp, 12 to 15 minutes. Let the pinwheels cool for a few minutes on the baking sheets before serving.

Sherry Temple

My sister and I learned early how to recognize a special occasion—if we were allowed to have a Shirley Temple, it was one. This is a grown-up version (shown on page 239), made boozy for adult merriment. Like the original, it calls for a bit of grenadine. Use a light touch and taste as you go—it can turn from subtly to syrupy sweet in an instant.

Batch It Up For a large group, scale up the ingredients to make the number of cocktails you'll need. Stir together everything except for the Prosecco and orange peel and keep in a pitcher in the fridge until you're ready to serve, for up to 24 hours. Pour ½ cup (120ml) into each glass, top with Prosecco, and add an orange twist.

Twists If you can, make the citrus twists just before you serve your cocktails. Once the peel is cut, the oils begin to leach out and some of the flavor and fragrance is lost. Plus, the twists start to shrivel and don't look as pretty.

MAKES 6 DRINKS

Peel from 1 navel orange

⅜ cup (90ml) freshly squeezed orange juice

⅜ cup (90ml) freshly squeezed lemon juice

⅜ cup (90ml) gin

⅜ cup (90ml) dry sherry

Grenadine, to taste

1½ cups (360ml) Prosecco

1 Slice the orange peel thinly to make twists.

2 Fill a cocktail shaker with ice cubes. Add the orange and lemon juices, gin, and sherry. Shake vigorously for 15 seconds and strain into 6 Champagne coupes or martini glasses.

3 Add a few drops of grenadine to each glass and top with ¼ cup (60ml) Prosecco. Add an orange twist and serve immediately.

Shirley Temple

For your smaller party guests, fill tumblers with **ice** and **ginger ale** (find a recipe for homemade ginger ale on page 268). Add about **a teaspoon of grenadine** to each glass (you want the drinks to be cherry red), stir gently, and plunk **a maraschino cherry** on top.

Red Wine Beef Stew with Parsnips and Carrots

Amanda turned me on to Mario Batali's recipe for beef in Barolo, which involves braising a whole brisket in an entire bottle of wine. I've never actually used Barolo (Dolcetto makes a fine—and more economical—substitute), and I prefer plain old stew meat to brisket because I'm not keen on the idea of wrestling a huge slab of meat into—and then out of—a pot of scalding liquid. Amanda's version on page 187 calls for short ribs, which work beautifully, too, but I like cubes of beef because there are no bones to deal with. I did take a nod from Amanda's recipe when I bumped up the carrots, though, and I've added parsnips to make this more of a one-pot meal. That said, mashed potatoes are rarely unwelcome, so you'll find a recipe for mashed potatoes and parsnips (page 251) this week as well.

Pick Your Protein Just as you can use different cuts of beef for this stew, it also works with similar cuts of lamb, veal, and even pork. You can even make it with chicken legs for a modified coq au vin. Just decrease the cooking time to 40 to 45 minutes and then reduce the sauce on its own for a bit longer.

Instead of buying precut stew meat, choose a whole piece of meat (like chuck roast or boneless lamb shoulder) and ask the butcher to cut it for you. This way, you can specify the size of the cubes, and you'll know the meat is all coming from the same cut.

SERVES 4 FOR 2 DINNERS

3 pounds (1.4kg) beef chuck, cut into 1½-inch (4cm) cubes (see note)

Kosher salt and freshly ground black pepper

3 tablespoons extra-virgin olive oil

4 ounces (115g) pancetta, diced

4 carrots, about 12 ounces/340g, peeled and sliced into ½-inch (1.3cm) rounds

3 medium (about 9 ounces/255g) parsnips, peeled and sliced into ½-inch (1.3cm) rounds

1 large yellow onion, diced

2 celery stalks, cut into ½-inch (1.3cm) slices

1 large clove garlic, peeled and smashed

2 cups (475ml) dry red wine

2 cups (475ml) beef stock

1 cup (240g) canned chopped tomatoes (preferably Pomi)

3 thyme sprigs

1 rosemary sprig (or ½ teaspoon dried)

1 bay leaf

1 Set out the beef for 20 to 30 minutes to take off the chill. Heat the oven to 350°F (175°C). Sprinkle the beef with salt and pepper. Warm 1 tablespoon of the olive oil in a large Dutch oven over high heat. Working in batches, add the beef, being careful not to crowd the pot. Cook the beef on all sides until browned, about 5 minutes. With a slotted spoon, transfer the browned meat to a plate and keep warm while you brown the rest.

2 Pour off all but about a tablespoon of the fat in the pot, turn the heat down to medium-low, and add the remaining 2 tablespoons of olive oil and the pancetta. Cook until it starts to crisp, about 5 minutes.

3 Add the carrots, parsnips, onion, and celery, and cook until they start to soften, about 5 minutes. Add the garlic and cook for a minute more.

4 Add the wine, stock, tomatoes, thyme, rosemary, bay leaf, and 2 teaspoons salt and bring to a boil over high heat. Add the beef, submerging it in the liquid. Cover, slide the pot into the oven, and bake until the meat is very tender, about 2 hours.

5 With a slotted spoon, transfer the beef to a plate. Bring the liquid to a boil over medium-high heat and cook until it reduces and is thick enough to coat a wooden spoon. Taste and adjust the seasoning, then return the meat to the pot. Let the stew cool slightly, discard the herbs, then cover and refrigerate in the pot.

6 **The day of:** Reheat the stew gently over low heat for 10 to 15 minutes.

Creamy Butternut Squash Soup with Sherry

My father has a bowl of hot soup for lunch probably 350 days out of the year. I usually reserve soup for colder weather (though, in summer, don't get in the way of me and my gazpacho!), and in the fall and winter I could easily eat it most days. I've been making the same basic butternut squash soup for years, with small tweaks here and there. It's smooth as velvet, as a proper winter squash soup should be. When I have a batch in my fridge, I truly feel armed for the week ahead.

To Swap or Not to Swap If you don't have sherry on hand, you can skip it or substitute brandy, Madeira, or Cognac. For a vegan version, use vegetable oil instead of butter and leave out the milk, cream, and crème fraîche. It will still be rich and delicious. I find that butternut squash makes a better soup than pumpkin (although cheese pumpkin behaves similarly to butternut squash), which can be watery and insipid.

A Peeling Trick for Butternut Squash One of my cooking pet peeves is the sticky orange film that coats my hands (and is impossible to scrub off) after handling peeled butternut squash. To minimize this, I hold onto the fat end of the squash, as close to the root end as I can without dropping it, and peel away from me and down the full length of the squash. Then I only have to touch the sticky part for a few seconds while I peel the last bits off the bigger end, and again briefly while I scoop out the seeds. A vegetable brush is an effective—and less painful—alternative to steel wool for removing any stubborn film from your hands.

SERVES 4 FOR 2 DINNERS, WITH LEFTOVERS

¼ cup (60g) unsalted butter

3 leeks, white and green parts, cleaned and chopped

7 to 8 pounds (3.2 to 3.6kg) butternut squash, peeled, seeded, and cut into 1-inch (2.5cm) cubes

Kosher salt and freshly ground black pepper

½ teaspoon freshly grated nutmeg

6 tablespoons (90ml) dry sherry, plus more for finishing

5 to 6 cups (1.2 to 1.4L) chicken or vegetable stock

2 cups (475ml) milk

¼ cup (60ml) heavy cream

Crème fraîche, for serving

1 Melt the butter in a 6- to 8-quart (5.5 to 7.5L) pot over medium-low heat. Add the leeks and cook, stirring with a wooden spoon, until softened, about 5 minutes (if they start to brown, add a few tablespoons of water).

2 Add the squash, 1 teaspoon salt, a few grinds of pepper, and the nutmeg and cook, stirring frequently, for 5 minutes more.

3 Add the sherry and cook until it is mostly reduced, a minute or two, then add enough stock to cover the squash (if you need more liquid, add a little water).

4 Simmer, partially covered, until the squash is tender, about 20 minutes. Turn off the heat and let the soup cool for at least 20 minutes.

5 If you plan to freeze the soup, blend it and freeze it without adding the milk and cream. This way, you'll avoid a possibly grainy texture when you defrost it. Otherwise, working in batches, blend the soup with the milk until creamy, adding some water if it seems too thick. Stir in the cream, taste, and adjust the seasonings. Store in the fridge for up to a week or in the freezer for up to 3 months.

6 If you've frozen the soup, defrost it in the fridge the night before you plan to eat it. **The day of:** Reheat the soup in a pot over medium-low heat, just until it simmers. Stir in the milk and cream if you haven't yet and return to a simmer. Taste and adjust the seasoning. Stir in another splash of sherry and add a dollop of crème fraîche to each bowl.

Sour Cream Mashed Potatoes and Parsnips

The first time I made mashed potatoes, my mother shared a vital piece of cooking wisdom: always add something with a little tang—sour cream, crème fraîche, buttermilk, Greek yogurt, what have you—to your mash. It gives it a gentle lift, rescuing it from the unrelenting heft of potatoes and butter, which can become tiresome on their own after a few bites. Ever since, I haven't (willingly) ignored my mother's mashed potato advice. This recipe calls for half parsnips and half potatoes, which makes for a mash that's less dense, with a pleasant vegetal punch. Like Amanda, I'm an advocate of using starchy cooking water in place of milk for mashed potatoes. It enhances the other flavors rather than muffling them. (See finished mash on page 246.)

SERVES 6, AS A SIDE FOR DINNER, WITH LEFTOVERS FOR CAKES (BELOW)

2 pounds (900g) parsnips, peeled and cut into 1-inch (2.5cm) chunks

2 pounds (900g) Yukon gold potatoes, peeled and cut into 1½-inch (4cm) chunks

Kosher salt and freshly ground black pepper

¾ cup (175ml) sour cream

3 tablespoons unsalted butter, at room temperature

1 to 2 tablespoons extra-virgin olive oil

1 Put the parsnips and potatoes in a large saucepan and add enough cold water to cover. Add 2 teaspoons of salt and bring to a boil over high heat. Lower the heat and simmer until tender, about 20 minutes.

2 Reserve 2 cups (475ml) of the cooking water, then drain the parsnips and potatoes and return them to the pot over low heat. Mash them, adding the sour cream, butter, olive oil, and a few splashes of the cooking water. Using a wooden spoon, stir the mash vigorously until it's smooth and creamy. If it seems dry, stir in more of the cooking liquid until you have a velvety consistency. Taste and adjust the seasoning. Cool and store in the fridge for up to 5 days.

3 **The day of:** Reheat the mash in a heavy saucepan over medium-low heat for 5 to 10 minutes, adding a little hot water to loosen it up. Don't forget to save some for the cakes (below)!

Mashed Potato and Parsnip Cakes

To make the cakes, beat **1 large egg per 8 ounces (225g) of leftover mash** and stir them together. Form the mixture into 3-inch (7.5cm) cakes (don't worry if they're loose—they'll firm up as they cook), coat them in **panko or other dry bread crumbs** seasoned with salt and freshly ground black pepper, and fry in **extra-virgin olive oil** in a heavy skillet over medium heat until golden brown, 2 to 3 minutes per side. Sprinkle with kosher salt and freshly ground black pepper and serve right away.

Soft Chocolate Almond Cherry Cookies

This was my entry for the Holiday Cookie Truck bake-off of 2015, where I eked out a victory against Amanda's chewy vanilla spice cookies with chocolate chunks (page 204). I was inspired by Pierre Hermé and Dorie Greenspan's World Peace Cookies, but I wanted a softer cookie, so I swapped most of the all-purpose flour for almond flour, and added some chopped dried cherries. The cookies are almost brownielike in texture, so they're still good on day five. I developed the recipe using weights for precise results, so if you're not using a scale, the measurements may seem a bit awkward. It will all pay off, though.

Not Overbaking Cookies It took me a while to absorb the importance of removing chewy or soft cookies (and cakes) from the oven before they look completely done. Like meat, they continue to cook out of the oven, so unless you're going for crunchiness (like on page 23), resist the urge to leave them in for "just one more minute."

MAKES ABOUT 3 DOZEN COOKIES

1 heaping cup plus 2 tablespoons (125g) almond flour

6½ tablespoons (50g) all-purpose flour

⅓ cup (30g) unsweetened cocoa powder

½ teaspoon baking soda

½ cup plus 3 tablespoons (125g) unsalted butter, at room temperature

⅔ cup (135g) firmly packed light brown sugar

1 cup (200g) sugar

1¼ teaspoons kosher salt

1 teaspoon pure vanilla extract

5 ounces (140g) bittersweet chocolate, coarsely chopped (⅓ inch/8mm or smaller pieces)

⅔ cup (135g) dried cherries, chopped

1 Whisk together the almond flour, all-purpose flour, cocoa powder, and baking soda in a large bowl. In the bowl of a stand mixer fitted with a paddle attachment, cream the butter on medium speed until light and fluffy, 3 to 5 minutes. Scrape down the sides of the bowl with a spatula.

2 Add the brown sugar, ¼ cup (50g) of the sugar, the salt, and vanilla and beat for 2 minutes. Scrape down the sides of the bowl. Add the dry ingredients, drape a kitchen towel over the mixer, and pulse on low speed for 2 seconds at a time about 5 times. Remove the towel and beat at low speed until everything is just combined. Scrape down the bowl again.

3 Add the chocolate and cherries and mix, just to incorporate. Cover the bowl and refrigerate for 30 minutes.

4 Heat the oven to 350°F (175°C). Line 2 baking sheets with parchment paper. Pour the remaining ¾ cup (150g) sugar onto a large plate. Form the dough into 1½-inch (4cm) balls. Roll the balls in the sugar and place them about 2 inches (5cm) apart on the baking sheets. (Or refrigerate them in a sealed container and bake the cookies as you need them.)

5 Bake for 10 to 12 minutes. The cookies should look dry on the surface but still be soft to the touch. Do not overbake. Cool on the sheets for 5 minutes, then transfer to racks.

6 The cookies will keep for a week in a tin on the counter. If you don't think you'll eat them within that time, freeze the baked cookies in a freezer-friendly zipper plastic bag for up to a month; thaw them at room temperature.

Peppermint Stick Ice Cream

Leftover candy canes are inevitable at Christmas. To use them up, soften **1 quart (950ml) of vanilla ice cream** at room temperature. Meanwhile, unwrap **12 candy canes,** put them inside two zipper plastic bags, and go at them with a mallet. Scoop the ice cream into the bowl of a stand mixer fitted with a paddle attachment. Add the crushed candy canes and **a teaspoon of good peppermint extract** if you have it. Mix on low speed until just combined, then refreeze.

THE WEEK AHEAD

THE RECIPES

Cabbage and Jicama Slaw 258

Fish Baked in Foil 259

Fish Salpicon 260

Noodle Soup with Fish,
Ginger, Cilantro, Chiles,
and Lime 260

Slow-Cooked Pork Tacos 263

Brothy, Garlicky Beans 264

Pasta e Fagioli 264

Green Rice 266

Lime Ice Cream 268

Lime Pie Ice Cream 268

Lime Ginger Floats 268

Broiled Grapefruits
with Lime 268

Ginger Syrup 268

Pickled Onions 86

HOW THEY COME TOGETHER

DINNER ONE

Fish Baked in Foil
Green Rice
Watercress with lime juice, olive oil, and cilantro
Lime Ice Cream

TO DO TODAY Reheat the fish and rice. Toss the watercress with fresh cilantro leaves, lime juice, olive oil, salt, and pepper.

DINNER TWO

Slow-Cooked Pork Tacos with avocado,
Pickled Onions, and sour cream
Cabbage and Jicama Slaw
Broiled Grapefruits with Lime

TO DO TODAY Warm the tortillas and pork and prepare the toppings for the tacos. Dress the slaw. Prepare the grapefruits, then broil them right before dessert.

DINNER THREE

Fish Salpicon
Cabbage and Jicama Slaw
Lime Ginger Floats

TO DO TODAY Make the fish salpicon. Dress the slaw. Make the floats for dessert.

DINNER FOUR

Pasta e Fagioli
Cured meats
Country bread
Lime Pie Ice Cream

TO DO TODAY Make the lime pie ice cream and keep it in the freezer. Make the pasta e fagioli and set out the cured meats and bread. Whip the cream for the lime pie ice cream before serving.

DINNER FIVE

Slow-Cooked Pork and Brothy, Garlicky
Beans with Pickled Onions
Green Rice
Watercress and celery with parsley and lime dressing
Vanilla ice cream with Ginger Syrup

TO DO TODAY Reheat the rice and warm some leftover pork taco filling and brothy beans together. Combine the watercress with thinly sliced celery and some chopped parsley, then dress with leftover lime dressing from the cabbage and jicama slaw (page 258). Drizzle the ginger syrup over the ice cream for dessert.

BROWN BAG LUNCHES

Noodle Soup with Fish, Ginger, Cilantro,
Chiles, and Lime
Pork, Pickled Onions, and sliced avocado
on a soft roll
Brothy, Garlicky Beans with a fried or
medium-cooked egg

GAME PLAN

TO MAKE OVER THE WEEKEND

Fish Baked in Foil

Cabbage and Jicama Slaw

Slow-Cooked Pork Tacos

Pickled Onions (page 86)

Brothy, Garlicky Beans

Green Rice

Lime Ice Cream

Ginger Syrup

AND AWAY. YOU. GO!

Your active cooking time this weekend will be about 3 hours.

- Start soaking the beans (page 264).

- Get the pork taco filling (page 263) on the stove.

- Wash and spin dry all the herbs and salad greens for the week and store them in the fridge.

- Make the ice cream base (page 268) and chill it in the fridge for at least an hour.

- Get the ginger syrup (page 268) on the stove.

- Heat the oven to 350°F (175°C). Assemble the green rice (page 266) and put it in the oven.

- Drain the beans and get them simmering with the rest of the ingredients.

- Freeze the lime ice cream, stirring every 20 minutes.

- Make the pickled onions (page 86) for the pork tacos, and slice the onion for the slaw (page 258). Refrigerate them both.

- Slice the cabbage and jicama for the slaw and store in the fridge.

- Make the dressing for the slaw (page 258) and refrigerate it.

- Once the rice is done, lower the oven temperature to 325°F (165°C). Prepare the fish baked in foil, then bake it (page 259).

- Strain the ginger syrup (page 268). Put everything in the fridge.

- Have a cup of tea and a cookie. You've earned it.

Don't have time for lots of cooking this weekend?
Make baked rice (page 83) in place of green rice. Skip the lime ice cream, ginger syrup, and slaw and supplement with your favorite store-bought ice cream and simple green salads. With these modifications, you'll shave off about half of your weekend cooking time.

GROCERY LIST

PRODUCE

Avocados, 4

Cabbage, 1 pound (450g)

Carrots, 3 large

Celery stalks, 1 bunch

Garlic, 18 cloves

Ginger, 2 (6-inch/15cm) bulbs

Grapefruits, 2

Jicama, 1 medium, about
1 pound (450g)

Limes, 25

Red onions, 2½ (2 large
and ½ small)

Yellow onions, 4 (2 medium
and 2 large)

Poblano chiles, 2

Scallions, 10

Serrano chiles, 4

Shallots, 4

Watercress, 2 bunches

HERBS

Cilantro, 3 bunches

Flat-leaf parsley, 1 bunch

Mint, 1 bunch

Rosemary, 1 sprig
(or ½ teaspoon dried)

Thyme, 2 sprigs

SPICES

Bay leaf, 1

Black peppercorns, 1 teaspoon

Coriander seeds, 2 teaspoons

Cumin seeds, 4 teaspoons

Dried oregano, 1 teaspoon

Ground ancho chile, 4 teaspoons

Ground chipotle, 2 teaspoons

PANTRY

Basmati rice, 4 cups (740g)

Canned chopped tomatoes
(preferably Pomi), 4 cups (960g)

Cider vinegar, 1½ cups (355ml)

Dijon mustard, 2 tablespoons

Dried white beans (such as
cannellini or navy), 2 pounds
(900g)

Extra-virgin olive oil, 1 cup
(240ml), plus more to have
on hand

Homemade or low-sodium
chicken stock or vegetable stock,
11 cups (2.6L)

Honey, 2 tablespoons

Hot sauce, for serving

Mayonnaise, for lunch

Red wine vinegar, 4 teaspoons

Rice vermicelli, 2 ounces (55g)

Short pasta, 4 ounces (115g)

Soy sauce, ⅛ teaspoon

Vegetable oil, 1 cup (240ml)

BAKING AISLE

Graham crackers, 3

Demerara sugar, ¼ cup (50g)

Sugar, 3½ cups plus
2 tablespoons (725g)

DAIRY AND EGGS

Unsalted butter, 6 tablespoons
(85g)

Heavy cream, 3½ cups (830ml)

Parmesan, for serving

Parmesan rind (optional)

Sour cream, for serving

MEAT AND SEAFOOD

Boneless pork shoulder (not too
lean), 4 pounds (1.8kg)

Fish fillets (such as striped bass,
snapper, branzino, etc.), 3 pounds
(1.4kg)

Selection of cured meats

BOOZE AND SUCH

Club soda, 1 (1L) bottle

FREEZER

Vanilla ice cream, for dessert

BAKED GOODS

Corn tortillas, 32 small

Country bread, 1 loaf

Soft rolls, 4

Cabbage and Jicama Slaw

Every stew or braise calls out for something crisp and fresh to balance it. This slaw is dead simple, and uses jicama, which is one of the best least-known vegetables there is. Jicama is bracing and just a little bit sweet. I find its natural crunch sort of addicting.

Make It Ahead Once you add the dressing, the slaw will start to lose its structure pretty quickly. I suggest that you mix it each time you serve it, using only what you plan to eat and storing the rest of the vegetables, herbs, and dressing separately in the fridge.

½ small red onion, thinly sliced

1 pound (450g) cabbage, any sort

1 medium jicama, about 1 pound (450g)

LIME DRESSING

6 tablespoons (90ml) lime juice

2 teaspoons finely grated lime zest

2 tablespoons honey

6 tablespoons (90ml) vegetable oil

2 teaspoons kosher salt

Freshly ground black pepper

½ cup (20g) loosely packed fresh cilantro leaves

½ cup (20g) loosely packed fresh flat-leaf parsley leaves

1 Soak the onion in a bowl of cold water for about 20 minutes to remove some of the sting. Drain the onion and store it in a container or bag lined with paper towels in the fridge.

2 Slice the cabbage thinly (you should have about 12 loosely packed cups/450g) and peel and julienne the jicama (you should have about 6 cups/450g). Keep them in a container or bag lined with paper towels in the fridge.

3 Combine the lime juice and zest, honey, vegetable oil, salt, and a few grinds of pepper in a jar with a tight-fitting lid. Screw on the lid and shake vigorously until emulsified. Taste and adjust the seasoning, then store in the fridge for up to 5 days. You'll be using this for salad as well as the slaw this week.

4 **The day of:** Combine half of the sliced cabbage, jicama, and onion in a large bowl. Coarsely chop ¼ cup (10g) each cilantro and parsley. Pour in about 3 tablespoons of the lime dressing and toss gently to combine. Taste and add more dressing if needed. Serve immediately. Repeat the second night you serve the slaw.

Fish Baked in Foil

This is an adaptation of a dish my husband and I had at a beachside resort in Kenya during our honeymoon. We were completely spoiled by impeccable seafood, fresh off the boat, every day. With a little cajoling, the chef agreed to give me a couple of his recipes. In this one, fish fillets get friendly with lime juice, olive oil, and cilantro before they're blanketed in onion and lime slices and then baked in foil packets. It works best with thinner fillets of fish, like striped bass, snapper, and branzino. I've also included a tip for preparing it with whole fish.

Foil Is Your Friend Baking in foil is a great way to capitalize on the even heat of the oven without falling victim to its dryness. The packet traps the moisture of whatever is inside it, which is especially handy for delicate, quick-cooking proteins like fish fillets or chicken breasts. To make the recipe with boneless, skinless chicken breasts, form individual packets for each breast instead of stacking them and bake at 375°F (190°C) for 25 to 30 minutes, until the internal temperature of the chicken reaches 165°F (74°C).

SERVES 4, WITH LEFTOVERS FOR
FISH SALPICON AND LUNCHES

¼ cup (60ml) freshly squeezed lime juice

2 teaspoons finely grated lime zest

½ cup (20g) coarsely chopped fresh cilantro leaves and stems

½ cup (120ml) extra-virgin olive oil

Kosher salt and freshly ground black pepper

2 large red onions, halved and thinly sliced

3 limes, thinly sliced

3 pounds (1.4kg) fish fillets (such as striped bass, snapper, or branzino)

2 tablespoons Dijon mustard

2 tablespoons unsalted butter, in small chunks

1 Heat the oven to 325°F (165°C).

2 Whisk together the lime juice and zest, cilantro, and olive oil in a bowl. Season with salt and pepper.

3 Stack 2 long pieces of heavy-duty aluminum foil, with the nonshiny sides facing each other. Make a ½-inch (1.3cm) pleat along one of the long sides, then fold the foil over twice more so that you join the two sheets securely together into one big sheet. Unfold and place the foil shiny side down on a flat surface. Repeat to create 2 more large foil sheets. Arrange several of the onion and lime slices down the center of each sheet, along the crease, creating beds roughly the same size as a fish fillet.

4 Lay a fish fillet on top of a bed of onion and lime and brush lightly with mustard. Place a couple of onion and lime slices on top of the fillet, followed by another fillet and a little more mustard. Repeat until you've used up one-third of the fish, finishing with a last layer of onion and lime. Do the same with the remaining 2 pounds (900g) fish on the other 2 foil sheets.

5 Start to fold up the edges of the foil, then drizzle one-third of the marinade over the top of each stack of fillets and dot with the butter. Fold and crease the foil into neat packages, leaving a little air between the foil and the fish. Place the packets on a rimmed baking sheet.

6 Bake until the fish is just cooked through, about 30 minutes. Serve half of the fish right away, storing the rest (minus the juices that collect in the packets) in the fridge for up to 3 days.

One Fish, Two Fish For a more dramatic dinner, try this with whole fish. Look for 2 fish that are the same size, about 1¼ pounds (570g) each. Ask your butcher to gut and scale them. Spread the insides of the cavities with mustard and stuff them with the extra onion and lime and the butter after creating the beds. Wrap them up and bake them as you would the fillets. Whole fish take a little longer to cook, 45 to 55 minutes.

Fish Salpicon

This is a great way to breathe new life into leftover seafood. Like a cooked ceviche wrapped in soft corn tortillas, it's a dish my husband and I first ate at Fonda, one of our favorite neighborhood restaurants in Brooklyn. I love how quickly it comes together on a weeknight, and the self-assembly component is another plus—especially for the cook! I typically use a white, flaky fish, but something heartier like tuna would also be nice.

SERVES 4

12 to 16 small corn tortillas

1 pound (450g) cooked fish (leftover from Fish Baked in Foil, page 259)

⅓ cup (13g) coarsely chopped fresh cilantro

4 scallions, white and green parts, thinly sliced

½ to 1 small hot chile (such as serrano or bird's eye), depending on your heat preference, seeded and finely chopped

Kosher salt

2 limes

1 or 2 avocados

Hot sauce, for serving

1 Heat the oven to 300°F (150°C). Wrap the tortillas tightly in aluminum foil and put in the oven to warm for 5 to 10 minutes.

2 Meanwhile, flake the fish with two forks, leaving some larger chunks, and put in a large bowl.

3 Add the cilantro, scallions, chile, and a few pinches of salt. Squeeze the juice of 1 lime over the top. Fold gently to combine everything. Taste and adjust the seasoning.

4 To serve, peel, pit, and slice the avocados and cut the remaining lime into wedges. Let everyone assemble their own tacos at the table, passing the hot sauce.

Lunch: Noodle Soup with Fish, Ginger, Cilantro, Chiles, and Lime

I got this great idea from Sophie Missing and Caroline Craig, the authors of *The Little Book of Lunch*. Put **2 ounces (55g) of rice vermicelli** in a 10- to 12-ounce (295 to 355ml) jar with a tight-fitting lid. Add **1 teaspoon grated fresh ginger, 2 thinly sliced scallions, ½ carrot,** julienned, **a few chopped fresh mint and cilantro leaves,** and ⅛ **teaspoon soy sauce** (or more to taste). Add ¼ **cup (50g) leftover fish** (page 259) in bite-size chunks. When you're ready to eat, pour in enough boiling water to cover the other ingredients and let sit for 3 minutes. Squeeze in the **juice of half a lime,** stir, and eat.

Slow-Cooked Pork Tacos

These tacos were inspired by a recipe I came across in *Fine Cooking* for chili con carne. I decided to make them with pork shoulder instead of beef, and I reduced the liquid and axed the beans to make more of a thick stew. Then, another thought: Wouldn't this be good wrapped in tortillas? And I might as well make some quick-pickled onions while I was at it. At this point it looked nothing like the original, but all recipes come from somewhere, right? Like most slow-cooked dishes, this is even better after a day or two.

Spice The taco filling calls for several types of chiles and chili powders. In a pinch, you can leave out what you don't have, but if you stock up on all of the ingredients you'll be rewarded with complex layers of flavor and heat. Feel free to adjust the amounts to match your tolerance for spice. Use 1 serrano instead of 2 and only 1 teaspoon of ground chipotle if you're feeling gun-shy.

SERVES 4, WITH LEFTOVER PORK FOR OTHER DINNERS AND LUNCHES

4 teaspoons cumin seeds

2 teaspoons coriander seeds

4 teaspoons ground ancho chile

2 teaspoons ground chipotle

1 teaspoon dried oregano

3 to 4 tablespoons vegetable oil

4 pounds (1.8kg) boneless pork shoulder, cut into ¾-inch (2cm) cubes (see tip about buying pork on page 165)

Kosher salt

2 yellow onions, diced

2 poblano chiles, seeded and finely chopped

2 serrano chiles, seeded and finely chopped

4 large garlic cloves, minced

3 cups (710ml) homemade or low-sodium chicken stock

2 cups (480g) canned chopped tomatoes, with their juices (preferably Pomi)

4 large limes

12 to 16 small corn tortillas

2 avocados

½ bunch cilantro, washed and dried

Sour cream, for serving

Pickled onions (page 86), for serving

1 Toast the cumin and coriander seeds in a small pan for a minute or two over medium heat, shaking the pan, until fragrant. (Be careful not to scorch them.) Finely grind the spices using a spice grinder or a mortar and pestle. Stir in both ground chiles and the oregano and set aside.

2 Warm 1 tablespoon of oil in a large heavy pot or Dutch oven over medium-high heat. Season the pork with salt. Working in batches so you don't crowd the meat, cook the pork until well browned on all sides, about 4 minutes total (add more oil as needed). Transfer the browned pork to a clean plate.

3 Lower the heat to medium-low and add another tablespoon of oil, the onions, chiles, and a few pinches of salt. Cook until softened, about 5 minutes. Add the garlic and cook for 1 minute more. Stir in the spice mixture and cook for another minute.

4 Return the pork with any juices to the pot, along with the chicken stock and tomatoes. The pork should be covered in liquid; if it's not, add a little water. Squeeze in the juice of 1 lime and add 1 tablespoon of salt. Bring the liquid to a boil, then turn down the heat, cover the pot, and simmer very gently for 1 hour.

5 Uncover the pot and continue to cook until the pork is tender and the sauce thickens, 30 to 60 minutes. Taste and adjust the seasoning. Let the pork cool and store in the pot in the fridge for up to 5 days.

6 **The day of:** Heat the oven to 300°F (150°C). Wrap the tortillas tightly in aluminum foil and warm in the oven for 5 to 10 minutes. Gently reheat the pork over medium heat for about 10 minutes and squeeze in some more lime juice. Peel, pit, and slice the avocados and cut 2 limes into wedges. Set out the pork with the avocados, lime wedges, a heap of cilantro, a small bowl of sour cream, and the pickled onions. Let everyone assemble their own tacos at the table.

Brothy, Garlicky Beans

One day when my pantry and fridge were looking particularly sad, I decided to throw all of my vegetable and herb scraps into a pot of beans, along with a Parmesan rind that had been skulking around for weeks. As the beans softened and plumped, they absorbed the flavors of this motley crew of aromatics. They were savory and mellow, leaving all of my previous bean efforts in the dust. Now I always make my beans this way. There's no need to feel wedded to the specifics: You can use onions instead of shallots, leeks instead of scallions, sage or parsley in place of thyme and rosemary, Pecorino rind rather than Parmesan, and so on.

Freezer-Friendly These beans freeze nicely. Keep them frozen in an airtight container for up to 3 months. The morning you plan to eat them for dinner, move them to the fridge to defrost.

SERVES 4 AS A SIDE, WITH EXTRA FOR
PASTA E FAGIOLI AND LUNCHES

2 pounds (900g) dried white beans (such as cannellini or navy), picked over and rinsed

8 cups (1.9L) homemade or low-sodium chicken stock or vegetable stock

2 large carrots, peeled and halved

2 celery stalks, with their leaves if you have them, cut into 3-inch (7.5cm) lengths

4 shallots, halved

4 scallions, trimmed

6 fat garlic cloves, smashed

2 thyme sprigs

1 rosemary sprig
(or ½ teaspoon dried)

1 handful flat-leaf parsley
(leaves and stems)

Parmesan rind (optional)

¼ cup (60ml) good olive oil, plus more for serving

Kosher salt

2 cups (480g) canned chopped tomatoes
(preferably Pomi)

1 To quick-soak the beans, put them in a large heavy pot and add enough cold water to cover by 1 inch (2.5cm). Bring them to a boil over high heat. Boil for 1 minute, then turn off the heat and cover the pot. Let the beans soak for an hour.

2 Drain the beans and return them to the pot. Add the stock and, if the beans aren't covered by at least 2 inches (5cm) of liquid, some water. Add the carrots, celery, shallots, scallions, garlic, thyme, rosemary, parsley, Parmesan rind, olive oil, and 3 teaspoons salt. Bring to a boil over medium-high heat. Lower the heat and simmer partially covered until the beans are nearly tender, 45 to 60 minutes. Add more water if the beans aren't covered at any time. Add the tomatoes and cook for 10 to 15 minutes more.

3 Remove the aromatics and vegetables (cook's treat!), taste the beans, and adjust the seasoning. Store in the fridge for up to 5 days.

4 **The day of:** Reheat the beans gently in a pot for 5 to 10 minutes.

Pasta e Fagioli

This is a simple shortcut to a classic dish. Cook **an ounce of short pasta** (I like trofie) per person, until just al dente. Warm **leftover beans** with **chicken stock** or water to make a thick soup, allowing about 1½ cups (355ml) of soup per person. Taste, adjust the seasonings, and add the pasta. Serve with a drizzle of **good olive oil** and **grated Parmesan.**

Green Rice

In the early days of Food52, one of our community members, Amreen Karmali, posted a recipe for shrimp biryani. I've made her bright, aromatic dish many times. First, you whir up a vibrant paste of chiles, garlic, and herbs that serves as a base for an amped-up pilaf. The same paste does double duty as a marinade for the shrimp that rest on top of the rice. Here, I've left out the shrimp and switched up some of the herbs and spices to make it a side dish (Amanda's take, opposite, includes shrimp). Try experimenting with the flavors. Dill and mint would be a nice alternative, and you could add a few cardamom pods or coriander seeds in place of the bay leaf.

Play with the Heat This recipe calls for black peppercorns, which are not removed before serving. If you like, you can substitute ¼ teaspoon freshly ground black pepper or tie the peppercorns into a small cheesecloth bundle for easy removal at the end.

Serrano chiles vary in size and heat. If your chiles are particularly large (or spicy), you may not want to add all of the paste to your rice.

SERVES 4 AS A SIDE FOR 2 DINNERS

½ bunch cilantro, washed and root ends trimmed

1 cup (40g) coarsely chopped flat-leaf parsley leaves

⅔ cup (30g) coarsely chopped mint leaves

8 large cloves garlic, peeled

2 serrano chiles, seeded

⅓ cup (80ml) vegetable oil

1 teaspoon black peppercorns

1 bay leaf

2 large yellow onions, finely chopped

Kosher salt

4 cups (740g) basmati rice

¼ cup (60g) unsalted butter, cut into cubes

4 teaspoons red wine vinegar

2 tablespoons extra-virgin olive oil

1 Heat the oven to 350°F (175°C).

2 Put the leaves and stems of the cilantro in the bowl of a food processor with the parsley, mint, garlic, and chiles. Pulse until you have a thick paste, adding a little water if you need to help things along, and scraping down the sides of the bowl a few times.

3 Warm the vegetable oil in an 8-quart (7.5L) oven-safe dish. Add the peppercorns and bay leaf and cook until fragrant, 2 to 3 minutes.

4 Add the onions and cook, stirring frequently, until they soften and start to brown, 8 to 10 minutes. Add half of the chile-herb paste and cook for 1 minute more.

5 Add 6 cups (1.4L) water and 1 tablespoon salt and bring to a boil. Stir in the rice and butter and return to a boil. Cover tightly with aluminum foil or a lid and bake for exactly 20 minutes.

6 Let the rice sit for 5 minutes. Uncover, fluff with a fork, and remove the bay leaf. Gently stir the vinegar, olive oil, and a few more spoonfuls of the chile-herb paste into the rice with the fork, tasting as you go. Adjust the seasoning. Let cool and store in the baking dish in the fridge for up to 5 days. Keep leftover paste in the fridge for up to a week, or in the freezer for up to 3 months.

7 **The day of:** Cover the dish in aluminum foil and reheat in a 300°F to 325°F (150°C to 165°C) oven for about 15 minutes, stirring halfway through.

Amanda's Fried Green Rice

Pour **1½ tablespoons of vegetable oil** into a large well-seasoned cast-iron skillet, nonstick pan, or wok with a lid, and place over high heat. Add **4 cups (515g) green rice** and spread it to the edges of the skillet, pressing it down lightly with a cooking spoon. Don't stir. When the rice is toasted and brown, after about 5 minutes, stir it, then spread and press it again. Rinse and repeat until the rice is good and crisp, adjusting the heat as needed. Transfer the fried rice to shallow bowls or a serving platter. Pour another **tablespoon of oil** into the pan and warm over medium-high heat. When the oil shimmers, crack **4 eggs** into the pan and season with salt and pepper. Let the eggs crisp on the bottom, then put a lid on the pan and steam just until the whites are cooked through, about 2 minutes. Place the eggs on top of the rice and pass **hot sauce** at the table.

Amanda's Green Rice with Shrimp

Cook the **green rice,** doubling the **cilantro** and leaving out the mint. Put the cooked rice in a small baking dish, covered with foil, into the fridge. **The day of:** Heat the oven to 300°F (150°C). Place the foil-covered baking dish in the oven and cook, stirring once or twice, until warmed through, about 20 minutes. When the rice is hot, remove it from the oven. Toss **1 pound (450g) medium shrimp** with **extra-virgin olive oil** and salt, then grill or broil them. Serve the shrimp over the rice.

Lime Ice Cream

I was six years old when my family went to the Bahamas on vacation, and we had the most delicious lime ice cream at dinner one night. It was intensely tart, with green threads of lime zest throughout. I plucked up the courage to ask for the recipe, which I transcribed onto a small slip of paper. The best part? You don't even need an ice cream machine to make it.

MAKES 1½ QUARTS (1.4KG)

3 cups (710ml) heavy cream

1½ cups (300g) sugar

¼ cup (25g) finely grated lime zest

⅔ cup (160ml) freshly squeezed lime juice

1 Combine the cream, sugar, and lime zest and juice in a large bowl, whisking until the sugar is dissolved. Cover and refrigerate until completely chilled, at least an hour.

2 Freeze the mixture in a wide, shallow container, stirring every 20 minutes, until creamy and frozen, about 2 hours. Cover the container. Don't be dismayed if the ice cream never gets really hard in your freezer—the texture should be airy and light.

Amanda's Riffs

"My family makes a very similar recipe, using lemon zest and juice, and milk instead of cream. Or try **Lime Pie Ice Cream:** Scoop **2 cups (475ml) of lime ice cream** into a bowl. Mash **3 graham crackers** into the ice cream. Mix well, then put the bowl in the freezer to firm up the ice cream while you eat. Whip **½ cup (120ml) heavy cream** until it just starts to hold soft peaks. Serve scoops of ice cream crowned with dollops of whipped cream. Or **Lime Ginger Floats:** Scoop **lime ice cream** into tall glasses. Top with **ginger ale** (see right)."

Broiled Grapefruits with Lime

Broiled grapefruit is a Southern tradition—one I stand firmly behind. The crisp, sugary crust shatters beneath your spoon like a good crème brûlée, but instead of the cloying richness of custard, juicy, slightly bitter citrus lies underneath. Traditionally eaten for breakfast, broiled grapefruit also makes a great finish to a meal, especially with a scoop of ice cream. To make grapefruit for 4, heat the broiler and position the rack 4 to 5 inches (10 to 13cm) from the flame. Cut **2 grapefruits** in half horizontally and slice a bit off the bottoms to allow them to sit flat on a baking sheet. Loosen the segments by cutting around the membranes and pith with a sharp knife. Sprinkle **1 tablespoon of demerara sugar** and a few grains of salt over each grapefruit half. Broil until deeply caramelized, 8 to 12 minutes. (Watch them carefully so they don't burn!) Let cool on the baking sheet for a few minutes, squeeze a little **lime juice** over them, and serve right away, with **lime ice cream** if you like.

Ginger Syrup

In a perfect world, I would have this simple, versatile syrup in the fridge at all times. To make 2 cups (475ml), thinly slice **2 (6-inch/15cm) bulbs of ginger** (don't worry about peeling it). Combine the ginger with 2 cups (475ml) cold water and **2 cups (400g) sugar** in a saucepan and simmer for 5 minutes. Let the syrup cool, then strain through a fine-mesh sieve and store in an airtight container in the fridge for up to 2 weeks.

You can use this syrup to make homemade ginger ale (stir **2 tablespoons ginger syrup** into **8 ounces/240ml of club soda**), or drizzle it over ice cream. Add it to cocktails or to boiling water for a soothing tea. It wouldn't be a bad idea to spoon some over your morning yogurt.

Tad's Friday Night Pastas

Rotelle all'Arrabbiata

During the early years of Food52, I worked most weekends. And on the weekdays, I would get home from work, spend some time with our kids, and just continue working on my laptop until bedtime. I rarely cooked or wanted to linger over dinner. My husband, Tad, and I refer to these years as the Dark Days.

One of the good things that came out of the Dark Days (in addition to Food52 thriving!) is that Tad got very good at making a few pastas. In 2013, the *New York Times Magazine* ran a recipe for Mario Batali's Penne all'Arrabbiata. I didn't even know Tad read the recipe pages until he served this dinner and revealed the source. Since then, he's easily made this recipe fifty times, and has added his own touches (bacon, for instance, and rotelle rather than penne) and adjustments (more tomato). He's also shifted to making this on Friday nights. Now that we're out of the Dark Days, and I have time to cook on the weekends and share dinner during the weekdays (though the evening laptopping fails to cease!), he has taken to cooking pasta many Friday nights to cut me a break. And his pastas have never tasted better.

SERVES 4, PLUS LEFTOVERS

Salt

8 ounces (225g) bacon, cut into ¼-inch (6mm) slices

¼ cup plus 3 tablespoons (105ml) extra-virgin olive oil

½ cup (130g) tomato paste

2 modest pinches of red pepper flakes (or as much as you like)

1¾ cups (420g) canned chopped tomatoes (preferably Pomì)

1 pound (450g) rotelle or other small pasta

Grated Parmesan, for serving

Ricotta toasts (page 20) with lemon zest and honey, for serving

1 Bring a large pot of generously salted water to a boil.

2 Meanwhile, spread the bacon in a large sauté pan over medium heat; brown the bacon and render the fat. Scoop out the bacon and set aside on paper towels. Pour off all but 1 tablespoon of fat from the pan, then add ¼ cup (60ml) olive oil to the pan and warm over medium heat.

3 Drop in the tomato paste and add the red pepper flakes; turn the heat to low and stir just until fragrant, about 4 minutes. Stir in the tomatoes and turn off the heat.

4 Drop the pasta into the boiling water and cook until truly al dente—you'll be cooking it a bit more with the sauce. Drain the pasta, reserving ¼ cup (60ml) of the pasta water.

5 Add the pasta, bacon, and the reserved pasta water to the tomato sauce, then stir and toss over medium heat until the pasta is well coated. Season with salt if necessary, then add the 3 tablespoons olive oil, tossing well. Serve immediately, with a sprinkling of Parmesan on top of each bowlful.

Leftover Pasta (Really) Tad has been known to pack the leftovers, dressed with extra olive oil, for school lunches. I was skeptical at first, but our kids love this pasta at room temperature—which means they'll probably survive college.

Vodka Pasta

Most vodka pastas are overwrought, with superfluous ingredients crowding out the magic that happens when you combine tomatoes, cream, and vodka. I fell in love with this recipe for its simplicity, its insistence on doing nothing other than letting the ingredients shine. This pasta also happens to be a perfect end-of-week recipe, demanding little of your pantry or you. It's become another one of Tad's signature dinners. You can use any small pasta; Tad suggests rotelle or small shells.

SERVES 4

Salt

7 tablespoons (100g) unsalted butter

Pinch or two (up to you!) red pepper flakes

¾ cup (175ml) vodka

1 pound (450g) small pasta (such as rotelle or small shells)

1¼ cups (300g) canned chopped tomatoes (preferably Pomi)

1 cup (240ml) heavy cream

1 cup (100g) grated Parmesan

1 Bring a large pot of generously salted water to a boil.

2 Meanwhile, melt the butter over medium heat in a saucepan large enough to hold the cooked pasta. Add the pepper flakes and vodka and bring to a boil. Lower the heat and simmer for 2 minutes.

3 When the pasta water boils, add the pasta and cook until al dente.

4 Add the tomatoes and cream to the sauce, bring back to a boil, then lower the heat and simmer for 5 minutes. Season with salt.

5 When the pasta is cooked, drain it and add it to the sauce. With the heat on low, add the Parmesan and mix thoroughly.

Zuni Pasta with Preserved Tuna

This recipe from Zuni Café in San Francisco was featured on Food52 by longtime columnist Nicholas Day. A writer, father, and home cook, he appreciated the simple beauty of a pasta dish that could be made with jarred tuna and ingredients from your pantry. The first time I made this, my family was skeptical. Where is the sauce? It's so monochromatic! But once they got over their pasta prejudices—an open mind means an open palate!—they became devotees. The red pepper flakes may be adjusted for the sake of any small humans in your household.

SERVES 4

Salt

½ cup (120ml) olive oil

1 tablespoon lemon zest

1 bay leaf

½ teaspoon red pepper flakes (or less—I often use just a pinch)

½ teaspoon freshly ground black pepper (optional)

2 garlic cloves, slivered

¼ teaspoon fennel seeds

14 ounces (400g) olive oil–packed tuna

¼ cup (35g) pine nuts

2 tablespoons capers, coarsely chopped

1 tablespoon rinsed and chopped preserved lemon

1 pound (450g) pasta (any short pasta shape you like; we prefer penne rigate)

1 Bring a large pot of salted water to a boil. In a small skillet, gently warm the olive oil, lemon zest, bay leaf, red pepper flakes, black pepper, garlic, and fennel seeds over very low heat for about 15 minutes, until the flavors infuse the oil. Then add the canned tuna, pine nuts, capers, and preserved lemon. Gently nudge apart the tuna and let it warm up but not cook.

2 Meanwhile, once the water boils, cook the pasta until al dente. Drain well and toss in a serving bowl with the tuna mixture.

Lunch: Zuni Pasta Niçoise Mix the leftover pasta with blanched **green beans, niçoise olives,** and a fresh infusion of **lemon juice** and **extra-virgin olive oil.** Top with **chopped hard-boiled egg.**

ACKNOWLEDGMENTS

Many people tested the recipes and menus in this book so that we could be sure we were accomplishing what we set out to. But there were no more valiant testers than our families, whom we eat with every week. Thank you to the dearest group of guinea pigs—and sometime sous chefs—we could ever hope for: Tad, Addison, and Walker, and Jonathan, Clara, and Henry. Thanks also to Dickyi Tenzin and Donna Herman, who care for our children's stomachs as ably as they do their hearts and minds.

When we first discussed the concept for this book with our editors at Ten Speed, none of us quite knew what we were getting into. We're so grateful to Hannah Rahill and Kelly Snowden for sharing our vision and sticking with us through several course changes, all in service of making this book as useful and inspiring as possible for anyone who needs to get dinner on the table every night. Our heartfelt thanks also go to Aaron Wehner, Michele Crim, David Hawk, and Margaux Keres at Ten Speed.

And now for the home troops: our talented team at Food52. We could not have produced this book without the serene energy and capable support of Ali Slagle and Kristen Miglore. Ali managed a maelstrom of Google docs and email communication in order to help us wrestle the book into shape, and also had a hand in much of the food styling. Kristen applied her keen eye to the finer details of the writing, photography, and overall style of the book.

Thank you to James Ransom (whom we've now worked with for more than five years!) and Alexis Anthony for coming up with an entirely new look and feel for the images in the book, and then creating them all. Our gratitude also goes to Carmen Ladipo for photo production, and to the multitalented Sarah Jampel for lending her food styling talents, and to C.B. Owens for the additional set of eagle eyes.

Many people tested these recipes or prepared them for photo shoots, giving us vital feedback along the way. Thank you to Josh Cohen, Derek Laughren, Erin McDowell, Emily Stephenson, Katy Peetz, Kenzi Wilbur, Stephanie Bourgeois, Samantha Weiss-Hills, Amanda Sims, Caroline Lange, Leslie Stephens, Angela Barros, Anna Gass, Deanna Curri, Emily Olson, Kate Knapp, Monita Buchwald, Sarah Green, and Victoria Ross.

And no Food52 cookbook could happen without our tremendously talented and generous community, whose cooking inspires us every day and whose exceptional recipes have helped us feed our families for years.

INDEX

Published in the United States by Ten Speed Press,
an imprint of the Crown Publishing Group, a division
of Penguin Random House LLC, New York.
www.crownpublishing.com
www.tenspeed.com

Ten Speed Press and the Ten Speed Press colophon are registered
trademarks of Penguin Random House LLC.

Some of the material in this work first appeared on the Food52 website.

Library of Congress Cataloging-in-Publication Data

Names: Hesser, Amanda, author. | Stubbs, Merrill, author.

Title: Food52 a new way to dinner : a playbook of recipes and strategies
    for the week ahead / by Amanda Hesser and Merrill Stubbs ;
    photography by James Ransom.
Other titles: Food 52 a new way to dinner | Food fifty-two a new way
    to dinner | New way to dinner | Food52.
Description: First edition. | Berkeley : Ten Speed Press, [2016] |
    Includes bibliographical references and index.
Identifiers: LCCN 2016022690 (print) | LCCN 2016024436
    (ebook) | ISBN 9780399578007 (hardcover : alk. paper) | ISBN
    9780399578014 (eBook) | ISBN 9780399578014 (E-book)
Subjects: LCSH: Cooking, American. | Seasonal cooking. |
    Dinners and dining. |
LCGFT: Cookbooks.
Classification: LCC TX715 .H57265 2016 (print) | LCC TX715
    (ebook) | DDC 641.5975—dc23
LC record available at
    https://lccn.loc.gov/2016022690

Hardcover ISBN: 978-0-399-57800-7
eBook ISBN: 978-0-399-57801-4

Printed in China

Design by Margaux Keres

10 9 8 7 6 5 4 3 2 1

First Edition